ECONOMICS I

Principles of Economics for Sustainable Development

By Dr. Edward Schellhammer

2nd Edition 2014, revised.
© **Copyright. Dr. Edward Schellhammer. All rights reserved.**

ISBN-13: 978-1478226734
ISBN-10: 1478226730

www.EdwardSchellhammer.com

Table of Contents

In Somnis Veritas for Economics I

Dreams tell the truth. Dreams stay above theories, ideologies and dogmas. During the last 33 years I had over 12,000 dreams about the state of humanity and the planet. I had estimated 3000 dreams about humans' evolution and all processes of the Archetypes of the Soul. Examples:

A voice: "Also for the rich people tomorrow, no risks will be covered."

An unknown town in Northern Europe. Everywhere men show their penis, some are partly and some completely naked, partly covered with cloth or plastic. Many have blown their penis up with air, technically enlarged, even some little boys. They show each other the 'marvelous' thing they have. Many women are totally excited over these men with big and large penises. Everything seems like carnival. I observe from a distance, find this disgusting, distasteful, an expression of the sick society.

One can ignite the entire world with one bomb.

Tornados. Floods. Waves up to 30 and even 100 meters. Massive. It destroys everything into 1000 pieces. I am somewhere, entirely in the light.

Young people don't want to learn, least of all about self-knowledge and reflection. Only by force.

An assembly. I tell the people: Not taking serious the values and realities of the psychical life is deadly for the entire collective.

In Zurich. Millions of very small maggots everywhere. They devour people's bodies.

Earthquakes. Floods. Masses of people falling into abysm. Agitations everywhere.

A huge ship like Titanic, but even bigger. 35,000 people are on it. It's sailing. It's night. Then, an incident, and the ship slowly sinks.

A big town such as Berlin: Neurotic people, psychopaths, amusement parks. Masses of monkeys dancing everywhere, people with drive disturbances, politicians, people from the show business, and also people from the culture.

All decadent!

I am standing on a bridge. There is a river underneath, flowing from a lake. It is raining incessantly. The water level is rising. I see that there is an enormous catastrophe approaching.

I receive a sword, a scepter, a globe and a cross; these symbols I compose into a circle-cross-Mandala.

I receive a goblet and I am summoned to search the mysteries of life in it.

A sun-like female figure draws me towards it, embraces me and I can feel its energy flowing through me like a strong current. Then I'm unified with this light, I am one with this sun. "This is the unio mystica", it is said.

I am in the Garden of Eden. It is indescribably beautiful. The paradise is mine. It is within me.

I am on my way to the universe; I must cross a bridge and I have to promise to go back to the people, then I meet God (a burning well); I can see pyramids of light, golden worlds and a huge golden circle-cross-Mandala shimmering on the eternal horizon. 'Death', who is the only witness of my journey to God, says: "Fulfilled is the word."

The truth and the Archetypes of the Soul are the primordial foundation and aim of science, human life, and society. 'Economics' doesn't have either of them! The entire social sciences do not have them. That's the scandalous drama of science. The absence of the truth and of the Archetypes of the Soul produces enormous destructive energy and developments in sciences and societies. It shows clearly that sciences do not take care of the archetypal, psychical and spiritual evolution of mankind nor do they have any respect for the creation. Such science is a sham. Such sciences dehumanize mind and soul, and eliminate the dignity of humans. Such sciences are infected with the most toxic virus ever existed: the dynamic code for regicide and deicide. In the end, it will irreversibly and unstoppably lead to the doom. It can happen within decades if drastic measures around the globe are not taken soon.

Dr. Edward Schellhammer

1. Structure of Global Problems

1.1. Humanity and the World in the Year 2050

All the economic systems of societies are now in a complex interrelation that mutually influences everything. The state of humanity and the planet will worsen exponentially, especially due to the rise of the earth population, the extreme exploitation of resources, and the manifold contamination. Minds will be dehumanized and bodies deformed.

We have to consider that the causes of the dire state of humanity and the planet today came in effect 10-20 years ago; and the damaging factors today we will experience in 10-20 years. This momentum, which is accelerating, is completely ignored today. All systems of human life have their own level of sustainability and are interdependent with each other.

Consider that today 2012:

You are 60-70 years old: you may live another 20-30 years and so you will experience the world in 2030-2040
You are 50-60 years old: you may live another 30-40 years and so you will experience the world in 2040-2050
You are 40-50 years old: you may live another 40-50 years and so you will experience the world in 2050-2060
You are 30-40 years old: you may live another 50-60 years and so you will experience the world in 2060-2070
You are 20-30 years old: you may live another 60-70 years and so you will experience the world in 2070-2080
You are 10-20 years old: you may live another 70-80 years and so you will experience the world in 2080-2090
You are 1-10 years old: you may live another 80-90 years and so you will experience the world in 2090-2100

If every human being on this earth continues living as usual and if unimaginable drastic economic, political and social measures are not taken globally within the next 6 years, then you must expect to experience the following picture of the world:

- The earth population will reach 12-14 billion at the end of the century; but there is not enough food and water.
- Poverty and misery in developing countries as well as in the Western world will increase dramatically.
- The distribution of wealth will take on new extremes: 0.5% super-rich,

9.5% well off and 90% brutal poverty.

- Unemployment and underemployment will reach 1.5-2 billion people; this is the systemic destruction of mankind.
- Physical and mental illnesses and deformed human beings will increase due to the all-embracing cocktail of contamination.
- Mental diseases from stupidity to naivety, narcissism to neuroticism and psychosis will increase, dehumanizing society.
- Human rights, ethics and human values already a basket case, will continue to be abused, destroying countries, people, and 'justifying' wars.
- Public education excludes most human realities, and does not include any real requirements necessary to master life.
- Big religions are the worst scam mankind has experienced in its history; extreme fanaticism is to be expected.
- Global lifestyles have fully lost their genuine culture; merely expressing compensation, lunacy or a fight for survival.
- Contamination increasing exponentially: Chemicals, pharmaceutics, fine dust in the air, soil, water, and food chain.
- Unimaginable mountains of human made waste and sewage from now 7 billion and later 12-14 billion people will destroy all human life.
- Increasing climate change will produce unimaginable natural disasters: drought, desertification, tornados, and floods, etc.
- Rising sea levels will steadily eliminate beaches, islands, land, immense deltas, and hundreds of big cities.
- All eco-systems are damaged and will be irreparably damaged and destroy all food chains and water reservoirs.
- Nature, all around the globe is already damaged and is increasingly destroyed, contaminated, and polluted to the point of no return.
- Natural resources are increasingly exploited, unrecoverable; most in less than 30 years poised to extinction.
- A huge number of species are disappearing and with that the complex balance of natural life will be destroyed.
- Natural catastrophes will become bigger and more frequent; and destroy huge areas, urbanizations and life.
- Inhumane living environments will suffocate most of mankind, transforming them into dehumanized creatures.
- Tourism will vanish due to financial collapses; leisure will mean 'hanging around', and crime will be the new sport.
- Decreasing agricultural land, poisoned by chemicals and over faming; food will be 95% industrialized for degraded humans.
- Transport and car traffic will absorb enormous resources; contaminating every living being and the entire planet.
- Energy demand will enormously increase and its production and use will

increasingly generate toxic emissions.

- The production of goods requires huge amounts of resources and produces unbelievable amounts of collateral toxic damage.
- The media in the hands of a small elite thoroughly brainwashes, manipulates, and dehumanizes billions of humans.
- Financial institutions and mega corporations are free to operate mad business practices with brutally disastrous consequences.
- Political systems will revert to acute authoritarianism; fascism, dictatorships, and police states with absolutely inhumane management.
- Politicians and all kind of leaders will be the enslaved protagonists controlled, managed, and paid for by the elite.
- Certain leaders, driven by religious psychosis, are ready to eliminate their own followers and billions more.
- State administrations with the help of technology will operate with a 100% control of their citizens 24/7 and with extremely rigid regulations.
- Central banks and rating agencies, already the main tools of the elite can and already do destroy entire countries and societies.
- Certain private banks are responsible for wars, hunger, misfortune and dire misery of billions of people.
- The astronomic levels of debt in the West cannot even be paid back in 200 years and will choke any efforts for real change.
- Militarism and immense wars will explode around the globe and produce frightening suffering and destruction everywhere.
- Law (national and international) will only serve the elite, the governments, and the corporations in order to rule humanity.
- Crimes and prison: crimes will be a daily occurrence with police forces and prisons run and managed by corporations for profit.
- Trouble spots around the globe will dramatically increase and produce irremediable suffering and hate.

→ Sustainability in perspective: today sustainability barely exists in any of the systems of human life and in the near future there will be absolutely no sustainability in any of the global systems that could enable humanity's evolution!

Diagram: Structure of Humanity's big Problems

It's all about economics. Even psychological and spiritual factors begin and end with economic factors. Even religion with its concrete institutions (churches, clergy, and teaching institutions) is an economic entity.

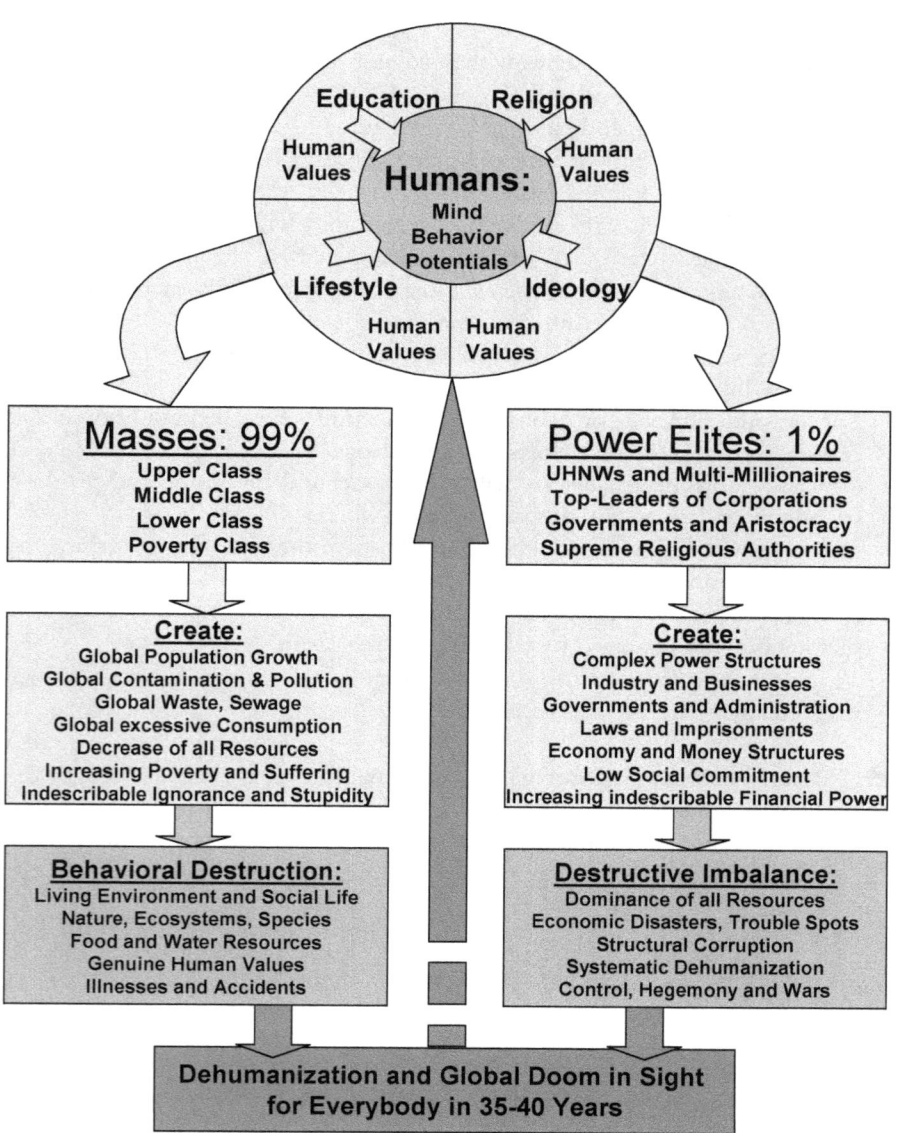

1.2. Key Topics of the State of Humanity and the Planet

Humans & Human Life
1. **Population (Structures):** Increase, urban growth, increase of needs, contamination, risks, sustainability
2. **Poverty and Wealth:** Hunger, lack of food and drinking water; causes; physical, psychical and social effects; distribution of wealth; structures of income
3. **Unemployment & Underemployment:** Lack of earning opportunities; costs and damages; impacts on humans
4. **Health (physical, mental):** Illnesses, disease, epidemics; accidents; lack of health care and pharmaceuticals
5. **Ethics and Human Values:** Lack of moral and respect for human values; the lost truth
6. **Human Rights:** Abuse, child labor, slavery, low wages, working conditions, attitudes of exploitation
7. **Education:** Illiteracy, public and vocational schools, universities; lack of holistic education, wrong education
8. **Religion:** Dogmatism, fundamentalism, superstition, deception, falseness, lies, brainwashing; power abuse, financial strength
9. **Life Style, Leisure, Sport, Culture:** Lack of culture, consumer mentality, superficiality, acute individualism

Nature and Environment

1. **Contamination & Pollution:** Drugs, detergents, fine dust; network of causes; chain of effects

2. **Waste and Sewage:** Garbage, electro-waste, nuclear waste, chemicals, package, toxic elements, recycling

3. **Climate Change:** Catastrophes, causes, economic consequences; long term effects

4. **Eco-systems:** Contamination, increase sea level; damages and consequences for nature and humans

5. **Nature:** Due to contamination and climate change; long term consequences; destruction of human life, and other species

6. **Resources:** Food and non-food; limited water resources; sustainability of natural resources and life style and consumption levels

7. **Species:** Complexity of importance for nature and food chain; consequences of decrease of species

8. **Catastrophes:** Droughts, desertification, deforestation, floods, tornados; heat waves, tsunamis and their damages

9. **Living Environment:** Over-construction; loss of natural environment; urban over crowding

Industry and Business

1. **Tourism:** Travel, Hotel diversification, Mass tourism, soulless tourism, heritage destruction, travel pollution

2. **Agriculture & Food Production:** Mass production, distribution, small farms, genetic engineering and over farming

3. **Transport and Traffic:** Car traffic, public and goods transport traffic; direct and lateral effects

4. **Energy Production:** Coal, nuclear power stations, green energy; damages and costs

5. **Goods Production:** Mass production, globalization; damages in businesses; elimination of small and medium sized businesses, environmental damages

6. **Media:** Brainwashing, manipulation, power of (misleading) information; propaganda, bias and fabrications

7. **Banking & Insurance:** Financial institutions, public debt, consumer debt, corporate debt, high earnings, credit, speculation

8. **Real Estate & Construction:** Megalomania, sale and rental prices, low quality, collapse of construction industry

9. **Businesses & Services:** Decrease of small and medium sized businesses; over regulation: tourism, leisure, etc.

Politics and Governments

1. **Political Systems:** Rules; democracy; efficiency; qualifications; abuse of taxes; cheating people, lobbying

2. **Politicians, Leaders, & Practices:** Abuse of power, world power aspiration, elites financial power, fabrications, weakness

3. **State Administration:** Quality and efficiency; regulations; totalitarianism, over-control; lack of professionalism

4. **Central Banks, Rating Agencies:** The people behind, the power, the effects, the legitimacy, the destructive effects

5. **Military and Wars:** Militarization, wars, civil wars; proxy wars, terrorism; economic and cyber war; false flags

6. **Law (national, international):** Lack of laws for nature; power interests; injustice; corruption; abuse of existing laws

7. **Crimes and Prison:** Mafia, corruption; crimes, violence, cheating, scams; prison life; political crimes; Ponzi schemes

8. **Trouble Spots:** Tensions, social unrest, riots, civil wars, causes and effects

9. **UN and Continental Institutions:** Lack of democracy, abuse of financial power, inefficiency

1.3. Human Factors Embedded Everywhere

People

- Billions of people are greedy, lazy, stupid, and never want a (national, global) all-embracing renewal.
- The majority of humans are brainwashed, poisoned and dehumanized: global or national renewal is not possible.
- The world is full of cowards, hypocrites, blabbers, false prophets, false politicians, false economists, and false priests.
- 6 billion people have deep inner pain and have lost faith; they can't put trust into any 'renewal project'.
- People would go crazy and rebel if the right to drive a car or use an airplane would be severely limited.
- Most people are submissive to authorities, trust and believe in them in an infantile psychical-spiritual way.
- People want illusions, are driven by illusions, fantasies, magical thinking; they admire 'smoke and mirror' tactics.
- People tend to project weaknesses, bad and evil character, amoral doing and the devil onto other people.
- People project their longing for redemption and salvation onto authorities, state institutions and religion, or onto consumption.
- People do not want to elaborate their redemption and salvation through psychical-spiritual development.
- People think they are good, accepted, esteemed and valuable if they blindly obey others and institutions.
- Unconscious complexes of individuals are transmitted within the family to the next 3-4 generations.
- People are obsessed with having a home, car, partner (etc.) with the hope to gain salvation and happiness.
- A majority of people are 'human robots', irreparably deformed, misshaped and distorted since prenatal time.
- A lot of people are running or speculating for fast money with the least possible effort or performance.
- Too many unemployed people reject learning, hard working, more working hours, or uncomfortable work.
- If the masses would dispose of much more money, they would only heat

up stupid and blind consumption.

- A huge majority of people are not well educated and extremely ignorant and lazy for a real democracy.
- Most people greedily want comfort, an easy life, fast results, cheap products, a lot of fun and distraction.
- To make oneself special with superficial self-presentation is more important than an integer character.
- The conceit to know what is fact, correct, just, right, and good (etc.) is an infecting pest around the globe.
- Owners of properties (homes, premises) reject a reduction of rental prices; preferring to leave them empty for years.
- The good will never win simply because it is good; and not a lot people want to live and strengthen the good.

Politics

- Politics as a core institution of society is never ready for critical self-reflection, pioneering projects, and renewal.
- People must be preoccupied with sorrow and fear so that leaders can operate in their own mad interests.
- People must be occupied with suffering in the soul so that the religion can operate in their own sick interests.
- People must be accommodated to regulations, norms, all kind of accreditations to be forced into obedience.
- The entire humanity is contaminated with a history full of evil and mad doing, of lies, falseness, fabrications, and wars.
- It is rarely possible to pursue a career with integrity, ability to love, the truth, and with good spiritual attitudes.
- Contamination, poverty and mega-cities are designed to degenerate, dehumanize, and weaken the masses.
- All kind of catastrophes are good because it strongly limits people's life and success, happiness, participation.
- Public education as a core educational institution is never ready for critical self-reflection and renewal.

Corporations and Businesses

- The cadre of economics and the big Western corporate groups are never ready for critical self-reflection and renewal.
- The media corporate groups would never inform humanity about urgent indispensable renewal, nor do they accept any educational responsibility.
- The big media will never give up their concepts of deceive, distortion, manipulation, and brainwashing (etc.).

- Media abuse freedom of speech to shape collective attitudes, to discredit individuals, institutions, and states.
- No super-pioneer, prophet or Messiah (Mahdi) will ever have the media power to reach humanity.
- Speculations in most big businesses: Investors are never ready to abdicate speculation profit or any 'casino-games'.
- Interests of loans and mortgages: Investors are never ready to abdicate highest possible profit; the entire interest-concept is pure money multiplier.
- Most owners of businesses are unable to deal with pioneering ideas, visions and reject any new sustainable concept.

Religion

- Religion as a core educational institution is never ready for critical self-reflection and renewal; they have lost the Archetypes of the Soul.
- Organized religion (The Church) has much more hidden power than most people could imagine: renewal not possible.
- The falsified, distorted and mad religions with sources in Abraham (Moses) reject any new prophet or Messiah.
- Most followers of a religion are addicted to a religious psychosis and will never give up dogmatic and fundamentalist belief.

Leadership

- The world is predominantly in the hands of psychopaths, megalomaniacs: renewal is not possible.
- The super-elite driven by a pseudo-religious mission and by psychosis are never ready for critical self-reflection and renewal.
- The Western world, economics and politics, is in the money grip of 6 families through banks: renewal is not possible.
- Politicians, economists, and leaders in other institutions of society have no time for personal further education.
- Constructive communication with psychopaths, megalomaniacs, psychotic or false and neurotic people is not possible.
- Politicians do not want to risk their career with pioneering projects and a new understanding of human life and society.
- Those who rule the world will never want an advanced democratic republic with informed and educated people.
- The state of humanity is purposely created by the ultra high net worth individuals (UHNWIs) to rule the world.
- Those who dispose of 80% of global wealth will never accept a balanced distribution of money and wealth.

Unemployment

- In many countries the rate of unemployment is disastrous: 8-25% and up to 30-50% of the youth do not have a job.
- Hundreds of millions worldwide do not have a job! Billions of people are underemployed or get a wage that does not allow for a humane life.
- 80% of working people in the industrial nations are scared of losing their job and see no future perspectives.
- Many well educated professionals are finding it difficult if not impossible to find a decent and suitable job or they are simply underpaid.
- For more and more couples, the creation of a family becomes a financial nightmare; love is gone and the relationship a permanent stress.
- Additionally, real estates, food, and consumer goods are all becoming more expensive; but the wages have stagnated or decreased since a decade.

Diagram: Consequences of Unemployment

Unemployment causes:

- Low self-esteem
- Decrease of self-confidence
- Permanent state of fear
- Distress
- Tense inner state
- Extreme frustration
- Sleeping disorder
- Unhappy state
- Bad mood
- Quarrels with the partner
- Alcoholism
- Depression
- Aggression
- Suicide
- Exaggerated smoking
- Passivity
- Isolation
- Feeling of shame
- Mentally low activity
- Emotional weakness

Unemployment causes:

- Loss of creativity
- Feeling down
- Despair
- Helplessness
- Discontentedness
- Emotional regression
- Compliance
- Conformance
- Tendency to obey
- Tendency to take orders
- Servility / submissiveness
- Mental disorder
- Psycho-somatic reactions
- Unhealthy eating
- Higher risk of accident
- Labor unrest
- Separations and divorce
- Destruction of family life
- No care for one's children
- Lack of care for health

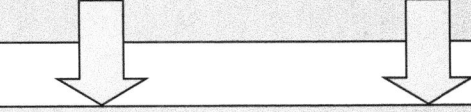

Impact in the psychical Organism:

Decrease of constructive thinking
Imbalanced interpretation
Ignored genuine inner needs
Disinterest in spiritual qualities
Preponderantly negative feelings
Very low power of and interest in love
Reduced control of perception
Disinterest in personal development
Strong defense mechanisms
No satisfaction or fulfillment

Economics

- Economics as a core institution of society (science, advice) is never ready for critical self-reflection and renewal.
- Economics' interest is preponderantly focused on 'as much profit as possible' disregarding the critical collateral substantial (world of nature and species) and humane effects.
- The super extreme economic power is not necessarily linked with the amount of wealth; but much more with the position of the power network in the decision-making entities.
- There are billionaires and CEOs that are simply protagonists on the scene without any specific power or participation on the level of supreme global aims and orders.

Conclusion

→ The state of humanity now is a result of, and expresses the titanic fight between the Archetypes of the Soul (the eternal inner human values) and the absence of them.
→ Economics with its enormous global power is the key contributor to the eradication of these eternal inner human values, taking humans to a new Dark Age and eventual extinction.

1.4. The Need for Human Values

The General Human Values

- To be on earth is a wonderful gift.
- The values of nature and species are priceless.
- The planet is the indispensable home for all living, an indispensable need to exist.
- The growing process from baby to old age is an amazing experience.
- Each human has a complex psychical organism with an immense potential.
- To have a home is a natural need for living, sharing life, and joy of life.
- Work is necessary to make one's living; work is also an inner need.
- Healthy food and drinking water are indispensable for living and health.
- Health care is a substantial need of humans and reduces immense suffering.
- Family life with true love is of immeasurable value and indispensable for all humans.
- Parental education and public education are a human need of highest importance.
- Social and environmental security is an inner need, facilitates peace and health.
- Culture is an unforgettable expression of performances, of experiences and learning.
- To love and being loved is supreme power and meaning of life, includes all human values.
- Friendship means sharing and gives strength, forms trust and promotes learning.
- Care about respect, learning, support, promotion, understanding is very valuable.
- Outright trust is a value like a diamond: beautiful, peaceful, pure, genuine, and powerful.
- Truth is of utmost value for humans to function well mentally and to perform successfully.
- Truthfulness is a key-value for friendship, for love, for a relationship, for a family life.
- Faithfulness is the essence of friendship, of a loving relationship, of a marriage.

- Hope is a fundamental attitude towards life, one's own forces and resources.
- Humans have an inner life they can discover, develop, express, shape, and use for good.
- People also have in their mind a spiritual intelligence of unlimited constructive potentials.
- Human's soul has a psychical pole of the other gender; balancing polarity leads to completeness.
- Sexual satisfaction between man and woman relaxes soul and body, reinforces love and health.
- A well functioning family is of paradisiacal value for children, parents; indispensable for society.
- Justice gives security, protection, stability, a frame of correctness and fairness in life matters.
- Balance is a key principle to make nearly everything in human's life work constructively.
- Peace has paradisiacal quality, in the mind and in real life; it's the result of spiritual development.
- Reliability allows for constructive living and working together; also makes politics valuable.
- Health is a value; mental health is superior and is expressed in realized human values.
- Ability to be responsible for oneself, for others, for any life or work issue is a high value.
- Understanding of oneself, of others, and of the human's life is the humane key for success.
- Participation creates foundation, strengthens interest, fairness, responsibility and cooperation.
- Authenticity means to become an authentic person, is meaning of life rooted in the soul.
- Sustainability is an indispensable factor for long term success and balance in life and society.
- Abilities and opportunities to learn for mastering life and creating things or events are invaluable.
- Experiencing the eternity of souls and their origin through dreams and inner growth is priceless.
- Respecting and living these human values are the unique foundation for sustainable global peace.

Work is a Human Value

Values of working - Working includes / means:

- Zest for action is a natural genuine human drive and need
- Is necessary for living a decent life
- Gives personal satisfaction and pride
- Gives meaning of life related to the person
- Promotes people to be responsible for their living
- Develops and strengthens personality
- Develops and strengthens professional knowledge and skills
- Need for working is a natural part of human's mind and soul
- Allows for the expression of personal talents, aptitudes and interests
- Allows to compete and increase result and salary
- Is (in most cases) also a stimulating social environment
- Promotes discipline, respect, creativity, communication, etc.
- Forms self-confidence due to the performances
- Is something like the 'second home' (second safe living environment)
- Makes a person more mature
- Allows to use one's energy and strength
- Offers many learning opportunities within the frame of the work
- Gives importance to the working person within the work field
- Gives an equilibrium to the family (personal) life
- Activates the mind and body, depending on the kind of work
- Gives a substantial extension to the psychological self-identity
- Can contribute something to society (and to other people)
- Gives stability in life and personal economic development
- Can live their own life with self-responsibility
- Work as a challenge is very stimulating for action
- Work makes people independent from pauper relief

Humanity has lost the Human Values

- 90-95% of humanity does not live human values or realizes them in a very rudimental way.
- Most leaders in all systems of societies and in all corporations ignore these human values.
- Religions do not prepare humans for living these human values; neither do they protect them.
- Human values are not real in life just like that; they do not grow automatically like grass.
- People cannot buy human values in the supermarket or inherit them from previous generations.
- Living human values is indispensable for the survival and evolution of humanity.
- It is the untouchable freedom of humans – 'Free will' - for humanity to

decide for or against these human values.

- Living human values is the result of holistic psychical and spiritual education, of performance, and learning.
- Living human values demands efforts, audacity, character qualities, humility, catharsis, and renewal.
- Living human values means living within the path towards complete psychical-spiritual fulfillment.
- To be a human requires learning, to shape, to strengthen, to respect, and to live human values.
- To be on earth is a wonderful gift; but humans must decide: to be mere human biomass or a divine creation.
- Give life to human values; make them real and sustainable in every day life and in the society!

1.5. Essential Fields of Economic Relevance

Thesis: Economics as a science must also genuinely address the following fields under economic view rather than just skim over them:

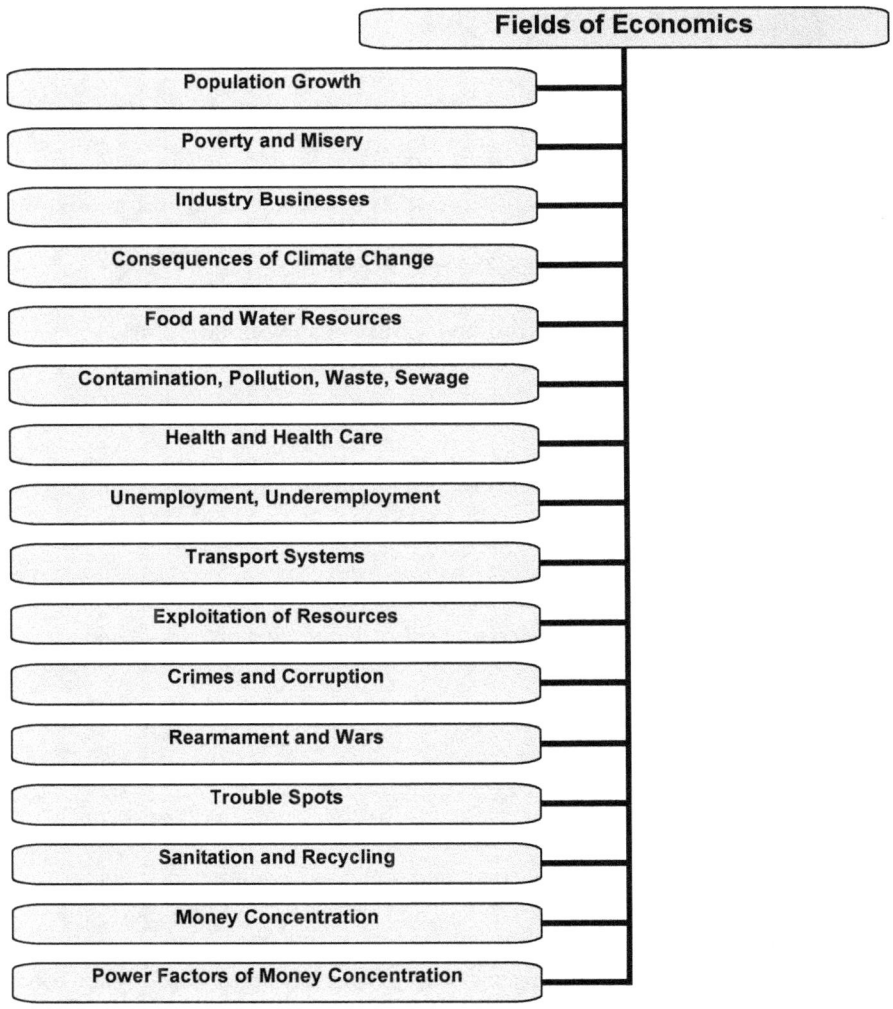

Fields of Economics

- Population Growth
- Poverty and Misery
- Industry Businesses
- Consequences of Climate Change
- Food and Water Resources
- Contamination, Pollution, Waste, Sewage
- Health and Health Care
- Unemployment, Underemployment
- Transport Systems
- Exploitation of Resources
- Crimes and Corruption
- Rearmament and Wars
- Trouble Spots
- Sanitation and Recycling
- Money Concentration
- Power Factors of Money Concentration

➔ Thesis: Economics as a science must have a global and time perspective of its parameters for 60-90 years as per the following presented perspective.

Earth Population Growth

2011: 7 billion people
2024-2027: 8 billion people
2037-2040: 9 billion people
2050-2053: 10 billion people
2090-2100: 12-14 billion people
80% live in Asia, Africa and South America
2050: 90-93% of the earth's population will live in Asia, Africa and South America

Other statistics calculate with higher figures and shorter periods (10-11 years per 1 billion). It doesn't matter if the world population will grow slower and reach 10 billion only in the years 2060-2065. It will happen; it will grow and reach an unsustainable level in 100 years. And already 10 billion people on earth are not sustainable, not even aiming for a lower life standard similar to those in the Western World during the mid twentieth century.

Population Fraction of Industrialized Countries (Western World)

1980: 25%
1990: 22.5%
2000: 20%
2010: 17.5%
2020: 15%
2050: 7-10%
2080: 5%

→ The Western world will be suffocated from the remaining 9 billion people in the years 2050-2060.
→ No Western army will be able to protect their citizens and wealth from the rest of the world population.

Food and Water

- 2.3-2.6 billion people malnourished, under-fed or starving.
- 1.3 billion people only dispose of dirty and contaminated drinking water.
- Today 4-5 billion people don't have enough food and drinking water.
- In 2012, 1 billion people more will suffer from hunger due to higher food prices.
- An additional 600 million people are at risk of famine due to climate change.
- For 3.2 billion people drinking water will be rare in the future.

Poverty and Misery

- Over 500 (600) million people live in absolute poverty.
- 4-5 billion people live under poor and very poor conditions.
- 50% of all children on earth (2.2 billion) live in poverty.
- 1.3 billion people earn less than US$1 per day.
- 50% of the earth population lives from less than $2.50 per day.
- 2.6 billion people live without proper sanitation.
- At least 80 million people in the EU are 'below the poverty line'. Countries with the highest poor population: France, Germany, Italy, Poland, Spain and the UK.
- 44 millions (or 14.5%) Americans live in poverty.

Global Warming and Climate Change

- The global average sea level will rise by at least 20-30 cm within 20-30 years. During the next 30 years the rise in Mediterranean Sea level will be 2 cm per year.
- Heat waves, drought, fires, rainstorms, floods, tornados, hurricanes, tropical cyclones become more frequent, more widespread and/or more intense.
- 300,000 deaths and 300 million people affected every year by global warming.
- Floods will affect 2 billion by 2050 due to climate change, deforestation, rising sea levels.
- 3.2 billion people will experience water shortages due to climate change.
- Estimated yearly costs of climate change damages (worldwide): over 1 trillion Euros.
- Heat waves with agricultural losses reached $15 billion.
- Climate change could cost the world up to 25% of its entire wealth.

Sewage and Human generated Waste

- 2.6 billion people live without proper sanitation.
- Sewage of 2.5-3.5 billion people goes to the soil, sea and oceans.
- Toxic chemicals per year: 650 million tons of sewage, 60,000 tons of mercury, 36.000 tons of phosphates dumped into the Mediterranean.
- 7 million tons of plastic debris, industrial chemicals, agricultural waste, petroleum, etc., end up in the oceans every year.
- Global emission of carbon dioxide will increase until 2030 by 40% up to 40,000 million tons (2006: 29,000 million tons).
- Traffic emissions: Tons of oil drops of vehicles go every day into the

nature (soil, drinking water): cancer, asthma, depressions, etc.
- Fine dust from cars, industry, oil heating, trains, chemical industry, oil industry, coal and gold mining, etc., produces illnesses (respiratory tract) and cancer.
- Antidepressants, blood pressure and diabetes medications, oral contraceptives, chemotherapy drugs, antibiotics, and 1000 medications more are in the water supplies.
- More than 3,000 million people suffer from illnesses and disease due to pollution and contamination.

Agriculture and Fishing

- Up to 30 million hectares of land (size of Italy) is lost each year to environmental degradation, industrialization and urbanization.
- Industrial agriculture has destroyed 200 million small farmer businesses.
- Wheat, grain, maize, rice, cocoa, fruit, sugar, staples, meat, and coffee are now the new fields for speculations with price increases of 15-40%.
- Fishes and sea fruits are 'eating' unimaginable chemical and drug residue cocktails.
- Fishing resources are rapidly decreasing because of excessive exploitation.
- Most resources are exorbitantly overexploited and within 40 years depleted.
- Most of the bees around the world are mysteriously sick and billions are dying every year. Bees pollinate over 90 types of vegetables, fruits and grain.

Contamination

- Oceans, seas, lakes, rivers and groundwater are contaminated by 50-90% of countless different consumed medications in urine and feces.
- Soaps, shampoos, hair products, cosmetics and perfumes contain chemicals that disappear down the drain by washing and showering, and go to the water in nature.
- Around 100,000 chemical products are used in Europe (and elsewhere). More than 700 carcinogenic elements are everywhere in the daily life environment.
- Heavy metal in high concentration we also found in animal bowels and sea fruits.
- Poisonous substances are in food, soil, air, water, sea, and reach the human's body.
- 3,000 corporate groups produce environmental damages of nearly $2 trillion each year.
- 60 % of the global ecosystems and over 40% of the oceans are heavily damaged.

- The loss of species is increasing at an alarming rate.

Nuclear Energy and Waste

- Nuclear waste is very dangerous for environment and humans.
- Nuclear storage always has a permanent risk.
- Nuclear waste – many hundred thousands of tons – must be stored, controlled, protected and administrated for 1 million years.
- Storage, repacking, and recycling nuclear waste will cost the following generations billions of dollars each year, over and over again.
- Nuclear electricity is the most expensive energy humanity is producing.

Road Traffic

- Road Traffic Accidents (RTA) result in 1.2 million deaths and 50 million injured every year.
- Over the last 50 years more than 60 (or: 100?) million people died and 2.5 billion people were injured due to RTA.
- In 2008, 380.000 people died in Europe as a result of fine dust from road traffic; and millions more around the globe.
- Pollution from cars and lorry traffic: exhaust gases, including fine dust (diesel), fine dust by abrasion tires, fine dust by abrasion driving surface, fine dust brake shoe; and traffic noise.
- Pollution also from: Trains, aviation, vessels, wrecks, oil tankers, and military vehicles.
- There are estimated 1.5-2 billion cars and other motor vehicles (e.g. lorry, van, etc.) in use worldwide; all producing pollution, contamination, accidents, etc.
- Within the next 20 years an estimated 1.5-2 billion additional cars will be produced around the globe!

World of Cars

- Raw material needed: Glass, steel, plastic, copper, lithium, aluminum, iron, plastic steel, wood, cotton, rubber, coconut fiber, chemical elements, detergents, oil, electricity, water, rare elements, paint, labor colors, leather, and much more, etc.
- Exploitation of prime resources produces (mines): destruction of environment, chemical and fine dust contamination, poverty, exploitation of people, illnesses (cancer), etc.
- Probably more than 1.5bn people are working within this chain from raw material exploitation to the owner of a car, the car maintenance and final recycling of the cars.

- 3-3.5 billion cars on this planet by the year 2050 are just unsustainable at every level.

Crimes and Corruption

- The revenue of organized crime worldwide is estimated at $2 trillion.
- World spending on illegal drugs per year: more than $300 billion.
- Corruption: $5 trillion, approximately 5% of the world's Gross Domestic Product (GDP).
- Around the globe 43% of companies are affected by economic crime (corruption).
- The financial damages of all kind of crimes worldwide are exorbitant: trillions of dollars!
- The administrative costs of all kind of crimes worldwide are exorbitant: trillion of dollars!
- The global prison costs are exorbitant: trillions of dollars!

Military and Wars

- Global military expenditure per year: $1.7 trillion [1]
- Global military expenditures in January 2011; means during one month: $3,200 million.
- Cost of Iraq War (2001-2010) plus war in Afghanistan: over $1 trillion.
- The US Military: 1,000 military bases in 130 countries and another 6.000 bases on US-territory.

Unemployment and Underemployment

- In many countries the rate of unemployment is disastrous: 8-30% and up to 30-50% of the youth do not have a job.
- Hundreds of millions worldwide do not have a job.
- More than one billion of people are underemployed.
- 80% of workers in the industrial nations are scared of losing their job and see no future perspectives.
- Many well educated professionals are finding it difficult if not impossible to find a decent and suitable job or they are simply underpaid.
- For more and more couples, the creation of a family becomes a financial nightmare.
- Additionally real estate, food, and consumer goods are all becoming more expensive.

---

[1] http://www.globalissues.org/article/75/world-military-spending

Politics and Leaders

- Most politicians have no comprehensive knowledge of the situation of their own people, of humanity and the planet.
- Most politicians have an idea of mankind from the Middle Ages.
- Most politicians are unable to think in complex networks, oriented in the past and the future.
- Most politicians are artists in exaggerating, understating, sweet talking, glossing over, lying, cheating, forging, seducing, manipulating, maneuvering and coming to terms.
- There are hundreds of thousands of CEOs, owners of corporate groups, politicians and religious leaders that have acted since centuries with their megalomania, paternalism, extreme greed, stubbornness, sick narcissism, arrogance, falseness and scrupulousness, perversion, amorality and a religious psychosis or political lunacy.
- Most politicians misuse God and religion for their perverse political games. They violate all the values that the earlier pioneers in their own people fought so hard to get.
- Most politicians do not want any truth. Therefore, they are never in the position to solve the big (economic) problems in their own country, let alone the critical state of humanity and the earth.

The Rich and the Rest

- The 20% richest population disposes of 75% of the global income.
- World's richest 1% own 40% of all wealth.
- The next decade the world needs 100 trillion more credit.
- 80% of the earth population lives on less than $10 per day.
- 1-1.2 billion people live in really good economic conditions.
- 3.4 billion people disposes of 1% of the world's wealth.

Mental Disasters

- The truth has lost; Lies have taken its place.
- That true good has lost; it can never win by itself.
- Love has lost; People are rotten to their innermost core.
- The inner Spirit of humans barely stands a chance anymore.
- All genuine human values are ignored.
- Billions are dehumanized and some rulers already converted into another monstrous species.
- All Archetypes of the Soul have been raped, abused, and completely destroyed.

- More than 6.5 billion people are brainwashed and deformed in their soul. They are trapped in dark psychical and spiritual labyrinths, in pathogenic narcissism, in neurosis or psychopathy, in obsession and greed, in lies and falseness, in political and religious psychosis, in stupidity, in arrogance and ignorance.

Conclusion for Economics

Considering the state of humanity and the earth we see the actual science of economics and the governmental management of the economy as nothing more than a children's playground. Or is it an absolute evil construction of monsters with a plan?

An economic science that ignores all of these dimensions of humans and economic reality, which certainly have an immense economic impact, is radically ignorant, absolutely irrelevant, and a waste of intelligence, time and of the trillions of Dollars and Euros it wastes at a very extreme human cost!

Diagram: Mere Prognosis or Prophecy?

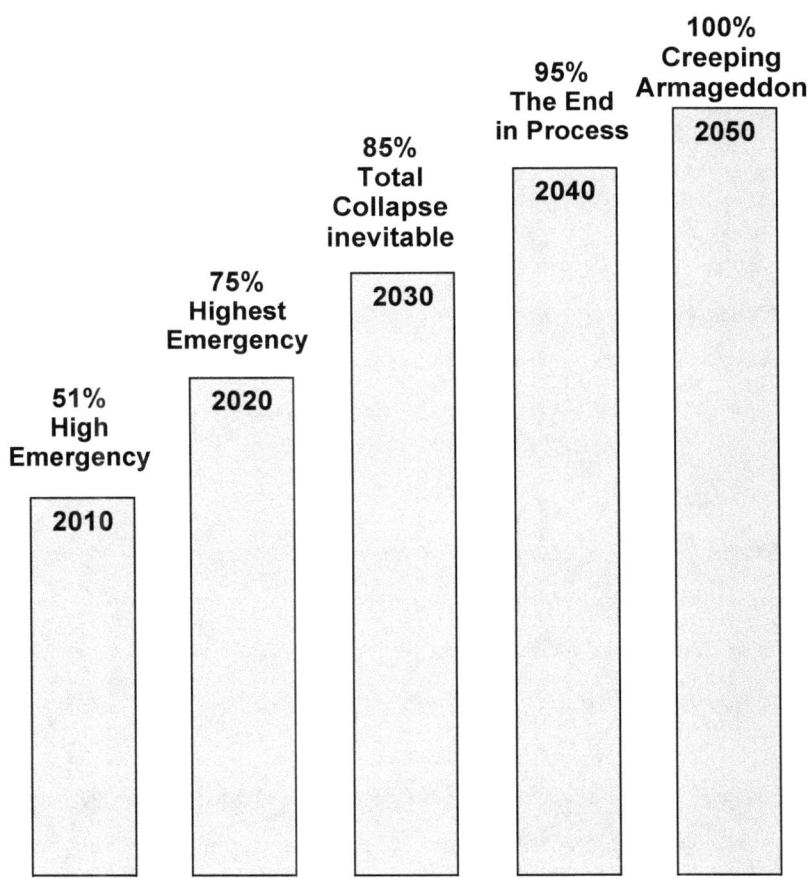

Comment: Obviously all the facts and figures detailed above change with the years and become quite different under the view of a single country's economy. [2]

---

[2] See: Schellhammer, Economics III

1.6. Letter from an Anonymous Billionaire

Dear Occupy Wall Street,

You appear so heroic, you call yourself patriotic, you shout and criticize, you divide and label into the 99% versus the 1%. You resist, you stay, and you will not call it a day. I hate to break it to you, but you haven't got the slightest clue about what really happened, what is really going on and what will definitely be next, let alone how to solve the big problems facing humanity.

Let's start where your problem lies: the 1%. Here is a reality check: The 1% made it to the 1% because they are smarter than you, meaner than you, bigger than you, stronger than you, more dedicated than you, more visionary than you, more strategic than you, more convinced than you or better informed than you... But most importantly, they made it because of you – the 99%! It is your fault!

You let it happen, you contributed, you supported, you admired, you worshipped, you followed, you bought, you were too lazy to ask, you were too naïve to question, you were too ignorant to look, you were too busy to find out, you were too stupid to do otherwise, you were too hypocritical to challenge... As the saying goes, "it always takes two to Tango".

Unfortunately, the 1% at the top (including myself) has zero interest in what only boils down to whining, winging, crying, moaning and pestering. So if you really want change, you really want a new era, start with yourselves! Everything you are doing up to now is merely a false alibi.

Let me give it to you black on white: Demonstrations, activism, hacking, protesting, rioting, shouting, gathering, donating, charity, believing, hoping, wishing or putting faith in others are all roads that lead to nowhere. If you really want to do something that leads to change, question yourselves, find out what you did, where you went wrong, what you contributed, what part you played and how your deficits, prejudices, stubbornness, ignorance and naivety paved the way for today's status quo.

All this aside, I will lay the cards on the table for you: There's something big in store… We have a problem; it's kind of a big problem. The problem has been apparent to us (the 1%) for a long time. The problem is global and it threatens both our planet and humanity as a species. The problem is simple: We the human race have destroyed the planet; contamination, pollution, environmental destruction, climate change, global warming, degrading food supplies, running out of resources, lack of drinking water, depletion of the ocean's fish reserves… As a human race we face a challenge and that is that with current resources and a population that has recently passed 7 billion people, it is only a matter of time before the whole system collapses – forever.

The intricacy of the matter however, is that although we've known for a long time, you the people, the 99%; are too stupid to listen, too greedy to give in, too stubborn to change, too obsessed to see alternatives, too lazy to learn. Somewhere in between we've had infiltrators on both sides that have played us out against each other. Effectively, the result has been that nothing could be solved and so the 1% got richer and the 99% poorer. The problem takes on a complexity when you go beyond borders. China, Russia, India, Brazil and other nations including those in Africa and the Middle East are suddenly getting 'wiser' and 'less tolerant'. Regardless of what you believe to know about history, the truth is probably far from what you have in mind. The reality is that you the 99% are actually the 1% when seen from a global perspective. You've lived nearly a century of joy, well being, pleasure, and all this worry-free – all at the expense of the rest of the world and ultimately at the expense of the planet.

Unfortunately, out of the 7 billion people living on this planet today, most if not 99.9% are too obsessed, too possessed, too brainwashed, too stubborn, too lazy, too ignorant, too stupid and too naïve to see the problem, let alone let themselves be guided to a solution. This leaves those at the top (around the globe) with only one solution; play you sheep out against each other. Decades of top-notch propaganda, false news, hyped up lies, hollow promises and delusional charades have been at work for one purpose and one purpose only – that is the Great War of the 21st Century, also to go down in history as World War 3.

Billions will die, power will shift and that which remains will be hard at work to ensure life can go on for the survivors in a new form. What can I say; you all were too busy, you all were too ignorant, you all were too quick to jump on a bandwagon... You asked for it and you will get it, all of you, regardless of race, religion, sex, age, or nationality... You are all responsible.

So my message to you is this: If you are really serious about changing the status quo then look, analyze, learn and put together the pieces. Free yourself from stupidity, narcissism, social norms, brainwashed ideas, naïve admiration, dogmatic indoctrination, prejudiced ideals, greedy wants, superficial values and questionable morals. Once you've figured it out, spread the message! All other roads lead to WWIII.

The good news is that the choice really is yours!

Sincerely,
Anonymous Billionaire

2. Economic Definitions

2.1. Some Definitions

Households

Countless dictionaries and books about economics relate the word 'economy' to the Greek word **'oikonomos'**, which means 'management of a **household'**. Mankiw & Taylor explain: "Household and **economy** have much in common ... A household faces many decisions ... a household must allocate its **scarce** resources among various members, taking into account each member's abilities, efforts and desires." [3] And the authors compare: "Like a household, a society faces many decisions ... once society has allocated people (as well as land, buildings and machines) ... it must also allocate the output of goods and services that they produce... It must decide (who gets what)." [4] **Economics** is the study how society manages its scarce resource." [5]

The term **'oikonomos'** [6] is used with different focuses: e.g. the one who manages a household, family, and the management of (all kind of) domestic affairs. What is a home without people? An empty home is not of interest to economics because no human needs and wants are there. Logically we can say: Aims and actors of all **household affairs** (**economics**) are humans and it is about their life. Therefore human's mind and human values must play an extremely important role in all matters of economics. Putting both components together, we can conclude: The narrower the understanding of humans is in the economic concepts and theories, the higher is the probability that such concepts and theories must fail in the real world.

Krugman uses the term **'housework'**, which is not necessarily the same as 'household'. [7] Maybe there is a slight difference between household and housework. Household includes the people and the goods, and housework preponderates the management of a household (by people).

We put the pieces together. 'Household' always means:

Economics = People + House + Management

---

[3] Mankiw (et al.), p. 2
[4] Mankiw (et al.), p. 2
[5] Mankiw (et al.), p. 2
[6] http://www.thefreedictionary.com/economy
[7] Krugman (et al.), p. 1

In a more general way the indispensable network is:

Economics = People + Basket of Goods + Management

Krugman describes the term **economy** as the "…system for coordinating productive activities … that create the goods and services people want and get them to the people who want them." The author specifies: "An economy succeeds to the extent that it, literally, delivers the goods."

"… **Economics** is the social science that studies the production, distribution, and consumption of goods and services". Krugman [8] And more about economics: "All economic analysis is based on a set of common principles…" [9]

Market economy is characterized by "… production and consumption are a result of decentralized decisions by many firms and individuals." [10]

Economics = Studies + Production + Distribution + Consumption + Goods and Services

Economy = A system + Coordinating + Productive Activities + Goods and Services + Needs and Wants

The "**command economy** … is a central authority making decisions about production and consumption." This boring difference is on an ideological level and an over-simplification of reality (of the past). It hides the fact that a direct or indirect governmental intervention in the free market is also a subtle 'command factor'. It is a fallacy to think that the 'free market' is really free. It is also a blatant idealization of market realities in the Western free market world. One should not be a coward and instead tell the truth about the economy: Money rules the economy! Who has the big money? And it is a distortion to say that everything in the planned market (up to 1991; in the Soviet Union) was really a planned matter.

"… people quite casually trust their lives to the market system." And the author comments: "The unplanned 'chaos' of a market economy turns out to be far more orderly that the 'planning of a command economy'." [11]
Colander has his special definition about economics: "Economics is the study of how humans coordinate their wants and desires, given the decision-making

---

[8] Krugman (et al.), p. 1
[9] Krugman (et al.), p. 2
[10] Krugman (et al.), p. 2
[11] Krugman (et al.), p. 2

mechanisms, social customs, and political realities of the society." [12] With 'coordination' he means: 1) What and how much to produce? 2) How to produce it? 3) For whom to produce it? [13] Part of the study is how these three problems are solved.

This definition presumes: People coordinate their needs and wants. Do they? How do they do this? We will analyze this coordination.

"Economics is all about how groups and individuals make choices and why they choose the things they do." And later on the author continues: "Economics is about human beings choosing among limited options to maximize happiness."

A bit later on he explains more about happiness: "Economists like to think of human beings as free agents, with free wills … people are fully rational and capable of deciding things on their own …The basic motivation driving most people most of the time is a desire to be happy."

Here the statements are completely hyped up: "Economics is all about how groups and individuals make choices." Does this statement really cover the reality of economics in the world? No! Absolutely not! Such a view misleads the reader and lets him run around in a dark labyrinth without exit; or let's say: the reproduction of such sick blabber in academic exams is the only exit. The next statement says that humans choose among limited options to maximize happiness. Again we identify here a very big lie. And the psychotic theatre continues: human beings have a free will; human beings are fully rational and capable of deciding… And the basic motivation is a desire to be happy. Such scientific statements are not only wrong, but manipulate the readers (students, 18-22 years old), but it also shows the perverse attitude of the authors in lying, cheating, deceiving and heating up a distorted picture about human beings. This is way beyond moral and integrity. [14]

Making Choices

"… people must make choices, sometimes difficult ones, is in the end what economics is about." [15]

"Every question in economics at its most basic level involves individuals making choices." [16] We consider this statement as a platitude. All the time and

---

[12] Colander, p. 4
[13] Colander, p. 5
[14] Antonioni, p. 27
[15] McDowell (et al.), preface xviii

at any moment in life humans take decisions, except when they sleep. 'Making choices' is primordially a topic of psychology. Whatever people do, every start of a movement involves making choices, including innumerable kind of movements that have nothing to do with economics. As everybody takes decisions all the time (when awake), it's logical that the entire humanity, today 7 billion people take decisions all the time and therefore the interactions between humans, whatever kind of interaction, we can see as a huge network of decision making processes.

"The key to a much better standard of living for everyone is trade." The author comments: "People divide task among themselves and each person provides a good or service that other people want in return for different goods and services that he or she wants." And: "There are gains from trade." And more explanation: "This increase in output is due to specialization: each person specializes in the task he or she is good at performing." That's why the economy as a whole can produce more.

This is a very strong statement! In other words the authors say: The way people make choice is what the economy is about. The economic experts unmask themselves here. Obviously: if economics knows the ways people (must) make choices, then they can manipulate these ways of making choices. The word 'must' is a sign what economics is about; for example: How can economics force people to make their choice towards a direction the market wants. Or: How can a study book about economics force (manipulate) the way of economic thinking of their students. We already identify with such definitions: The link between humans and the goods and services consists in needs and wants and choices. [17]

Economics = People + Needs and Wants + Choices

Above that we can already conclude: a majority of the content in classical books about economics we can forget; it's not about economics. What then is it about? We will find it out. But we will never find it visible in the classical books and theories about economics; maybe we will find it hidden in the safe of the IMF or the World Bank. The devil likes covering himself behind the small details.

'Individual **Choice**' is the core of economics: "… decisions by an individual about what to do and what not to do." [18] The author shows another view of

---

[16] Krugman (et al.), p. 1
[17] Krugman (et al.), p. 11-12
[18] Krugman (et al.), p. 4

economics: "Fundamentally (economics) is a **way of thinking** about the **world**." And: "Our basic premise is that a small number of basic **principles** do most of the heavy lifting in economics..." [19] We have here another approach to determine economics:

Economics = Choice + A way of Thinking + Principles + World

We will explore step-by-step the 'way of thinking about the world'. One line is formed by the authors of some classical economic books (used to teach students). The way the authors deal with words (terms) shows us how they think about the world. Another line is marked by the consumer's mind and behavior: How mind and behavior is 'working'. And a third line is given through the fact of astronomic damages of humans, of humanity, of the world and the planet with its ecosystems due to the capitalistic understanding of economics ('the households').

A new element must be added to economics: "**The invisible hand** ... (means) the way in which the individual pursuit of self-interest can lead to good results for society as a whole." [20] We will discuss this strange 'invisible hand' (Adam Smith) later on here.

We identified the following mixture of definitions about economics:

Economics = People + House + Management
Economics = People + Basket of Goods + Management
Economics = Study + Teaching + Research of all areas of economics
Economics = Production + Distribution + Consumption + Goods and Services
Economics = People + Needs and Wants + Choices
Economics = Choice + A way of Thinking + Principles + World
Economics = To add: The Invisible Hand

And the Economy refers to a country or area and is determined with:

Economy = System + Coordination + Productive Activities + Goods and Services + Needs and Wants

---

[19] McDowell (et al.), p. 1
[20] Krugman (et al.), p. 3

The Lines that give Direction

- Way of using words together with thinking in economics
- How the mind and behavior of people is operating
- The world with its raw resources, goods and services
- Benefits and damages produced by the implemented economics
- Ways of interactions (correlations) of all components

We could also regroup the world of economics:

- The 'Household' is the living area of people practicing a certain 'Management' of their life.
- The 'People' have 'Needs and Wants', have a 'Way of Thinking and Choosing', and 'Consume'.
- The 'World' is the source of all 'Raw Resources' and is the environment for living (the households).
- The 'Basket of Goods' is a certain amount of 'Goods and Services', always 'scarce' (limited).
- The Goods and Services need a well organized 'Distribution' network.
- There are the 'Fields of Production' (consist in labor, education, intelligence, etc.; later on to explore)
- There are 'Principles' expressing the ways these groups are operating and interacting.
- The 'Economy' is any area as a unity encompassing all the real matters of economic interest.

The Positive Approach

'Positive' is related to the way of practicing science and means: "… the study of what is, and how the economy works." [21] Or: "Positive economics focuses on facts and cause-and-effect relationships." [22]

The Normative Approach

'Normative' means "the study of what the goals of the economy should be." [23] Or: "Normative economics incorporates value judgments about what the economy should be like or what particular policy actions should be recommended to achieve desirable or certain aspects of the economy." [24]

---

[21] Colander, p. 18
[22] McConnell (et al.), p. 7
[23] Colander, p. 18
[24] McDonnell (et al.), p. 7

The Political Approach

Political economy, also called 'art of economics' is the "application of the knowledge from the economic science." [25] The application here is related on the one side to knowledge and on the other side to the goals of the normative economic science.

Colander makes it clear: "Politicians, not economists determine economic policy." [26]

From this point of view we have three sections of economics that form a unity. If we take away for example the normative approach, we will have a highly reduced understanding of economics and the real economy. If we take away the political approach, the economy becomes an uncontrolled chaotic economy and economic science. If the positive (descriptive) approach fails, then it produces misleading and highly reduced pictures about what economics is in the concrete global economy.

Therefore we can conclude a premise for the economic science: Economic science must always include all three perspectives. De facto this does not happen; not in reality and not in the classical scientific books used today in the university's programs of economics and business (as we elaborate here)!

Does everybody agree now with this premise for the science of economics?

Critical Questions

If a government with astronomic debt depends on private economic institutions (banks, investors), who have the say about the goals of political economy?

If the politicians are formed under the terms of economic science, without understanding all the ideological traps and neurotic constructions, how do they take decisions in the economy?

If a majority of economic experts are rather neurotic, narcissistic and distorted in human values, how is their way of thinking and with that how do they understand and develop economics?

If politicians have (which they need) economic experts, trained by the classical

---

[25] Colander, p. 18
[26] Colander, p. 19

economic studies, how do the politicians shape an action in the economy and how do they take decisions?

If the concentration of immense amounts of money leads to a specific group of people how do they influence the economy and the study programs of economics?

If the claim 'highest profit with lowest cost' becomes a premise of the business world and of economics, how is the science of economics constructed?

If politicians and ministers are psychically and spiritually not developed and if they have an archaic understanding of what a human is, how will they determine the goals of the economy?

Diagram: The World of Economics at First Sight

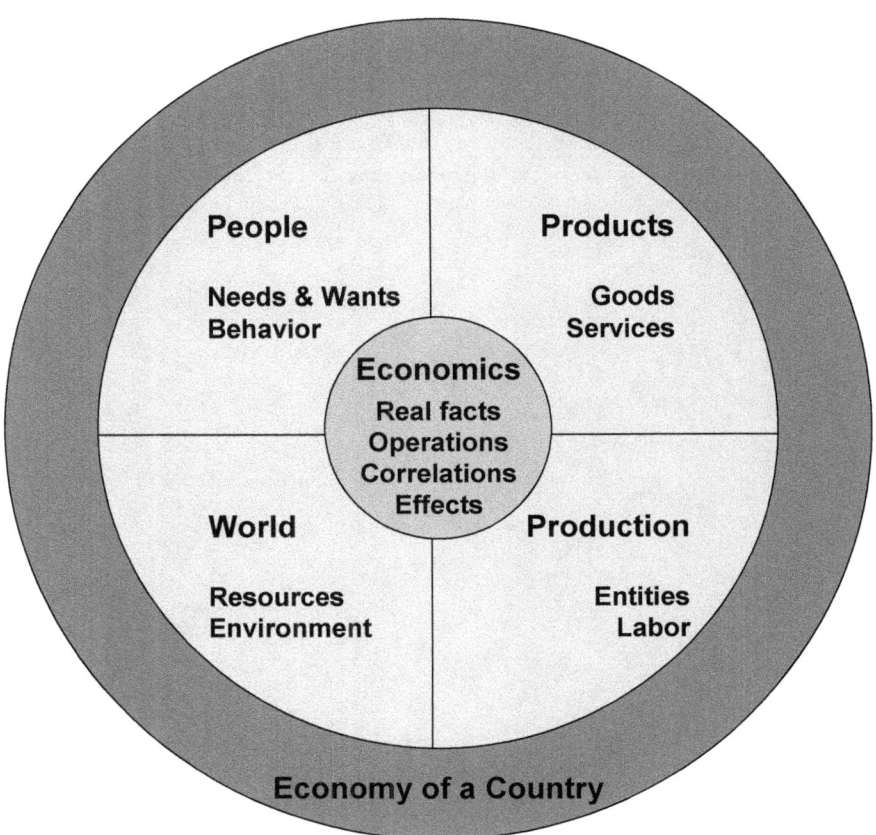

Fundamental Facts

- The world can exist without humans.
- The world with everything is limited.
- Human's life is limited.
- The planet isn't for an unlimited amount of people
- Humans have a mind and human values.
- Humans have needs and wants.
- Human's economic behavior is decisive.
- Products and services are for humans to use.
- Production is not possible without humans.
- Production is not possible without resources.
- Production processes occur within an entity.
- Economics is for humans and their life.
- Humans are the actors of economics.
- Humans are the beginning and goal of economics.
- Humans are responsible for all effects of their doing.

Conclusion

➔ Economics must consider all these fundamental facts!
➔ It doesn't make sense to destroy humanity and the planet!

2.2. The Elements of Manifold Economic Definitions

Everybody can find on the internet and in many books about economics a variety of definitions and descriptions about 'economics' and the 'economy'. In this chapter we summarize and categorize the manifold elements forming part of such definitions.

Fundamental Aims

- Identifying and allocating scarcity
- To satisfy the demand for goods and services

General Areas

- The components of a system or structure in the economy
- The interplay between the components of a system or structure in the economy
- The real areas: business entities, location, area, country or other terrestrial areas

Substantial Fields

- Manufacturing, production, trade, services
- Raw resources and land resources
- Distribution (Allocation)
- Consumption of goods and services
- Finances, investments, income, expenditure
- Labor

Human Activities in the Substantial Fields

- Establishing structures and tools (for the aims)
- Production and services
- Money related to production and services
- Management of aims, structures and processes

- Management of natural resources
- Decision making processes
- Distribution (allocation), exchange
- Consumption of goods and services
- All kind of internal activities
- Research and development

Normative-operational Meaning

- Careful, orderly, efficient, skillful management
- Avoiding collateral damages (no externalities)
- Economizing costs
- Optimizing profit
- Avoiding waste of time and effort
- Sparing and restrained use of (i.e. resources)
- Achieving maximum effect with minimum effort
- Equilibrium in a micro- or a macro-system
- Determining how scarce resources are allocated
- Saving money by spending less
- Free-market or planned market

Systemic Principles

- Demand and supply between participants regulate the system
- Individuals and society decide about scarcities
- The limitedness of everything on this planet
- Trust between the participants makes everything work

Exterior Frames

- Sociology
- History
- Anthropology
- Geography
- Government

Re-Construction of Economics

A science has a structure, starts always with a general description of its entire field. Some fields are huge, and others small, but indispensable. Many parts of a science are linked with elements or fields of other sciences. There are always different methodical ways how to proceed in exploring the field of a science (as an introduction). We could start with the most important fields or the most fundamental principles, or the essential terms that the science uses.

As for economics we could start with some elemental facts, quasi axioms that form the economic system. The most important entities (fields, systems, pillars) of economics and the modern economy are: [27]

- Money (Monetary Systems, Money Flow; primordial Good for all)
- Electricity (Energy; is a primordial Good for all Entities)
- Raw Resources (vivid, non-vivid, food and non-food)
- Labor (Manpower, Worker, Management, Education)
- Consumers (Needs, Wants, Demand, Mind, Behavior)
- Production (Goods, Services) and Offers on the Market
- Distribution (Allocation), Scarcity Incidents (local, regional, national)
- Trade and Sale Proceedings (includes: Price Management)
- Government (Ethics, Rules, Regulations, Laws, Control)
- Government's Needs, Wants, Possessions, Spending
- Environment (Planet with all the Ecosystems and the Societies)
- Structures and Power Holders of Entities (operating these Systems)

An economy doesn't work properly if one of these systems would fail or gets ignored by the economic science. For all these entities special terms, parameters, and ways of interdependences (structures) exist. We will conclude from all the following critical analysis that economics must re-structure itself in such a way because there are misuses of terms, hidden ideological premises, lack of transparence of meanings; useless and misleading lump-sum parameters, additionally many ignored human factors, human values, ethical importance, ignored very costly collateral effects, and everywhere a confusing chaos in the constructions.

---

[27] http://www.theyrule.net

2.3. The Masters of the Economy

Key Industries depending on Oil/Gas, Electricity, and Banks

Thesis: The key industries provide society with the goods people and the government need and want. They all depend on oil/gas, electricity, and banks. The key industries are an immense source of making high profit. As money rules the world, the masters of the economy primordially rule the sectors oil/gas, electricity, and banks.

Conclusions about Profit:

→ The higher the collective demand, the higher the profit
→ The higher the mass production, the higher the profit
→ The higher the mass consumption, the higher the profit
→ The lower the wages and conditions of production, the higher the profit
→ The lower the prices of raw materials, the higher the profit
→ The lower the environmental respect, the higher the profit
→ The more extensive robot operation, the higher the profit
→ The broader the mass media marketing, the higher the profit
→ Corporate groups aim at any cost for highest possible profit
→ Corporate groups tend to expand and aim to increase of profit
→ The bigger the independence from governments, the higher the profit

- Society works only with oil/gas, electricity and especially with the banks.
- If these industries depend on loans from banks, the banks have a say.
- The banks have a say over oil/gas industry and electricity industry.
- The owners of the banks, the oil industry and the electricity form a united power.
- This united power also holds power in most of the key industries which is proven.
- The rulers own the banks and the industry and therefore dictate governments.
- An estimated 500 rulers and 6000 managers rule the entire capitalistic coalition and most of the world (proven!).
- It works only with a corresponding education, brainwashing and manipulation.

- If there is little, low or no demand, then demand must be created or stimulated.

A government with high debt is not free and therefore is not a democracy!

The Large Families that Rule the World [28]

Some people have started realizing that there are large financial groups that dominate the world. Forget the political intrigues, conflicts, revolutions and wars. It is not pure chance. Everything has been planned for a long time.

Some call it 'conspiracy theories' or New World Order. Anyway, the key to understanding the current political and economic events is a restricted core of families who have accumulated huge amounts of wealth and power.

We are speaking about 6, 8 or maybe 12 families who truly dominate the world. Know that it is a mystery difficult to unravel.

We will not be far from the truth by citing Goldman Sachs, Rockefellers, Loebs Kuh and Lehmans in New York, the Rothschilds of Paris and London, the Warburgs of Hamburg, Paris and Lazards Israel Moses Seifs Rome.

Many people have heard of the Bilderberg Group, Illuminati or the Trilateral Commission. But what are the names of the families who run the world and have control of states and international organizations like the UN, NATO or the IMF?

To try to answer this question, we can start with the easiest: inventory, the world's largest banks, and see who the shareholders are and who make the decisions. The world's largest companies are now: Bank of America, JP Morgan, Citigroup, Wells Fargo, Goldman Sachs and Morgan Stanley.

Let us now review who their shareholders are:

Bank of America: State Street Corporation, Vanguard Group, BlackRock, FMR (Fidelity), Paulson, JP Morgan, T. Rowe, Capital World Investors, AXA, Bank of NY, Mellon.

JP Morgan: State Street Corp., Vanguard Group, FMR, BlackRock, T. Rowe, AXA, Capital World Investor, Capital Research Global Investor, Northern

---

[28] http://english.pravda.ru/business/finance/18-10-2011/119355-The_Large_Families_that_rule_the_world-0/ - 18.10.2011

Trust Corp. and Bank of Mellon.

Citigroup: State Street Corporation, Vanguard Group, BlackRock, Paulson, FMR, Capital World Investor, JP Morgan, Northern Trust Corporation, Fairhome Capital Mgmt and Bank of NY Mellon.

Wells Fargo: Berkshire Hathaway, FMR, State Street, Vanguard Group, Capital World Investors, BlackRock, Wellington Mgmt, AXA, T. Rowe and Davis Selected Advisers.

We can see that now there appears to be a nucleus present in all banks: State Street Corporation, Vanguard Group, BlackRock and FMR (Fidelity). To avoid repeating them, we will now call them the 'big four' Goldman Sachs: 'The big four,' Wellington, Capital World Investors, AXA, Massachusetts Financial Service and T. Rowe.

Morgan Stanley: 'The big four,' Mitsubishi UFJ, Franklin Resources, AXA, T. Rowe, Bank of NY Mellon e Jennison Associates. Rowe, Bank of NY Mellon and Jennison Associates.

We can just about always verify the names of major shareholders. To go further, we can now try to find out the shareholders of these companies and shareholders of major banks worldwide.

Bank of NY Mellon: Davis Selected, Massachusetts Financial Services, Capital Research Global Investor, Dodge, Cox, Southeastern Asset Mgmt. and ... 'The big four.'

State Street Corporation (one of the 'big four'): Massachusetts Financial Services, Capital Research Global Investor, Barrow Hanley, GE, Putnam Investment and ... The 'big four' (shareholders themselves!).

BlackRock (another of the 'big four'): PNC, Barclays e CIC.

Who is behind the PNC? FMR (Fidelity), BlackRock, State Street, etc.

And behind Barclays? BlackRock?

And we could go on for hours, passing by tax havens in the Cayman Islands, Monaco or the legal domicile of Shell companies in Liechtenstein. A network where companies are always the same, but never a name of a family.

In short: the eight largest U.S. financial companies (JP Morgan, Wells Fargo,

Bank of America, Citigroup, Goldman Sachs, U.S. Bancorp, Bank of New York Mellon and Morgan Stanley) are 100% controlled by ten shareholders and we have four companies always present in all decisions: BlackRock, State Street, Vanguard and Fidelity.

In addition, the Federal Reserve is comprised of 12 banks, represented by a board of seven people, which comprises representatives of the 'big four,' which in turn are present in all other entities. In short, the Federal Reserve is controlled by four large private companies: BlackRock, State Street, Vanguard and Fidelity. These companies control U.S. monetary policy (and world) without any control or 'democratic' choice. These companies launched and participated in the current worldwide economic crisis and managed to become even more enriched.

To finish, a look at some of the companies controlled by this 'big four' group: Alcoa Inc. / Altria Group Inc. / American International Group Inc. / AT&T Inc. / Boeing Co. / Caterpillar Inc. / Coca-Cola Co. / DuPont & Co. / Exxon Mobil Corp. / General Electric Co. / General Motors Corporation / Hewlett-Packard Co. / Home Depot Inc. / Honeywell International Inc. / Intel Corp. / International Business Machines Corp / Johnson & Johnson / JP Morgan Chase & Co. / McDonald's Corp. / Merck & Co. Inc. / Microsoft Corp. / 3M Co. / Pfizer Inc. / Procter & Gamble Co. / United Technologies Corp. / Verizon Communications Inc. / Wal-Mart Stores Inc. / Time Warner / Walt Disney / Viacom / Rupert Murdoch's News Corporation / CBS Corporation / NBC Universal

The same 'big four' control the vast majority of European companies listed on the stock exchange. In addition, all these people run the large financial institutions, such as the IMF, the European Central Bank or the World Bank, and were 'trained' and remain 'employees' of the 'big four' that formed them. The names of the families that control the 'big four' never appear.

The Elite Controls the Global Economy
(It's not just a conspiracy theory!)

Bankers really do control the world! That's according to Swiss researchers who, in an exhaustive scientific study, mapped out a blueprint showing the real architects of global economic power.

From freemasons to the Council on Foreign Relations to Bilderberg, the belief that secretive groups control the world's economic and political systems are possibly as old as human civilization itself.

But while Occupy Wall Street protestors may be slightly exaggerating in calling themselves the 99 per cent, a recent study conducted by the Swiss Institute of Technology in Zurich shows that they aren't too far off the mark.

Drawing from a 2007 Orbis database, which lists 37 million companies and investors spanning the globe, the researchers focused on 43,000 transnational corporations and the share ownership which connected them. Based on their analysis, the Swiss team found that a core of companies, the majority of which are in the banking sector, yield excessive power over the global economy, the weekly New Scientist magazine reports.

Within this group, 1,318 companies with intertwined ownership structures were on average connected to 20 other companies.

Representing some 20% of global operating revenues, the study also shows this group of 1,318 controls the bulk of the largest blue chip and manufacturing firms. In terms of the real economy – the part which produces actual goods and services – they take in some 60% of global revenues.

The team was further able to break down this group into what they described as a 'super-entity' of 147 companies that controls some 40% of the network's wealth.

"In effect, less than one per cent of the companies were able to control 40 per cent of the entire network," says James Glattfelder, one of the researchers behind the study, as cited by the New Scientist.

And when it comes to the top 50 groups within the super-entity, more than a few would be familiar to those who have been camping out in downtown Manhattan over the last month.

Bank of America Corporation, Morgan Stanley, Goldman Sachs Group Inc, Merrill Lynch & Co Inc, and JP Morgan Chase & Co were included among the top 25.

Quick to dismiss criticism that they are merely concocting another conspiracy theory, Glattfelder insists that their research is evidence-based.

"Reality is so complex, we must move away from dogma, whether it's conspiracy theories or free-market," says James Glattfelder. "Our analysis is reality-based", he said, as cited by the weekly.

Money Makes Money

The most recent study of the Swiss researchers builds on past economic theories, which also recognized such systemic concentrations of wealth.

In 1906, an Economist named Vilfredo Pareto discovered that around 20% of the population in his native Italy controlled around 80% of the land. This observation has come to be known as Pareto's Principle.

Pareto also found that while individual ratios of wealth and control might vary from country to country, the actual distribution is always the same. That is to say, natural wealth, regardless of human effort, tends to accumulate rather than spread around. That accumulation leads to wealth condensation, a theory more commonly understood as the idea that money makes money. And if less than one per cent of the surveyed companies control 40% of the network, it appears that a slim few have managed to concentrate an astronomical level of wealth into their few hands.

For the researchers, however, the issue of wealth concentration is less important than how deeply the network is integrated.

As the 2008 financial crisis has shown, when a relatively small group yields tremendous power over the global economy, their mistakes will ripple across the world.

Ultimately, those invested in studying the network which controls the bigger part of our world economy hope that through greater understanding, they will be able to make the financial system more stable.

For example, Yaneer Bar-Yam, head of the New England Complex Systems Institute, has suggested taxing firms if their interconnectivity becomes excessive in order to discourage risk, the New Scientists reports. Others have proposed global anti-trust laws to help regulate the level of connectivity.

One question not answered by the study is just how much political power the financial elite are able to wield. John Driffill, a macroeconomics expert at the University of London, told the New Scientist that the interests of 147 companies would most likely be too diverse to sustain collusion.

But while the capitalist network which controls our economy might not be an active conspiracy, they will inevitably have some interests that correspond. The desire to fight any attempts to regulate the network most likely remains a point they can all agree on. [29]

The Rich 'one percent' in the USA

Fortune 500 has issued a list of S&P 500 companies along with their 2010 financial details. Along with American billionaires and millionaires, the 500 companies are believed to form a main part of the 'One Percent' rich in America. Recent anti-Wall Street protesters blame the One Percent for their desperate economic situation. (Forbes 2011)

Who is the One Percent in America?	Diversified Financials	Commercial Banks
The following are the largest full-service global investment banks which usually provides both advisory and financing banking services, as well as the sales, market making, and research on a broad array of financial products including equities, credit, rates, currency, commodities, and their derivatives.	The following are the top eight diversified financials in the U.S. in terms of revenue in 2010.	The following are the top ten commercial banks in the U.S. in terms of revenue in 2010. Fortune 500
1. Bank of America	1. Fannie Mae .... $153.82 billion	1. Bank of America $134.19 billion
2. Barclays Capital	2. General Electric ...... $151.62 billion	2. JP Morgan Chase $115.47 billion
3. Citigroup	3. Freddie Mac .... $98.36 billion	3. Citigroup .... $111.05 billion
4. Credit Suisse	4. INTL FCStone .... $46.94 billion	4. Well Fargo .... $93.24 billion
5. Deutsche Bank	5. Marsh & McLennan ...... $10.93 billion	5. Goldman Sachs Group $45.96 billion
6. Goldman Sachs	6. Ameriprise Financial ..... $10.04 billion	6. Morgan Stanley .... $39.32 billion
7. JPMorgan Chase	7. Aon .... $8.51 billion	7. American Express .... $30.24 billion
8. Morgan Stanley	8. SLM .... $6.77 billion	8. US Bancorp .... $20.51 billion
9. Nomura Securities	**Oil & Gas Equipment, Services**	9. Capital One Financial ..$19.06 billion
10. UBS	The following are the top U.S. firms active in oil and gas equipment and services in terms of revenue in 2010. Fortune 500	10. Ally Financial .... $17.37 billion
11. Wells Fargo Securities	1. Halliburton .... $17.97 million	**Aerospace & Defense**
Petroleum Refining	2. Baker Hughes .... $14.41 million	The following are the top ten U.S. corporations in aerospace and defense in terms of revenue in 2010.
The following are the top ten U.S. petroleum refining firms in terms of revenue in 2010. Fortune 500	3. National Oilwell Varco ..$12.15 million	1. Boeing .... $64.30 billion
1. Exxon Mobil .... $354.67 billion	4. Cameron International ...$6.13 million	2. United Technologies .... $54.32 billion
2. Chevron .... $196.33 billion	**Motor Vehicles & Parts**	3. Lockheed Martin .... $46.89 billion
3. Conoco Philips .... $184.96 billion	The following are the top ten U.S. manufacturing	4. Northrop Grumman ......

[29] http://rt.com/news/global-elite-economy-conspiracy-427/
http://arxiv.org/PS_cache/arxiv/pdf/1107/1107.5728v2.pdf
http://www.theyrule.net/

4. Valero Energy .... $86.03 billion 5. Marathon Oil .... $68.41billion 6. Sunoco .... $35.54 billion 7. Hess .... $34.61 billion 8. Murphy Oil .... $23.34 billion 9. Tesoro .... $20.25 billion 10. Holly .... $8.32 billion	companies of motor vehicles and parts in terms of revenue in 2010. 1. General Motors .... $135.59 billion 2. Ford Motor ....$128.95 billion 3. Chrysler Group .... $41.94 billion 4. Johnson Controls .... $34.30 billion 5. Goodyear Tire & Rubber ..$18.83 billion 6. TRW Automotive $14.38 billion 7. Navistar International ... $12.14 billion 8. Lear .... $11.95 billion 9. Paccar .... $10.29 billion 10. Oshkosh .... $9.84 billion	$34.75 billion 5. Honeywell International.. $33.37 billion 6. General Dynamics .... $32.46 billion 7. Raytheon .... $25.18 billion 8. L-3 Communications ..... $15.68 billion 9. ITT .... $11.15 billion 10. Textron .... $10.52 billion

American Millionaires

The number of Americans who are millionaires is about one percent of the population.

Of the 435 members of the House, 244 current members of Congress are millionaires – that's about 46 percent and that includes 138 Republicans and 106 Democrats, according to the Center for Responsive Politics, a nonpartisan watchdog group that tracks money in politics. In fact, there are probably many more millionaires in Congress, since lawmakers don't have to include the value of their family home and other details. [30]

In 2010, the average winner of a House race spent $1.5 million for his/her campaigns. The average Senate winner spent close to $10 million. Closely contested races are much more expensive. And about half of that money, on average, comes from an elite group of very wealthy donors.

Wealthy Americans have more access to lawmakers than most regular voters and constituents do, according to the Center for Responsive Politics. [31]

---

[30] http://abcnews.go.com/blogs/politics/2011/11/47-of-congress-members-millionaires-a-status-shared-by-only-1-of-americans/
[31] http://www.npr.org/2011/09/20/140627334/millionaires-in-congress-weigh-new-tax-on-wealthy

The median net worth for a current member of the U.S. House of Representatives was $725,000 in 2009, according to the Center for Responsive Politics, and the media net worth of a U.S. Senator was $2.4 million. Open Secrets!

The richest member of Congress is Darrel Issa, whose net worth was valued between $156 million and $451 million. Open Secrets!

Here is a list of the 20 wealthiest current members of Congress and their average net worth, according to the Center for Responsive Politics, based on their financial reports covering calendar year 2009. [32]

The rich members of Congress [33] [34]	Top Donors to Obama in 2008 [35]	American Billionaires [36]
1. Rep. Darrell Issa (R-Calif.) $303m	The following table lists the top donors to Barack Obama in the 2008 election cycle.	The following is a list of top 20 American billionaires issued by the Forbes 400 in 2011.
2. Sen. John Kerry (D-Mass.) $238m		
3. Sen. Mark Warner (D-Va.) $174m	1. University of California .$1.6m million	1. Bill Gates from Microsoft .... $59 billion
4. Rep. Jared Polis (D-Colo.) $160m	2. Goldman Sachs .... $1 million	2. Warren Buffet Berksh. Hathaway .$39bn
5. Sen. Herb Kohl (D-Wis.) $160m	3. Harvard University ....$0.85m million	3. Larry Ellison from Oracle .... $33 billion
6. Rep. Vernon Buchanan (R-Fla.).$148m	4. Microsoft Corp. .... $0.83m million	4. Charles Koch from diversified ....$25 billion
7. Rep. Michael McCaul (R-Texas) $137m	5. Google Inc. .... $0.80 million	5. David Koch from diversified .... $25 billion
8. Sen. James Risch (R-Idaho) $109m	6. Citigroup Inc. .... $0.70 million	6. Christy Walton from Wal-Mart ...$24.5 bn
9. Sen. Jay Rockefeller (D-W.Va.) . $98 m	7. JPMorgan Chase & Co. $0.69m million	7. George Soros from hedge funds . $22 bn
10. Sen. Richard Blumenthal (D-Conn.) $94m	8. Time Warner .... $0.59 million	8. Sheldon Adelson from casinos .$21.5 bn
11. Sen. Dianne Feinstein (D-Calif.) .. $77m	9. Sidley Austin LLP ......$0.58 million	9. Jim Walton from Wal-Mart .... $21.1 bn
12. Sen. Frank Lautenberg (D-N.J.) ...$76m	10. Stanford University ....$0.58 million	10. Alice Walton from Wal-Mart $20.9bn
13. Rep. Nancy Pelosi (D-Calif.) $58m	11. National Amusements $0.55 million	11. S. Robson Walton Wal-Mart $20.5 bn
14. Rep. Gary Miller (R-Calif.) $51m	12. UBS AG .... $0.54 million	12. Michael Bloomberg LP .... $19.5 n
15. Sen. Bob Corker (R-		

[32] http://www.rt.com
[33] http://www.rollcall.com/50richest/
[34] http://www.opensecrets.org/pfds/overview.php
[35]   http://www.guardian.co.uk/world/2008/nov/08/barackobama-wallstreet-bankers-campaign-donations-goldmansachs
[36] http://www.forbes.com/billionaires/list/

Tenn.) $50m	13. Wilmerhale Llp .... $0.54 million	13. Jeff Bezos Amazon.com .... $19.1 bn
16. Rep. Diane Lynn Black (R-Tenn.) $49m	14. Skadden, Arps et al ....$0.53 million	14. Mark Zuckergerg Facebook ......$17.5 bn
17. Rep. Rodney Frelinghuysen (R-N.J.) $43m	15. IBM Corp .... $0.52 million	15. Surgey Brin Google .... $16.7 billion
18. Rep. Richard Berg (R-N.D.) $39m	16. Columbia University .. $0.52 million	16. Larry Page from Google ..... $16.7 billion
19. Rep. Nita Lowey (D-N.Y.) $39m	17. Morgan Stanley .... $0.51 million	17. John Paulson hedge funds .. $15.5 billion
20. Rep. Kenny Marchant (R-Texas) .$38m	18. General Electric .... $0.49 million	18. Michael Dell from Dell ..... $15 billion
	19. U.S. Government ...... $0.49 million	19. Steve Ballmer Microsoft .... $13.9 billion
	20.Latham & Watkins .... $0.49 million	20.Forrest Mars candy .... $13.8 billion

This data does not include the wealth disparity in China, Russia, India and Brazil or the vast inequality of wealth in other countries.

➔ Multi-millionaires and billionaires are the rulers of the economics and indirectly also the rulers of the politics!
➔ Therefore: These people with their concentrated amount of money at disposal must be a parameter of economics (science)!

The Lesson of the Titanic

The cause of this disaster was not the iceberg. It was the arrogant and narcissistic captain that didn't listen to all incoming warnings and it was the madness of megalomania: the biggest, the best, the most efficient, and the first super-luxurious-liner. No human and no technique can ever dominate the energy of the momentum of a dynamic entity or (and especially) of the momentum of interrelated dynamic entities.

Today the luxurious liner is called 'capitalistic economy' (or 'economics') that also has a multiple momentum nobody can stop anymore. Ant it will lead to the doom of these capitalistic constructions. The causes are the neurotic, narcissistic, psychotic and megalomaniac captains together with those blinded and stupid masses who can never have enough needs and wants at the cheapest possible price with the most minimal work.

Other Sources:
a) Academic Study Books: See Literature
b) Internet:

http://www.thefreedictionary.com/economy

http://www.investorwords.com/1652/economy.html

http://en.wikipedia.org/wiki/Economy

http://www.investopedia.com/terms/e/economy.asp

http://www.businessdictionary.com/definition/economy.html

http://geography.about.com/od/urbaneconomicgeography/a/sectorsecono my.htm

http://oxforddictionaries.com/definition/economy

http://www.comparativepoliticseconomics.com/definitionofeconomy.html

http://en.wikipedia.org/wiki/Economic_sector

http://en.wikipedia.org/wiki/Quaternary_sector_of_the_economy

http://en.wikipedia.org/wiki/Quinary_sector_of_the_economy

http://www.recycoil.com/rmse_pdfs/quinary_economic_sector_white_pape r_aaron_perry_rmse_2009.pdf

2.4. Microeconomics and Macroeconomics

Microeconomics

"Microeconomics (is) the study of individual choice under scarcity, and its implications for the behavior of prices and quantities in individual markets." [37] And another definition: "Micro-economics is the study of how households and firms make decisions and how they interact." [38]

"Microeconomics is the part of economics concerned with decision making by individual costumers, workers, households, and business firms." [39]

Microeconomics is about "how individuals make decisions and how these decisions interact." [40]

In the words of Colander "microeconomics is the study of how individual choice is influenced by economic forces." [41] A micro-approach begins with the details, the little parts, and explores from there to the whole. The invisible hand is one of the most essential operators in microeconomics.

These definitions include:

- Focus on factors concerning local economy: market, consumer behavior, decisions made by firms and individuals
- Understanding the decision-making process of firms and households
- The interaction between individual buyers and sellers
- The factors that influence the choices made by buyers and sellers
- Patterns of supply and demand and the determination of price and output in individual markets
- Supply and demand and how individual businesses make their price-management

---

[37] McDowell (et al.), p. 15
[38] Mankiw (et al.), p. 31
[39] McDonnell (et al.), p. 7
[40] Krugman (et al.), p. 3
[41] Colander, p. 15

Both fields together are interrelated and form a unity:

"Micro-economics and macro-economics are closely intertwined." [42]

Macroeconomics

"Macroeconomics (is) the study of the performance of national economies and the policies that governments use to try to improve that performance." [43] And another definition: "Macro-economics is the study of economy-wide phenomena." [44]

"Macroeconomics is the branch of economics that is concerned with overall ups and downs in the economy … Macroeconomics is concerned with economic fluctuations, such as recession, that can temporarily slow down the economic growth." [45]

Colander's description: "Macroeconomics is the study of the economy as a whole. It considers the problems of inflation, unemployment, business cycles, and growth … Macroeconomics analyzes from the whole to the parts." [46]

"Macroeconomics examines either the economy as a whole or its basic subdivisions or aggregates, such as the government, household, and business sectors." [47]

These definitions include:

- The state of a country or region in terms of the production and consumption of goods and services and the supply of money
- Information about unemployment, national income, rate of growth, gross domestic product, inflation and price levels
- Movement and trends in the economy of a country
- Getting a basic knowledge of how the economic world in an specific area is working

---

[42] Mankiw (et al.), p. 31
[43] McDowell (et al.), p. 15
[44] Mankiw (et al.), p. 31
[45] Krugman (et al.), p. 4
[46] Colander, p. 15
[47] McDonnels, (et al.) p. 6

2.5. The Sectors of the Economy

a) Primary Sector: Raw Material
Mining, agriculture, farming, grazing, hunting and gathering, fishing, forestry, and quarrying. Processing of the raw material associated with this sector is also considered to be part of this sector.

b) Secondary Sector: Manufacturing
Metal working and smelting, automobile production, textile production, chemical and engineering industries, aerospace manufacturing, energy utilities, engineering, breweries and bottlers, construction, and shipbuilding.

c) Tertiary Sector: Services
The service industry: Retail and wholesale sales, transportation and distribution, entertainment (movies, television, radio, music, theater, etc.), restaurants, clerical services, media, tourism, insurance, banking, healthcare, businesses, legal and professional services.

d) Quaternary Sector: Intellectual activities
Intellectual activities including government, culture, entertainment industry, libraries, scientific research, education, research and development, financial planning, media, and information technology.

e) Quinary Sector: Intellectual Power
Decision-making elite, top executives or officials in fields such as banks, government, science, universities, nonprofit, healthcare, culture, and the media; in general: experts stewarding our planet.

f) Unofficial Sector: Domestic Activities
Another section is required with work that refers to domestic activities such as those performed by stay-at-home parents, homemakers, nanny and cleaning help. These activities are not measured by monetary amounts.

g) Black Economy:
Unknown extension of activities, incl. corporate crimes that go undetected.

Sources [48] [49]

---

[48] http://geography.about.com/od/urbaneconomicgeography/a/sectorseconomy.htm
[49] http://en.wikipedia.org/wiki/Economic_sector

2.6. The Principles of Economics

A – The 7 Principles of Economics from McDowell (et al.): [50]

1. The Scarcity Principle: "Having more of one good thing usually means having less of another." Preface page xviii

2. The Cost-Benefit-Principle: "Take no action unless its marginal benefit is at least as great as its marginal cost." Preface page xviii

3. The incentive Principle: "Cost-benefit comparisons are relevant not only for identifying the decisions that rational people should make, also for predicting the actual decisions they do make." Preface page xviii

4. The principle of comparative Advantage: "Everyone does best when each concentrates on the activity for which he or she is relatively most productive." Preface page xix

5. The principle of increasing Opportunity Cost: "Use the resources with the lowest opportunity cost before turning to those with higher opportunity costs." Preface page xix

6. The Efficiency Principle: "Efficiency is an important goal because when the economic 'pie' grows larger; everyone can have a larger slice." Preface page xix

7. The Equilibrium Principle: "A market in equilibrium leaves no unexploited opportunities for individuals but may not exploit all gains achievable through collective action." Preface page xix

➔ I will prove that these principles are not principles and in most cases not even scientific statements.

B – The 10 Principles of Economics from Mankiw (et al.): [51]

1. People face trade-offs

---

[50] McDowell (et al.), preface xviii-xix
[51] Mankiw (et al.), p. 4-15

2. The Cost of something is what you give up to get it

3. Rational people think at margin

4. People respond to incentives

5. Trade can make everyone better off

6. Markets are usually a good way to organize economic activity

7. Governments can sometimes improve market outcomes

8. An economy's standard of living depends on its ability to produce goods and services

9. Prices rise when the government prints too much money

10. Society faces a short-run trade-off between inflation and unemployment

➔ I will prove that these principles are not principles and in most cases not even scientific statements.

C – The 12 Principles of Economics from Krugman (et al.): [52]

1. Resources are scarce.

2. The real cost of something is what you must give up to get it.

3. "How much?" is a decision at the margin.

4. People usually exploit opportunities to make themselves better off.

5. There are gains from trade.

6. Markets move to equilibrium.

7. Resources should be used as efficiently as possible to achieve society's goals.

8. Markets usually lead to efficiency.

---

[52] Krugman (et al.), p. 10-17

9. When markets don't achieve efficiency, government intervention can improve society's welfare.

10. One person's spending is another person's income.

11. Overall spending sometimes gets out of line with the economy's productive capacity.

12. Government policies can change spending.

D – 3 Principles of Economics from Colander:

Colander discusses some principles in the context of single topics. Some of his highlighted statements could also be seen as principles, but are not declared as such. We focus on three examples:

1. "The principle of rational choice tells us to spend our money on those goods that give us the most marginal utility per dollar." [53]

2. The principle of increasing marginal opportunity cost: "In order to get more of something, one must give up ever-increasing quantities of something else." [54]

3. The principle of diminishing marginal utility states that, "after some point, the marginal utility, received from each additional unit of a good, decreases with each additional unit consumed." [55]

E – Principles in Economics from McConnell:

A principle according to McDonnell is: "A very well tested and widely accepted theory is referred to as an economic law or an economic principle – a statement about economic behavior or the economy that enables prediction of the probable effects of certain actions." Later on the author says: "Economic principles are expressed as the tendencies of typical or average consumers, workers, or business firms." [56]

And he continues: "Economic principles are generalizations relating to economic behavior or to the economy itself."

---

[53] Colander, p. 235
[54] Colander, p. 28
[55] Colander, p. 233
[56] McConnell (et al.), p. 6

➔ I will prove that these principles are not principles and in most cases not even scientific statements.

Why do we have here a different amount of principles? Are there more principles in the economic science? Did the authors choose their subjective opinion or their personal hobbyhorse? Or do these differences reflect different understandings of economics as a whole? Where does it lead, if the same science is based on 8, or 12, or 15 principles, and one day on 30 principles? There are certainly 100 principles within the entire economic science.

Such differences lead to different constructions, to different importance, and to different foundations. It hides the fact that principles are also simply a result of scientific explorations (or calculations) that could be revised (falsified) one day. What happens, if some or all these principles are wrong (or partly wrong) and lead to distorted results (constructions of knowledge)? Such a proceeding is not a scientific proceeding; it's an ideological proceeding pretending to be based on rock-solid foundation.

What is a 'principle'? A simple look at some relevant dictionaries (to find in the Internet) shows us for example: [57]

- A fundamental, primary, or general law, or rule, or truth from which others are derived
- A basic or essential quality or element determining intrinsic nature or characteristic behavior
- A basic, supreme and primordial condition for the existence of a fact, concern, matter
- A rule or law concerning the functioning of natural phenomena or mechanical processes
- A natural regularity of a phenomenon and not a correlation of a probability level (e.g. of 0.95%)

We would conclude from such general understanding of 'principle' that a principle in the economic science must be fundamental, not traceable to more fundamental conditions and of intrinsic nature for all possible cases within the corresponding topics and its existential conditions; and never simply a correlation with a higher or lower probability or a fact that is reducible to more fundamental facts or laws. A principle also includes the potential to be a primordial foundation that allows a complex theory to be built upon it.

➔ A principle is not simply a description of a fact or a correlation between

---

[57] http://www.thefreedictionary.com/principle

two or more variables.

Also a law, an intrinsic nature, a mechanical process (in social sciences: an interrelation, correlation), an essential quality or element, or an idea that has been demonstrated as true (theorem) must and can be proven.

Principles are a result of (social) science and all results of social science can change in the future due to new knowledge. Therefore they are all proven 'fundamental theses' or unchangeable facts.

The above mentioned economic principles are not fundamental and unchangeable rules or laws in the sense of intrinsic 'natural phenomena'.

'Laws' in social science are not the same as laws in physics! Principles in economics are not mechanic, supreme or primordial, and not even general rules.

'Principles' or 'laws' in social science are simply evident and unchangeable facts, factors or elements; e.g. 'people behave', 'people live', 'people have a thinking capacity', 'people have a consciousness', 'everything on earth is limited', etc. The statement 'people chose rationally' is never a principle: some do chose rationally, some not; and even rational decision depends in most cases on many other factors.

If a principle shows a 'proven' way how a variable 'A' naturally is, or is interrelated (correlated) with a variable 'B', then we have in the science of economics hundreds of such 'principles'. It does not make sense to refer to such a nature or such interrelations as 'principles'.

A principle can be a social rule. But this is something else; it does not express a fundamental knowledge, and is much rather a normative statement.

How do we have to understand the economic principles about consumer behavior if these patterns of behavior are already the result of brainwashed, manipulated and dehumanized people? How do we have to explain the consumers that do not follow the programmed consumer behavior? If a majority of people indeed confirm with their behavior some principles, can these confirmed principles be defined as 'law', or 'natural'?

The self-justification of economic principles is a very dangerous matter. It leads to a wrong pathway and includes lies, deceit, cheat, sheep behavior, coded mass humans, and economical equalization – a pre-condition for ruling the world through economics and economy.

First, economics creates principles that are the foundation to achieve their supreme goals. Then they shape the masses into the direction of their principles. And finally they get their principles confirmed with surveys. The principles become the 'natural laws' of economic science.

We conclude: A social science can not start with 'principles'. A social science must start by describing and legitimating the fields it claims to be a subject or a topic of this specific science. If a science starts with (social) principles, then it leads to canalized thinking, explorations, and corresponding results. Starting with principles implicitly sets a certain amount of ideological premises as the infallible foundation of the science. It becomes a belief that can't be questioned anymore. All following constructions (of economics) are based on such irrevocable 'facts'. Such a proceeding is a dangerous manipulation at the beginning of determining and understanding a scientific field. It leads in the real world to immense damages and failure.

Colander understands 'modern economics' as a 'combination of deduction and induction' together. Economics starts with a set of self-evident principles. The principles are the assumptions that people are rational and self-interested. Principles are the result of discovered patterns in data. A theory is "a logical deduction based on those principles." [58]

Economics = Data + Principles + Theories

Such an understanding of social science is extremely short-sighted. What are economic data? Are principles the result of theories or premises of theories? Are human factors also an economic data? Are human values an economic data? Who determines the relevant human factors and human values? Does it make sense to develop an economic science without the human factors and without the essential human values?

Colman gives an indirect answer: "To think like an economist involves addressing almost all issues using a cost/benefit approach." [59] What are cost parameters for human factors and human values? Except from some problems with 'externalities' and 'welfare' or 'wellbeing' the above cited authors mention in their books we could not find any clarification or extensive exploration. Therefore the definitions about economics are extremely ideological, manipulated and deceiving.
The term 'principle' also means 'rule' and is in this context a normative

---

[58] Colander, p. 5-6
[59] Colander, p. 6

(social) term. The word 'principle' also has a connotation of mainly, principally, essentially, basically, mostly, cardinally, especially, etc. The above mentioned economic principles express sometimes a rule, sometimes a simple fact, sometimes an interrelation, sometimes a fundamental issue.

→ The sloppy use of the term 'principle' is unspeakable and very manipulative, means ideological and not scientific.

We must put the scientific economic game on the table: Heavy big (and expensive) books of highest quality, immense amounts of pages, colored, and glossy printing, countless examples (blabber stories) and endless exercises confirming and reinforcing the principles, extremely complex statistics and graphs, with the background of famous universities and their immense (partly historic) buildings, and we have the infallible science for young students that don't have the self-confidence and the relevant knowledge to question such highest accredited authority. They all don't have any other option but to study (copy) and believe in the huge amounts of junk, and to go through the exams suffering a lot in understanding (better: memorizing and copying) the immense amount of deceptive principles, probability theories, formulas, statistical constructions, and neurotic statements. Isn't it in the core the same with religion?

Colander gives us a hint: "Economic reasoning, once learned, is infectious… It will influence your analysis of everything, including issues normally considered outside the scope of economics." [60]

The author becomes a magic trainer of robots: "People trained in economics think in a certain way. They analyze everything critically; they compare the costs and the benefits of every issue and make decisions based on those costs and benefits." [61]

→ A joke: Students become critical when they study economics.

Cynically we must comment: That's why we have a majority of CEOs, managers, members of boards of directors, and members of governments that are psychopaths, megalomaniacs, and ignorant towards human factors und human values. And that's why we have the economic crisis and all the wars since World War I. And that's why we have a significant increase of the destruction of the planet with all its resources, and the poverty around the globe. Due to such understanding of economics these powerful people throw

---

[60] Colander, p. 6
[61] Colander, p. 6

babies, the young generation, the weak people, the poor, the handicapped people, the failed people, the elderly people, the human values, and the truth about human life and any psychical-spiritual meaning of life into the boiling water. The infection starts with the economics' baptism, means: starting to study economics.

This we could understand as a principle: Greed is un-satisfying if the inner source of greed is not solved. Greed is shaped already in the prenatal time depending on the life condition of the mother and her greed in general. Latest when the mother starts giving her milk to the baby, the ability (inability) to accept frustration (not having immediately or having irregularly satisfied a need, or can't get the want without understanding) is shaped. The oral neurosis is shaped.

Assumptions – Premises

Theories and models are based on assumptions, also called 'premises'. A premise is a statement that is assumed to be true for the purpose of an argument from which a conclusion is drawn. In other words: it is a proposition that is accepted as true in order to provide a basis for logical reasoning. [62] Colander gives us three examples: [63]

- Individuals behave rationally
- That what consumer choose reflects what makes them happiest
- The invisible hand

The science of Psychology has extensively explored that individuals behave preponderantly irrational. Psychology also documented in many ways that happiness does not depend on the amount of wealth, goods and services; and especially untrue is the idea: the more goods people have, the happier people are. And we will explore in different contexts this invisible hand and discover: there is no invisible hand, not even a finger of a hand. Such premises are useless and misleading. Such premises are not science! It's simply ideology.

In Chapter 3 we will explore the economic principles and their terms.

---

[62] http://www.thefreedictionary.com/premise
[63] Colander, p. 14

Diagram: A First simple Overview of Economics

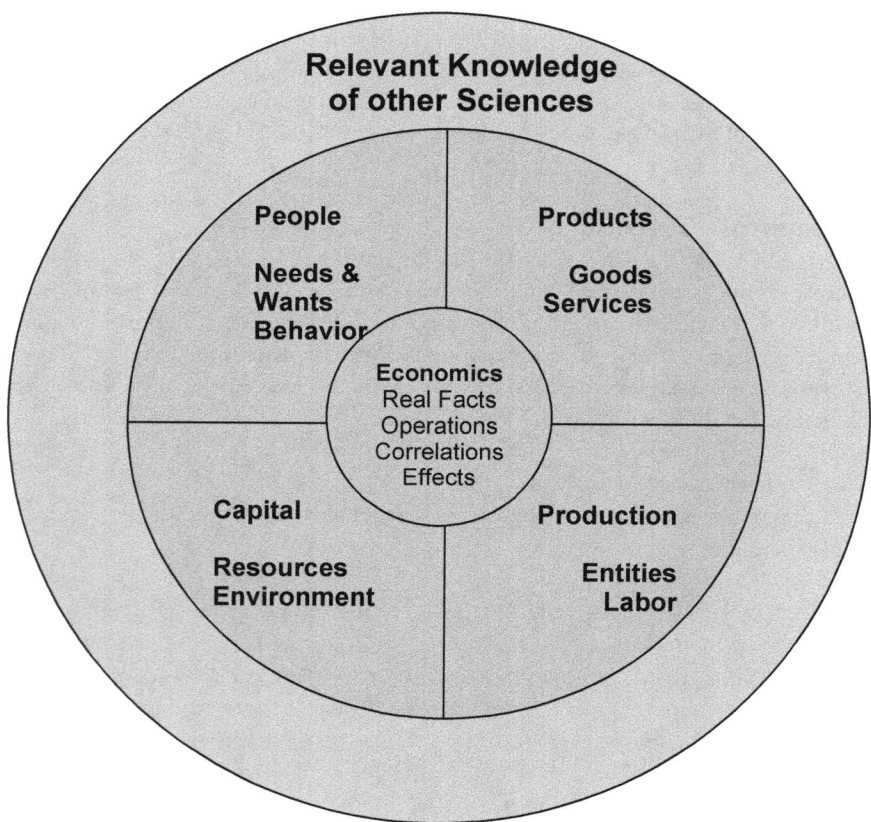

The Market Frame of Economics

All the following groups are fully linked with economic factors. These factors are of fundamental importance for economics.

The allocation, the price management, and the offers of goods must be seen within the following buyer-seller frame:

- There are the people: consumers buy = buyers
- There are the products/services: producers sell = sellers

- There are different budget groups of buyers
- There are different price groups of goods from sellers

- There are different people groups of buyers
- There are different product-groups from sellers

- There are different groups with time at their disposal for shopping
- There are different groups with time at their disposal for selling

- There are different price-baskets of goods for the different budgets
- There are different price-groups of products from sellers

- There are perishable products of short duration for the every day life
- There are products of long duration for years

- There are products of interest to the masses of humans
- There are products only for totally specific interests

- There are products that need only a short time to buy
- There are products that need significantly more time to buy

- There are sale locations within a short distance from the buyers' home
- There are sale locations with a significant distance from the buyers' home

- There are locations with a short radius of high concentration of dwellers
- There are locations with a big radius of low concentration of dwellers

- There are sale locations that require spending money to go there
- There are sale locations where people can walk to go there (no costs)

- There are sale locations with additional services for leisure activities

- There are sale locations without additional services for leisure activities

All these frame components influence the general consumer behavior, the decision making process, the amount of money people spend, the success of sales, and the collateral effects burdened to the community. Not one of the principles the authors mention in their books refers to these market frame conditions of the market. We assume that this neglect is intentional due to the profit psychosis, and to hide the 'invisible hand'.

Who gets most of it is of highest economic importance and it has two sides: on the one side the consumer's needs and wants; and on the other side: who can sell and make as much profit as possible. The market frame is an indispensable concept to understand the market dynamics and find the efficient solution – or better: the best sustainable solution.

Market Organization

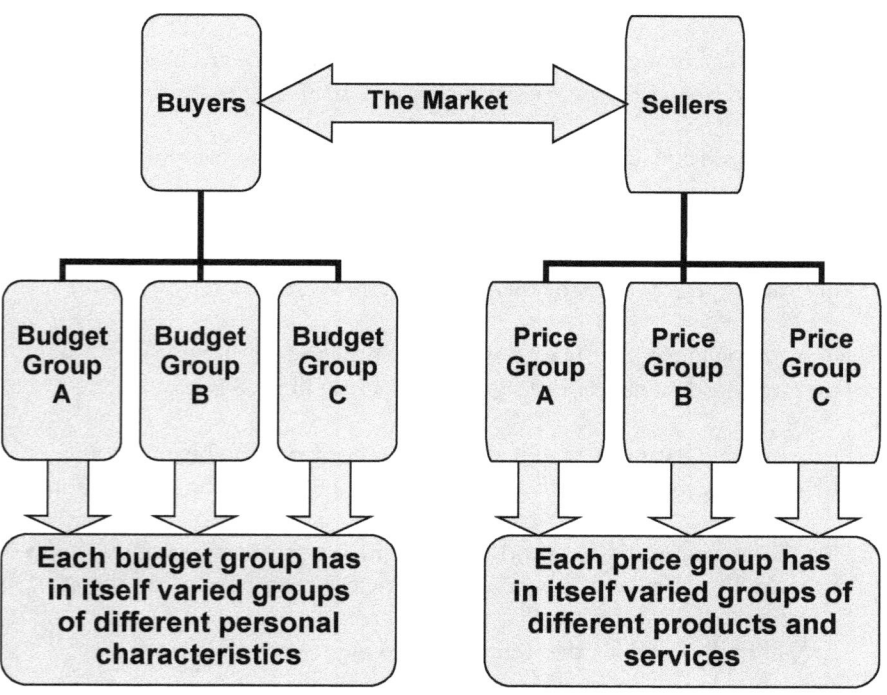

Conclusion

→ Before economics as a science can start thinking about consumers' behavior, it must organize the structure of market frames.

→ Before economics as a science can start thinking about consumers' behavior, it must organize the principles of the market frames.

→ To put all goods and services people buy in one basket is idiotic and nonsense.

→ To put all the consumers in one pot is stupid and nonsense.

Budget Groups

Budget determines the amount of money people can spend for goods.

Rent Mortgage Fixed Costs	Taxes Social Security *	Water Electricity Heating Fixed *	Consumption Budget Furniture Long term fixed *	Consumption Budget Daily Goods Internal Flexibility

Comment:

* Rent or mortgages are stable; indexed on the CPI and on interest rates; there is no individual flexibility.
* Taxes and social security are determined in relation to the wages; there is no individual flexibility.
* Water, electricity and heating have a minimum of necessity; mostly can't be reduced by 30-50%.
* Purchased furniture normally is in use for over 10 years; purchase is time-focused.
* The car-psychosis drastically limits the flexibility in the consumption of daily goods.
* Consumer goods for everyday life have a significant internal flexibility (quality, brand on same price level).

The principles of the authors we presented above do not reflect any of the behavior consequences that are involved in the internal basket of daily goods. For the masses there is not much flexibility in choosing quality products from the 10,000 goods on the market. Their flexibility (decision making) moves around the price level of their possibilities. Not many people can at any time choose between a steak for 20€ or sausages for 7.50€

The choice at the margins is a joke if we consider the minimal flexibility that the masses have in their decision making and no consumer calculates with the opportunity cost parameter.

The manifoldness of goods is not simply a matter of 'unlimited option'. Most people have only a small range of goods they can choose:

- A kilo of organic apples that costs 3€ is not the same as the apples that cost 1€ per kilo.
- A bottle of wine with a price of 20€ is not the same as a tetra pack of wine that costs 0.85€
- A pair of shoes that cost 300€ is not simply equal to a pair of shoes that costs 10-30€.
- Those who can buy shoes on a level of 500€ will never buy 20 pairs of shoes for 25€ each.
- Buying a car consists not only in the money needed to get it; the follow-up costs are significant.
- Having a car reduces the monthly budget for goods with a minimum of 250€ per month.

Opportunity Costs

Opportunity	Opportunity	Opportunity
Buying a car with a leasing of 350€ during 3 years	Going for Holidays with the airplane for 2,500€	Going to the Cinema for 15€
Alternative	**Alternative**	**Alternative**
Buying a cheaper car with a leasing of 150€ during 3 years	Spending holidays at home and exploring the cultural and natural area; total travel costs 500€	Going to get a pizza and a bottle of wine
Additional opportunities	**Additional opportunities** **For the same amount of costs**	**There are more Alternatives**
During 3 years, each month 200€ left for innumerable shopping: Books, DVDs, CDs,	Buying some books, DVDs, CDs, going to the gym every day, buying plants, some new	Buying (and reading) a book Making a present to a friend

presents for partner, flowers, a further education, short excursions once every 2-3 months, small toys for the children, some accessories every 2-3 months, finding a new hobby, giving attention to healthy food ('bio-food'), etc.	decoration, inviting friends for a party, going to museums, etc.	

Conclusion

→ Products and services are always related to the amount of money people can spend. Credit can help!

→ The lower the wages, the less money the masses of people have for consumption. Credit can help!

→ Most people have a limited amount of money to purchase products and services. Credit can help!

→ The volume of production in a country depends on the amount of money people can spend. Credit can help!

→ The higher the rent or mortgage rate per month, the less money people have for consumption. Credit can help!

→ The higher the taxes and social security costs, the less money people have for consumption. Credit can help!

→ The higher the costs for water, electricity and heating, the less money people have for consumption. Credit can help!

Consumers' Time Use

Shopping time determines the extension of shopping activities.

Sleeping and Rest	Working plus Travel to Work	Household Management	Leisure No Cost	Time for Shopping

The time that working people have for shopping is of highest importance for the market and therefore for economics as science. This topic of highest importance is never mentioned in the principles of economics. There must be a reason here that the super intelligent experts neglect this fundamental condition of the market.

→ The more people need to sleep and want to rest, the less time they have for shopping.

→ The more time people need for work and travel to work, the less time they have for shopping.

→ The more time people spend on household (cleaning), the less time they have for shopping.

→ The more people like to spend time with cost-free activities, the less time they have for shopping.

→ The more people have an interest in learning for life (books), the less time they have for shopping.

→ The more people are interested in a creative hobby, the less time they have for shopping.

→ The more people take time to meditate twice a day, the less time they have for shopping.

→ The more people take time to interpret their dreams, the less time they have for shopping.

→ The more people feel the importance of genuine inner needs, the less time they have for shopping.

→ The more people are aware of the superficial lifestyle, the more they think about their consumption.

→ The more time parents take to communicate with their children, the less time they have for shopping.

→ The more time couples take to communicate with each other, the less time they have for shopping.

→ The more time people spend surfing the Internet, the less time they have for shopping.

→ The more time people spend on Facebook, the more they lose the connection to the real life.

→ The more time people watch TV, the more they can be brainwashed for consumption.

→ The more people are brainwashed for consuming, the less time they spend on rational decision making.

→ Optimization of time use (calculating 'time is money') at a certain level breaks the human being.

2.7. The Complexity of Economics

Based on common understanding and general descriptions of economics and economy we identify the following essential fields and components: [64]

a) Systems of Economics

- Microeconomics and its Data
- Macroeconomics and its Data
- International Economy
- Consumers, Consumption and Scarcity (Needs, Wants)
- Production
- Service
- Trade
- Small and medium sized Businesses
- Structures and Function of big Corporations
- Structure and Function of small Businesses
- Markets and its Elasticity, Monopoly
- Labor Market, Manpower, Unemployment
- Competitive Market
- Monetary, Financial Systems, Banking
- Public Goods and Resources
- Tax Systems and Fiscal Policy
- Internal Norms, Rules, and Regulations

b) Work and Business

- Manufacturing
- Services
- Trade
- Industry
- Tourism
- Mining
- Agriculture
- Animal Breeding

---

[64] Taken from Krugman (et al.), McDowell (et al.), Mankiw (et al.)

- Banking
- Black Market

c) Management

- Communication
- Negotiation
- Management and Team Work
- Administration and Accounting
- Allocation of Resources
- Price Management
- Technology (i.e. IT, Methods, Statistics)
- Distribution, Transport
- Marketing (Public Relations and Media)

d) Exterior Frames

- Sociology and Culture
- Anthropology and Welfare
- Psychology and Education
- Ethics and Human Rights
- Laws, International Laws
- Health Science
- Political Science (Governments)
- Environmental Science
- Geography
- History

e) Indicators Measuring Economic Activities

- Consumer Spending
- Foreign Exchange Rate
- Gross Domestic Product
- GDP per capita
- Gross National Product
- Stock Market
- Interest Rate
- National Debt
- Rate of Inflation
- Recession
- Depression
- Deflation

- Unemployment
- Balance of Trade

We add here a selection of global problems with high economic implications:

f) Economics and Global Problems

- Failure of Businesses
- Wealth, Wages and Poverty
- Shrinking Middle Class Businesses
- The Power Concentration of Money
- Unemployment and Recession
- Depression
- Externalities and Collateral Damages
- Monopoly
- Corruption
- Globalization
- Inequality and Imbalance
- Unrest and Wars
- Neurotic, psychopathic and psychotic rulers
- Scarcity of Resources
- Growth of World Population
- Power of the Media

Definition of the Economic Science

→ The field of the economic science must cover all active and passive entities, factors and variables that form part of the economic life.
→ All relevant external influences must also form part of the economic science.
→ The primordial task of economic science is a precise and useful organized description of all economic realities.

Diagram: The Macro System of Economic Topics

We take a selection of the above categorized key words forming the economics and economy we have collected from general descriptions about economics and economy, and reorganize the topics:

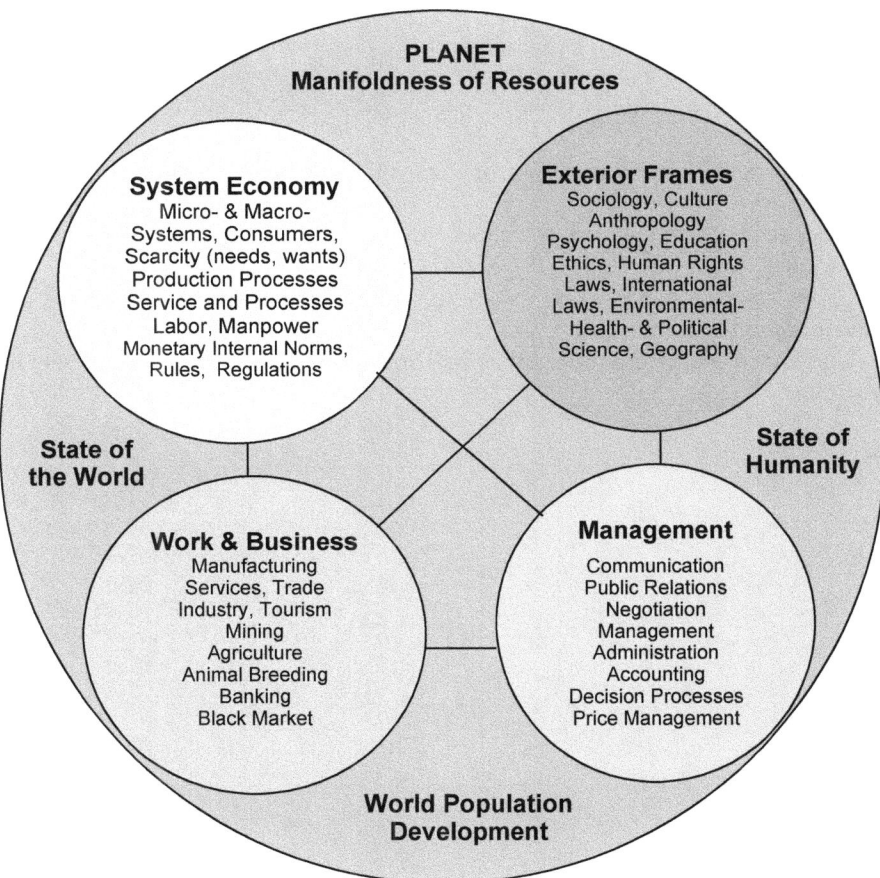

Theses: In a first overview we can conclude some theses about economics:

1. Economics is inevitably correlated with humans, processes, resources, and the planet.
2. Economics as a scientific system has essential pillars that determine the internal structures.
3. The Economy cannot exist and work without being connected with relevant exterior frames.
4. Economic realities can't operate and can't be developed without a skillful management.
5. Increasing economic entities change from a certain level on its functions and effects.
6. Increasing world population from 7bn up to 10bn will enormously affect the economy.
7. The state of the world is frame and condition to practice or develop economics.
8. The state of humanity is an essential factor that determines the development of economies.
9. The indicators of the micro-systems form the macro-system, the society as a whole.

3. Essential Economic Terms

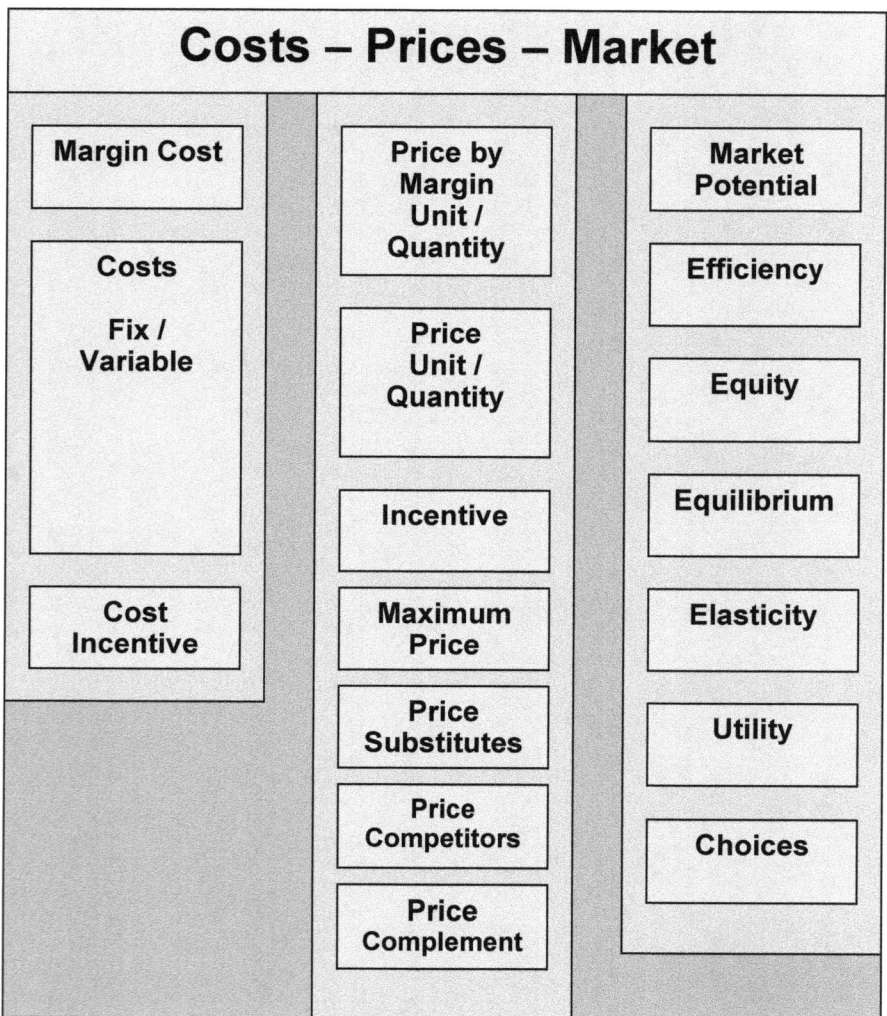

Costs – Prices – Market

| Margin Cost | Price by Margin Unit / Quantity | Market Potential |

Costs
Fix / Variable

Price Unit / Quantity

Efficiency

Cost Incentive

Incentive

Equity

Maximum Price

Equilibrium

Price Substitutes

Elasticity

Price Competitors

Utility

Price Complement

Choices

3.1. Scarcity

'Scarcity' is one of the most important and fundamental keywords in the concepts and theories of economics. The entire system of economic theories and concepts (Free Market Concept) crashes down if this term is not rock-solid in its meaning related to a concrete reality. We first want to describe the traditional meaning and importance taught by the classical economic science; and then we develop a critical analysis of the word, its meaning and functions in an economic theory or concept.

Mankiw & Taylor explain the term 'scarcity'; summarized: Economics reflects how society manages its scarce resources and its allocations. Economics allocates people, land, buildings, machines and the output of goods and services. Many forces and trends have an effect in human's needs for goods and services; and in consumer behavior and the economy of a country as a whole. The authors conclude: "The behavior of an economy reflects the behavior of the individuals who make up the economy." [65]

"The Scarcity Principle: Having more of one good thing usually means having less of another." [66]

McConnell says it in his way: "Scarce economic resources mean limited goods and services. Scarcity restricts options and demands choices. Because we can't have it all, we must decide what we will have and what we must forgo." [67]

In our words: The way an economy of a country functions (not: 'behaves') expresses the behavior (not: 'function') of individuals who shape the real world of economics (not: 'make up the economy'). It's a simple fact: humans make Economics (science, theory, concepts) and humans also create the world of the Economy (of a country) in the real world.

Logically we must and we will have a very close and precise look at these humans and their behavior. We can even say: Humans are the most important factor in the theory and real world of economics and economy. It is

---

[65] Mankiw (et al.), p. 2-3
[66] McDowell (et al.), preface xviii.
[67] McConnel (et al.), p. 4

absolutely impossible and useless to develop a theory of economics as long as we don't have a very precise picture about humans. Without an accurate understanding of humans such a theory would be wrong already in its foundation and therefore such economics must fail as a science and as a practical orientation or interpretation. Most mathematical models of economics would be useless instruments that mislead economic leaders as well as governments.

Scarcity means in Krugman's definition: "Resources are scarce". Krugman mentions some examples: limited income, limited time, limited labor, limited supply, limited land, limited buildings, limited capital, limited products and services, limited natural resources, and limited human capital (education, skills, intelligence), and even clean air and water. "A resource is anything that can be used to produce something else." The core element 'scarce' means: "There is not enough of the resources available to satisfy all the various ways a society wants to use them." And more: "The scarcity of resources means that society as a whole must make choices." [68]

Krugman says: "Overall spending sometimes gets out of line with the economy's productive capacity." [69] We can understand this principle as a scarcity problem. But is this statement a principle? It is not a principle! It describes a fact that can occur sometimes. And there is nothing that says that this 'must' happen sometimes due to whatsoever. A very sloppy principle!

Also the authors McDowell (et al.) found the economics with the principle of scarcity: "Scarcity is a fundamental fact of life. There is never enough time, money or energy to do everything we want to do or have everything we would like to have. Scarcity simply means we must choose." And: "Scarcity makes trade-offs necessary." Logically the authors conclude: people must choose. [70]

"For better or worse, most people have virtually unlimited wants." [71] This is an extreme exaggeration and expresses a hidden psychotic idea.

A way of new economic thinking could be about the statement "We never have enough time …" is a subjective way of looking at the time factor. We could say it in another way: We always have enough time … because nothing is in a hurry (in general) and nothing forces us to always optimize time in everything. There is no ontological law that says that humans must force the

---

[68] Krugman (et al.), p. 5
[69] Krugman (et al.), p. 16
[70] McDowell (et al.), p. 10
[71] McDConnell (et al.), p. 8

factor time to the extreme; not in sexual encounter, not in having lunch, and not in the economy. Maybe one day human's science will be able to reduce by 50% the natural demand for time spent sleeping; and then we would have much more time for economic issues. A better way could be: if humans balance the demand for money and energy with the limited time factor, then there is more than enough time for everything humans need and want. There is plenty of time on earth for humans. Let's see the problem with a picture: Humans never have enough muscles to heave a stone of 500 kg. But humans can divide the stone into 20 smaller stones of 25 kg each and go ahead slower by heaving one stone after another. And then it works fine. But it costs more time.

Colander introduces the term 'scarcity' in his ways: "Inevitably individuals want more than is available, given how much they're willing to work." That means: "In our economy there is a problem of scarcity – the goods available are too few to satisfy individual's desires." [72]

Is it really inevitable that individuals want more than is available? Are there goods (and which goods?) that are not available in the Western economies? There are thousands of goods available for all kind of needs, wants and desires. And if an individual can't get what he wants, then it's a problem of accessibility (distance to get it). Yes, as people are very greedy due to many reasons (not naturally!), many people want more than they can afford. If we relate this problem to the hours of work per week and with that to a possible increase of wage, then the problem again looks different. This is not a scarcity problem; it's a problem of greed and readiness to work or of lack of working places. But Colander says it clearly: "goods available are too few to satisfy individual's desires. Too few? Yes, certainly in Africa, Asia, and elsewhere; but not in the United States and in Europe.

"The quantity of goods, services, and usable resources depends on technology and human action." The author says that there is always a scarcity as new wants are constantly arising. We consider this as a result of external influences, and not as a natural need. The author's solution: coercion – limiting people's wants and increasing the amount of work (to get their wants). This statement sounds like an ideological support of the production sector: produce more, and more, and more … (hidden: for profit) and get paid less and less.

The problem remains: Who says what is too few? Desires can be shaped, formed, re-directed, and the 'how to' satisfy desires must be managed through

---

[72] Colander, p. 5

education. Every baby must learn that it can't have what it wants satisfied at any desired moment. Therefore, it's a matter of education – de facto a matter of failed education.

Scarcity

We can conclude from the author's understanding: Economics is essentially based on scarcity. The keywords in this context are 'scarcity', 'decision making' and 'allocation' (Mankiw & Taylor). But everything on earth is limited in some ways. Obviously the term 'scarcity' must be determined within this general fact and must be related to the specific circumstances and cannot be related only to this general limitation of resources on earth.

"Society has limited or scarce economic resources, meaning all natural, human, and manufactured resources that go into the production of goods and services." [73] The author gives a list including factories, farms, buildings, equipment, tools, machinery, transport means, and communication facilities.

We could say: every human, every household, every business or institution on earth always has scarce economic resources. Such a way of saying creates a wrong view, a wrong approach, and wrong suggestions: "Wee need more economic resources." This is the starting point of a hungry, insatiable monster that is always preoccupied with food and eating. It is a hidden purpose of capitalistic economics to permanently heat up more needs and wants. This is the product of a very sick mind. Production machinery and sales should never stop and growth is a permanent 'must'. This is psychotic! Here they create a suck that drags down humanity into the abyss. And they have pre-packed it into 'scientific' statements, principles and theories.

Let's take an example to show how experts in economics manipulate their terms, principles and thesis: "Scarcity is why you can't have everything, even if you're the richest person in the world. Even if money's not scarce, time and /or physical resources will be…Sadly, scarcity is a fact. Too little time and stuff exists to satisfy all our desires, so people have to make hard choices about what to produce and consume."

You can't have everything: Is there a mentally healthy human being on earth who really wants everything? No! But the statement 'you can't have everything' is a negative message and easily causes a subtle frustration. It suggests that it would be wonderful if humans could have everything. The sentence 'even if money's not scarce' is an illusion and therefore manipulative.

---

[73] Mc Connell (et al.), p. 10

The author continues with 'time ... resources (are scarce)'. The way it is said provokes the normative idea: 'time must be used in the most efficient way to make money; each unused or uncounted second is a loss of money or a loss of happiness'. The message is clear to all businesses: Use each second in the best way to get the most you can. In other words: each unused second is a loss of possible money (profit).

This is a very perverse understanding of human life and of working. Greed here is not the only motivation factor. There is a compulsion to count every second of any human activity and to canalize and control activities for a given goal (profit). The question here is: is it really only about profit? Or is the essential aim to control every second of labor activity? The next statement 'too little time and stuff exists' is simply not true for the Western world. It suggests nearly a panic: run to get as much as you can, we never know if there will be a serious shortage (scarcity). We continue: 'to satisfy all our desires'. Do humans really need to satisfy all imaginable desires? Here the psychotic drive has an infectious effect.

The sad messages continue: 'people have to make hard choices'. It's so hard to make a choice! That's a joke! It's totally overheated; and shows us another sign of the psychotic mission of capitalistic economics. More stupidity is not possible. The ideological dimension of such statements makes people crazy. But as the book is for dummies, it's anyway not important. It's their fault if they take such junk into their head and do not understand all the hidden implications due to a lack of profound and critical thinking or due to lazy-minded attitudes in general.[74]

Therefore let's explore the term 'scarcity' to get a deeper and more complete understanding of its meaning and function in the system of economic theory.

Where is there a real scarcity in the Western world? 50% of the population lives in big towns, cities and mega-cities. There are immense shopping malls and shopping centers. Smaller urbanizations (small towns, villages) have in most cases a shopping center within a radius of 50 km. Most developments in rural and mountain areas are connected with villages and cities. There might be a problem with accessibility respectively public transport to the world of shopping areas with 10.000 and more products and services around. Even for products and services of very high living standard the consumers (middle and upper class) will find what they need and want. In a majority of arising delivery problems, the causes lie in the logistic. The question arises: Why does the concept of 'scarcity' get the highest importance and even take the starting

---

[74] Antonioni, p. 14

position in developing economic concepts and theories?

The capitalistic economic theories focus primordially on the Western world. A focus on developing countries would change the entire science of economics a lot, because there is indeed an existential scarcity in many developing countries or areas of such countries. But this is another matter.

As a defense argument in the interest of the 'scarcity' – committed authors we could interpret, they think about Africa, Asia, and other developing countries. There are 5 billion people around the globe that live with real scarcity. But this would be a very cynical argument as the capitalistic world is stealing all their resources and contributing a lot to the scarcity in these countries.

An embarrassing question in this context arises: Are the philanthropic projects of the Rothschild's, Goldman Sachs and Co (aiming to reduce scarcity in developing countries) pure alibi projects to save the reputation of their 200 year-old businesses? And for individuals such as Warren Buffet, Bill Gates [75] and others the question would be: Are these individuals committed to scarcity matters in the interest of a self-catharsis of their conscience (and their family)? An even more important question would be: Are the IMF, Goldman Sachs or other financial institutions really interested in re-building the economy in countries (e.g. Greece) or is it their aim to destroy entire countries?

There are other questions about such philanthropic commitment: Do they really not know about the dire state of humanity and the planet? Do they really not know that the momentum of all factors damaging humanity, the world and the planet will lead within 40 years to a doom beyond imagination?

Considering the state of humanity and the planet, these people carry water to the sea and their good will actions will not save humanity and the planet as long as there are elites behind the scene ruling (and blackmailing) governments in order to gear up towards the total destruction of the planet and towards the elimination of humanity within decades.

Either these philanthropists are naïve or indeed their philanthropic projects serve only to protect their reputation and to cover the hidden interests of their own super-elites' interests. This is not conspiracy and neither a hypothesis. Herein lays the very explosive real problem of economics.

A critical approach towards economics is not simply about psychopaths in the

---

[75] McConnell (et al.), p. 8

economy and the governments. It's about evil itself: today there are humans already beyond a state of dehumanization; they converted into incarnated evil monsters – an inhumane species of up to today in the history of humanity unseen destructive (economic, political, and religious) power.

Economics must explore and reveal these worlds if it does not want to be impeached to be a collaborator of these monsters like 'Saurus' (The Lords of the Rings) and his soldiers. The protagonists in the economy and in economics as a science must take and declare position about where they stand and want to stand. And their position must be proven with real facts. This is a normative statement that is indispensable and must be placed before developing a concept or theory of economics and before acting in the economy of a country and in the world as a whole. [76]

Scarcity has Different Meanings

- Something is sensibly limited
- In short supply
- Short of, scant of, tight
- Rare and infrequent
- Spare, sparely, meager
- More meager
- There is not enough of something
- There is a shortage / tightness of something
- There is a marked deficit of something
- There is a lack of something absolutely indispensable
- The demand is higher than the supply
- The supply is higher than the demand

➜ The word 'scarcity' itself does not express the general fact that everything on earth is limited.
➜ Within an economic theory the word 'scarcity' expresses a lack of supply related to a demand.
➜ 'Scarcity' includes a time frame from a day up to months or years; or forever.

Scarcity also has Other Dimensions

- Scarcity can be the result of excessive (blind and greed) wants or needs of something.
- ~~Unexpected, important and urg~~ent need in the collective produce scarcity.

[76] Antonioni, p. 14

- There is a day, a week, a month, several months or a year (or more) of a local scarcity.
- There is only a location or a specific population experiencing a scarcity of something.
- If everybody cares about the right use of this something, then there could be enough resources.
- The lack of something in general does not have any individual damage (health, life, well-being)
- There is always here and there and more in the future a limited nature of society's resources.
- Not all goods people need or want can be produced and distributed due to limited resources.
- The opposite of scarcity: abundance, opulence, and more than enough, for good living standard.
- Abundance can lead to stocks of goods and services that can't be sold anymore.

Scarcities can Produce Damages

- The lack of something has no notable impact for human's life.
- The lack of something produces serious damages on health, life, and well-being.
- The lack of something produces damages in the economy (businesses).
- The lack of something produces social problems and unrest in society.

Conclusions

→ Scarcity doesn't mean that all needs and wants of all people on earth must be satisfied.
→ Scarcity doesn't mean that everybody everywhere in a country is affected from it.
→ Scarcity of food and water is not the same as scarcity of luxurious cars, iPhones, or sex toys.
→ It doesn't make sense to use the term 'scarcity' without the corresponding context.
→ Depending on the context, the meaning gets completely different importance or urgency.
→ Depending on the context, completely different conclusions may be appropriate.
→ The fact of a scarcity doesn't logically lead to individual or collective damages.
→ The fact of a scarcity doesn't logically lead to necessary measures to

increase the resource.
→ The fact of a scarcity due to blind and greedy demand can be answered with new behavior.
→ A specific scarcity can be solved by redirecting the demand towards alternatives.

In a certain way it is strange and weird that Mankiw & Taylor (and other authors) start their foundation of economics with the topics 'scarcity and allocation'. In the last 20-30 years Europe and the United States (and other capitalistic countries) have not experienced an all-encompassing scarcity. These countries have not experienced serious problems with the allocation of goods and services. Scarcity has always been real in some areas in the Western world and certainly much more in many developing countries or areas. This is here and there sometimes unavoidable up to a certain level.

Allocation is without doubt also a topic of economics; but it does not make sense to give to this issue such a fundamental importance in developing the picture of economic science. It may be simply a problem of logistics. The topics of scarcity and allocation are simply a specific problem of an economy in addition to many other economic problems in a country, mostly linked with political structures and corruption.

Why do these authors not start with a simple exploration and systematic organization of all the economic systems and sub-systems in a country? 'Scarcity' is not a logical starting point to describe the science of economics. It is also strange, that the authors start with describing their 7 to 10 or more economic principles as if they would be eternal basic axioms. Such an understanding is nonsense and very manipulative. Principles are a result of scientific research and analysis. There must be a serious reason or hidden interest of such a proceeding in developing the house (structure) of economic science. We will find it out later.

Diagram: Scarcity = Lack of Supply related to Demand

Scarcity is always related to Entities that have a Need or Want

- Living (primary needs: having a home, food, water, etc.)
- Improving life standard (secondary needs: not indispensable wants)
- Production processes (tools, resources)
- Manpower (amount and qualities)
- Services (amount and qualities)
- Institutions (e.g. NGOs)
- Government with its responsibilities
- Products, consumer goods (amount and qualities)
- Tools for ways of distribution (e.g. sale, trade, money)
- Production entities require a specific amount of needs or wants
- Production entities have a time frame and a frame of size
- Scarcity in general has a time frame and a frame of size

Conclusions

→ Scarcity can be related to the tools the production processes need to operate.
→ Scarcity is always related to needs and wants of humans and institutions.
→ Needs can't always be understood as indispensable needs for living life or for production.
→ Wants are not understood as indispensable needs for living life or for production.
→ Scarcity is not limited to indispensable resources and tools for living life.
→ Certain needs (requirements) of societies are, determined by the level of modernity.

Necessity and Indispensability

- There are indispensable and necessary basic needs related with living life.
- There are indispensable and necessary needs related to requirements of society's institutions.
- Wants are never indispensable and necessary elements related to living life.
- Wants are never indispensable and necessary elements related to the economic life.
- There are artificial needs and absolutely exaggerated and unnecessary or meaningless wants.
- There are artificial needs and unlimited want that destroy humans, human life, society and the planet.

Scarcity of Money

- There are 4-5 billion people that don't have enough money to live a humane life.
- Also in the capitalistic world there are more than 100 million people living at or under the poverty line.
- There are countries where scarcity of goods and scarcity of money at the same time is looming.

→ Scarcity is also a term to apply for money needs (and wants).
→ Scarcity of (indispensable) goods and money at the same time is a very serious concern.

Conclusions

→ Depending on the necessity, the meaning gets completely different importance or urgency.
→ Depending on the necessity, completely different conclusions may be appropriate.
→ The thesis "scarcity requires increase of production/services to satisfy the demand" is not a general logical consequence, but much more an ideology.
→ From another view: Businesses need and want consumers. In that sense here also we can identify a 'scarcity'.

Diagram: Fields of Possible Scarcity

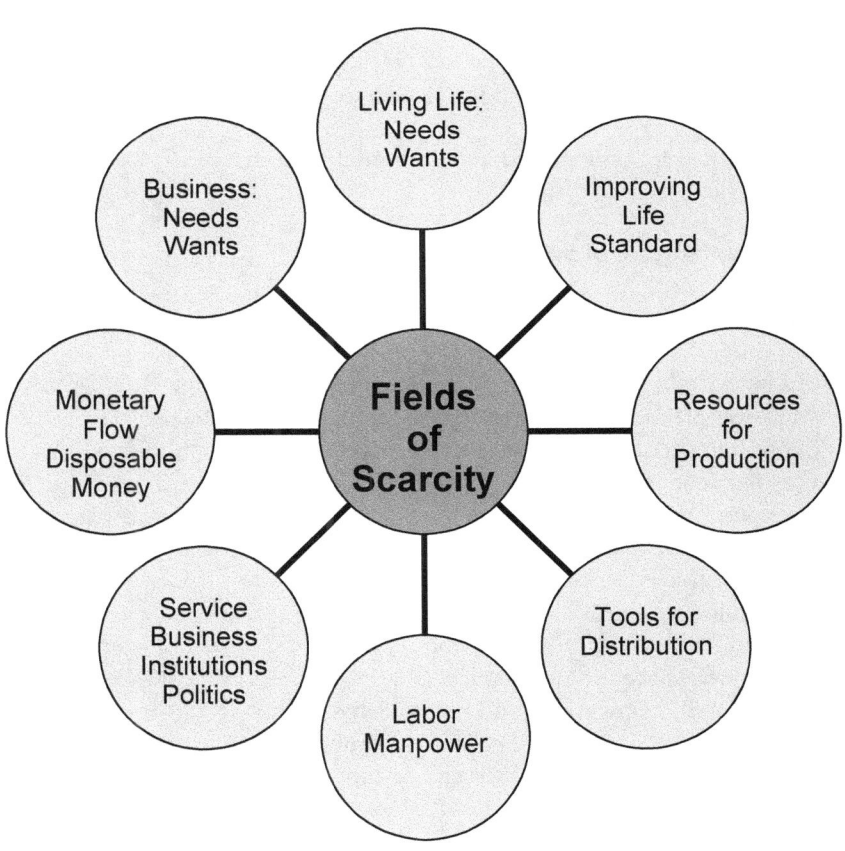

Causes of Scarcity by different Entities, Conditions and Incidents

- Individuals
- Institutions
- Governments
- Society
- Nature
- Life
- Circumstances (e.g. catastrophes, weather conditions, wars).

Conclusions

→ The factors that produce scarcity are heterogeneous depending on entities and incidents.
→ Scarcity must be understood and answered with measures depending also on such factors.

New Understanding of Scarcity

- Scarcity is also a result of personality factors, culture, education, lifestyle, role models, social networks, etc.
- Individuals do not take rational decisions because they don't know or don't respect their real genuine needs. Greed is unlimited.
- Economic theory cannot simply be understood as a complex entity that aims to satisfy all needs and wants.
- Economic policy destroys itself, humans, societies and the planet if it does not consider collateral effects on nature, social structures, and human's mind.
- Economics as science and practical tool for satisfaction of needs and wants must be all-round sustainable.
- The critical base of economics is how people are educated, shaped, conditioned, brainwashed, and manipulated.
- Unlimited and artificial needs and wants at any time and always immediately cannot be the essential duty of economics as science and tool.
- The norms and rules of economics must first be related to the indispensable needs of humans and society.
- The norms and rules of economics must be related to the limitedness of the planet's resources and to the evolution of human beings.
- The psychical-spiritual needs of all humans are subsequent to the satisfaction of the basic needs for a basic life standard, including genuine human values.

- Obsolescence practices and cosmetically polishing goods (e.g. car models) create unnecessary needs (demands) and often scarcity (e.g. 'limited edition').

Extended Interpretation

→ There is always, for all eternity, a scarcity of goods and services as people are greedy and never fully satiable and have endless variations of (new) needs and wants.

→ The market as well creates new (unnecessary) needs and new wants. And the market uses all marketing tools to stimulate such new needs and wants.

→ Scarcity must be equilibrated in its interpretation and assessment with the term and reality of 'abundance' and with the primary indispensable needs to live life.

→ Scarcity as an economic concept must include the need and wants of having money, necessary for at least living a humane life (and being a consumer).

→ Scarcity is a term with a strong emotional negative connotation, in most cases producing unspoken preoccupation, anxiety, existential fear, and sometimes even a sense of panic.

→ Scarcity is an appellative term appealing for something (a decision, an action) on the sides of the consumers and the businesses or the governments.

→ Scarcity in many contexts has got a lot to do with human's greed and irrational consumption behavior; psychological factors must be considered in the use of this term.

→ Scarcity as a term related to a lack of demanded goods and services does not logically imply the necessity to answer with more production and services.

→ Scarcity is an ideological term used and manipulated in favor of capitalistic interests and presumes a variety of conditions and aims that are not natural axioms.

The term scarcity is confusing and used in an inappropriate way. We would recommend finding a new terminology for this complex factor of economics.

Scarcity understood as limitedness of something on the market is a natural phenomena, always given in any households and in any country. 'Scarcity and allocation' as a systemic unity must be seen as follows:

On the one hand any system, an individual or a household (e.g. family) or an institution, has a limited amount of money at its disposal to pay for goods and services and therefore they all must select. The amount of money starts with penniless people or institutional entities with billions of dollars (Euros) at their disposal.

On the other hand we have the world of goods and services: there are countless goods and services in an average sized country; or in a small country or special area there may only be a minimum of goods and services. Some goods are indispensable for living; other goods are for the expansion of the quality of one's living standard and for all kinds of wants in general. Furthermore, part of this systemic unity is the decision process to choose between certain amounts of options. Choosing is not simply about this good or an alternative good; it also means: today this and tomorrow another good.

'Scarcity and allocation' as a systemic real unity leads to the questions: Does economics as a complex theoretical concept have a duty to provide proven efficient models for a balance at least at the level of humane life and basic wellbeing? Or does it only serve the capitalistic interests: the ways to manipulate (brainwash) people to decide for buying these or other goods and services to get highest possible volume of business and profit. In other words: What is the interest of economics to include the factor of wellbeing in its systemic theory? And how is wellbeing understood in this concept? Scarcity is a stupid material concept of greed and excludes human values and the genuine needs of the inner life of people.

Assessment

→ Having more of one good thing usually means having less of another, is not a principle.
→ The concept of scarcity is vague, a platitude, and not even elaborated in a scientific way.
→ The term 'scarcity' is a chewing gum that becomes after a while very distasteful and useless.
→ Nobody would want a medical science that in the long term destroys people, society and the planet.
→ Nobody would buy a new car that does not work properly; 100% inspections must periodically control the efficiency; sometimes specific measures are required and indispensable.
→ The world of car and air traffic and trains is planned, regulated and controlled with extensive measures; economic realities and theories not at all.
→ There is no instance (authority) that controls, regulates and punishes any failure and abuse of economic realities or its concepts (economic science).

It is absolutely impossible and unthinkable that all humans on earth live today and tomorrow on an economic level e.g. like Germany, especially considering the growth of the world population: 7 billion, 8 billion, 9 billion, 10 billion, and more.

→ Scarcity can globally never be unlimitedly satisfied, not even in the Western world! Increasing scarcity is forever guaranteed!

What can we learn from the use of this term 'scarcity' in economics?

It is strange, but also very insightful that 6 different classical books about economics (published from highest scientific authority) start their foundation with the topic 'scarcity'.

First, it is confusing as the word has very different content (meaning), depending on the context of its use. In a certain way this term is distorted; into something irrational is in the description and use of this term. Secondly people can make many different interpretations or conclusions depending on the meaning they focus. Thirdly who ever use this term and whatever the context is or whoever criticizes the use of the term or the principle of scarcity, the term is always right. And above that is the classical pattern we know about perversion (from Sigmund Freud), a drive that allows any distortion and rectification for its action.

But there is more. Given that all authors start their theory of economics with it, I could describe this as follows:

At the beginning everywhere there was scarcity, a lack of everything that makes life comfortable. Even the humans are scarce in knowledge, mind functions, behavior, language, enlightenment, understanding (the world and their existence); there was a very simple social life, and first archaic handmade tools for hunting and fishing, making a shelter. Everything was scarce, pitiful, depressing, fearful, mean, miserable, dirty, rough and bitter, wild, drive and instinct related, magic and sordid; also the man, the woman, and their children: a shameful and embarrassing creature, at that moment an anthropoid, not far away from monkeys. Obviously we can also say: everything they had for living their life (a household) was very limited and uncomfortable, except the undiscovered world of plenty of resources. Seen in that way, we are at the beginning of the evolution of humanity or in the middle of a myth and of the archaic religion. – We are here also at the beginning of a theory of economics!

We have revealed here the first roots and verbal tools of a scam – economics! More explorations in this book will lead to the unveiling of the most horrifying inhumane monster humanity has ever experienced and created.

Our advice for students of economics is: examine very carefully the terms used in any concept, principle, theorem, thesis, or theory of economics before you continue with examinations of the graphs presented in these 'scientific' books because in the graphs lie the most devilish traps.

Nevertheless, the right and transparent use of the word 'scarcity' has an importance in human's life and in economics. Thus the word scarcity indeed has an important practical meaning also for the economy. An existing scarcity of existential importance must be understood and managed in an appropriate way!

Subsequently we offer a new conceptual diagram about the above discussed topic that replaces the concept of 'Scarcity' from Mankiw & Taylor.

Diagram: Management of Scarcity

Dealing with a Scarcity

- Identify the human factors (rational, irrational, unconscious)
- Identify the importance and urgency based on needs and consequences
- Analyze sustainability and risks (damages) of scarcity
- Focus on genuine needs including genuine inner needs
- Weigh and balance the appropriateness of wants
- Include all round the human values as an indispensable factor
- Relate scarcity to motives and claims of the required lifestyle
- Put it in perspective to the limitedness of everything
- Explore the connotations: emotional, rational, systemic
- Identify the manipulations of needs and wants (e.g. marketing)
- Consider education and redirecting given needs and wants
- Take appropriate conclusions and multi-dimensional actions

3.2. Allocation (Distribution)

The Concept of Allocation

The concept of scarcity includes allocation as described by Mankiw & Taylor. We stress out the core element: "Economics allocates people, land, buildings, machines and the output of goods and services." We prefer to use the word 'distribution' for the following considerations.

Another component of allocation is the value that consumers give to the goods and with that the consequences for production and supply, and contingency, including price politics. We elaborate these aspects in Economics II (allocation and efficiency).

Indeed, especially the distribution of goods in an economy is a decisive key structure. All people in the Western world know well the hundreds of thousands of shopping centers; many are immense in size. These shopping centers and shopping malls are the main targeted locations of the distribution network. Consumers go there to buy for their needs and wants. An immense network of transport and storage form the link between production and sale locations. It is a topic of economics to create the best possible or the most efficient conceptual structures.

Shopping centers and shopping malls concentrate ten thousand and more products and guarantee with their locations the best possible access for customers. Indeed it seems that shopping centers and shopping malls are the best tool to guarantee the availability of all products offered from production entities for all consumers. But let's have a closer look at these business entities; we must admittedly generalize a bit and operate with the word 'shopping center'.

Shopping centers have 200, 500, 1000 or more units used as well-defined surface for the sale of the different goods. These surfaces are rented out to a firm that sells; partly it is the production company itself that rents a surface. This means: the corporation owning the shopping center gets a significant amount of money per year, alone from renting surfaces. The seat of the corporations is in most cases not at the location of the shopping center. Logically, a huge amount of money leaves the location and goes to the location of the seat of the corporation.

Most firms that have rented a surface do not sell the products of local producers. And they also have their seat at a location different from the shopping center's location. This means: the money they get in through the sale goes to another location (partly of the production). A majority of the customers are living in the municipality of the shopping center. They work in the municipality or in the extended area. The money they bring in to this shopping center (buying goods and services) goes away from the location. However, some of the people working as sellers in these shopping centers get a wage – a low wage plus a little commission per sale they make.

Given that most people are sheep and considering the fact that a shopping center may make shopping easier as most products can be found in the same place, these customers go less and less to local shops and businesses. The rental prices of premises in a shopping center are high. Local businesses can't afford such rental prices. As a consequence hundreds if not thousands of local businesses have an enormous decrease in income and many must give up. This happened in the past and it significantly happens today with the economic crisis. If the customers living and working in the municipality could find their products in a hundred or more local businesses, a significant cash flow would remain within the municipality.

The consequence is that an enormous amount of money leaves the municipality and goes to another location where the seat of the shopping center corporation is established. We reveal herewith that shopping centers are economic monster octopuses. One corporation seat gets hundreds of millions of dollars (or Euros) and hundreds if not more than a thousand businesses are destroyed. Without the shopping center these smaller or bigger businesses could all benefit from the local market (demand) and most of the money would remain within the municipality or the wider area.

Conclusion: Shopping centers decimate the entire local middle class businesses and with that the local economy. But now the middle class is shrinking and therefore is also disappearing from an active democratic political field. They have lost motives and interest. Where does the profit of the corporations land? Sure is: a few owners of the corporation of the shopping center make immense profits and another few top-managers get an immense wage plus bonuses. Additionally to that we must see that there are a few corporations that own a hundred or several hundreds shopping centers in a country. Therefore an astronomic amount of money is sucked away from the local areas and directed to the location of the main headquarters and the CEOs, the top-managers, the members of the board, and the investors. This business concept creates a complete imbalance in the economy of an area or a whole nation. If we talk about allocation, we must see this network of critical effects as well.

Another perspective of allocation to consider is: The distribution of goods for Europe and United States starts in Asia, as the production is established there (wages 20-30$ per month). The network of global transportation is also in the hands of the same investors (owners). The production fields are under direct or indirect control of the same investors. The entire cash flow from the production to the consumer via global transportation ends up in the hands of the investors and its top-managers. This is called 'globalization', an economic topic to be analyzed later on (and in other projects from the author).

At least: This economic complexity is an example of the fulfillment of the Western (capitalistic) economic theory about scarcity and allocation. The holy message from the classical economic experts is: "There is scarcity, therefore a production problem and an allocation problem. We solve it all."

Remember the statement: "Economics allocates people, land, buildings, machines and the output of goods and services." We could see it from another economic view: Economics allocates money (profit) between investors, owners, and investors that exploit resources, manpower, and the local economy, at the cost of social, environmental and natural destruction. The goods and services are only a tool to enormously increase the money concentration (on a level of trillions of dollars or Euros). And this money concentration is also only a tool for hidden global or continental political interests of the elites. Economics and all people should never forget or ignore: Money rules the world! Money rules the households, the businesses, the big corporations, the CEOs, the politicians, and the governments. And to bring it to the point: Money rules the imperialistic wars.

Allocation Understood as Logistic Distribution

The big corporations that produce millions of goods need a perfect all-area covering network of distribution and a corresponding logistics network.

Lorries, trains, vessels, airplanes, and container ships are the main vehicles that transport the goods all over a country. A collateral effect is the contamination and the immense masses of trucks (lorries) driving on the roads, for example from Finland to Gibraltar or to Greece.

One thousand big corporations could be transformed into one million medium sized businesses and the allocation problem would be in a majority of local or regional dimension.

The other Dimension of Allocation

The allocation principle requires and claims the goal that all possible goods and services must be distributed and accessible for everybody. All resources must be used the most efficient way (efficient in time, resources, labor, costs, management, etc.) to satisfy people's needs and wants. This reflects absurd greed, envy, and jealousy of global dimension. It is not realistic. It breaks the basic principle of human life: never can a human possess everything, nor can he have access to everything and this always in the shortest possible time at minimal costs. It is against the fundamental humane life with its immanent conditions and limitations. It excludes collateral costs and is not founded within the frame of genuine inner human values and the psychical-spiritual longing and fulfillment of humans.

With the needs and wants of humans this principle shall simply justify the capitalistic principles, which are in the interest of those who already possess wealth and power in super extreme abundance. It also hides the intended concentration of economic and governmental power over the entire world. The allocation principle shall justify the control over everything and the unlimited production for unlimited profit.

The dynamic becomes a psychoanalytical dimension: the never satiable unsolved inner complexes. It's much worse than the obesity of a 300kg man: imagine one day the obese man has a weight of 1,000 kg and later 10,000 kg without end in the increase of his volume and weight. That's capitalism in its purest goal, acting, and effect. Where does it lead for the man with 500kg or 5,000 kg? It leads to a monster far beyond a dehumanized human biomass, and in the end to self-destruction. If we adapt this picture for humanity as a whole, it leads to the complete destruction of the planet and to the elimination of humanity.

3.3. Rational or Irrational Decisions

Mankiw & Taylor explain a first principle: "Making decisions requires trading off one goal against another." [77] Another trading off society faces is between efficiency and equity." [78] And: "**Efficiency** means that the society is getting the most it can from its scarce resource. **Equity** means that the benefits of those resources are distributed <u>fairly</u> among society's members." [79] Read this sentence again: 'fairly'! And be aware: Money is also a good to be distributed.

"Trade-offs are at the heart of rational decision-making." [80] 'At the heart' means: in the core, in the innermost, in the essence. What is at the heart of rational decision-making? A need? A want? What kind of needs and wants? But the thinking process itself is neither a need nor a want because thinking is a rational function with some important and supportive sub-functions. Within these rational processes we find the roots of the ways how thinking processes come into existence. Rational thinking processes depend on a complexity of sub-functions and this complex activity leads to decisions. Magical thinking must also be mentioned. Most people cannot distinguish between these two ways of thinking, probably not even the economists. We will explore this later on here - it leads us consequently to the 'heart'.

"In studying choice under scarcity, we shall usually begin with the premise that people are rational, which means they have well-defined goals and try to fulfill them at best they can." [81] The authors admit: "In using the cost-benefit framework, we need not presume that people <u>choose rationally all the time</u>." [82] And the authors shortly explain: "Choice involves compromise between competing interests." [83]

Let's have a closer look at the decision-making processes and the efficiency:

Meaning of Rational Decision Making

- ~~People know what they need~~ (primary needs).

[77] Mankiw (et al.), p. 4
[78] Mankiw (et al.), p. 5
[79] Mankiw (et al.), p. 5
[80] McDowell (et al.), preface xviii
[81] McDowell (et al.), p. 6
[82] McDowell (et al.), p. 21
[83] McDowell (et al.), p. 5

- People know what they need (secondary needs).
- People know why and what for they have their wants.
- People know what they want and why they want it (wants).
- People are able to distinguish between genuine needs and wants.
- People are able to sustainably manage their entire life for health.
- People are able to sustainably manage their financial resources.
- People are able to set priorities and urgencies in their needs.
- People are able to set priorities and urgencies in their wants (wishes).
- People are able to rationally distinguish between options of a product (or service).
- People are able to identify compensatory needs and wants (wishes).
- People's ability to take rational decision includes ability to previously understand.
- People are able to control allurement and seduction (media, marketing, sale communication).

Assumption

- → People are at least able to identify their indispensable basic needs (food, water, etc.).
- → People are not able to appropriately manage all needs and wants in a rational way.
- → People don't know the unconscious compensatory forces of many of their purchases.
- → People can't control their entire consumer behavior in a sustainable way.
- → People do not relate their needs and wants with the 'working before buying' attitude.
- → People are bombarded with countless suggestions for purchases on a daily basis.
- → People are exposed to countless influences from the media, environment and social groups.
- → People are lured, seduced, and manipulated into having artificial needs and wants.

Irrational Components of Decision-Making

- Unconscious deficits from the past and present
- Lack of present satisfaction (compensation)
- State of frustration and anger
- Physical state (e.g. hunger)
- Exciting environment (e.g. people, weather)
- Individualism, egoism and narcissism

- Responsiveness to allurement and seduction
- Emotional responsiveness (i.e. atmospherics in the shopping center, music, smells etc.)
- Projection of unreal expectations
- Weak self-esteem and self-confidence
- Dependence on social appreciation
- Addiction and psychical compulsions
- Compensation drive to create inner balance

Stimulating or Forcing a Demand

- Obsolescence practices
- Uplifting a good with cosmetic details
- Yearly new fashion products
- Professional door to door pressure selling
- Selling appliances that require batteries (for the battery production)
- Miserable quality of products
- Electronically limiting the working life time of a device (e.g. printers)
- Aggressive telephone marketing
- Nag factor at inconvenient/embarrassing locations (sweets at the check-outs)

A decision making process is exposed to many internal and external influences. People are in many contexts simply forced to take a specific decision. The concept of rational decision is therefore rendered redundant making it a theoretical laboratory product of complete insignificance for the sale of the majority of goods and services.

The narrow Decision Making Concept

- An individual may take decisions alone; in important matters maybe even seek advice from mum or dad or a friend.
- A couple may discuss decisions with strong arguments, sometimes ending in a fight.
- A family may have never ending family conferences about important decisions.
- A banker may run to the whorehouse after work and not take rational decisions.
- If parents want to take a decision with their teenager children, it will end in 'fuck you!'
- A single person in psychotherapy may want to explore some decisions concerning the purchase of sex toys.

- And those who run for drugs don't take decisions, nevertheless, the drug business is billions of $.
- Elderly people take it easier and especially slower in taking decisions over an amount of some Euros.
- How can a single person take rational decisions in a shopping center faced with a thousand choices of different clothes and shoes?
- It is today known that children are brainwashed in a way (TV) that the parents purchase what the children decide.

And more:

Goods and services are not simply goods and services. Taking a decision about apples A or apples B or C is not the same as taking a decision about a car or a new computer. Taking a decision about a specific psychological therapy is not the same as buying psychological books. Taking a decision about marriage is not the same decision as taking a decision about going for holidays to Greece or to the Maldives.

Do these scientists when they develop (or teach) such a decision making concept, have any idea about realities? Do they really think, that the realities they have in their 'screen' (consciousness) and in their heavy books cover the real world of decision-making? Or is this economic theory simply a way to deviate student's attention from the highly planned strategic 'invisible hand' of the market that is there to habitualize 'irrational' behavior? Is this the scientific level created by the super reputation of Harvard, Oxford and Co.? And such an economic science is accredited from accredited institutions that are also accredited from governments (or religion)! Is the world naturally mad or is it being driven to madness?

Critical Conclusion

→ The hidden assumptions of this concept of rational decision-making are ideological, idealistic, reductive, artificial, distorted, exaggerated, and simply wrong.
→ This concept of rational decision- making is stupid and manipulative.

The following lists show the reality.

Diagram: Rational and Irrational Factors of Decision Making

Factors for irrational decision making	Factors for rational decision making
State of frustration	Ability to think thoroughly
General emotional state	Ability to analyze minutely
Unconscious deficits	Listening and carefully weighing information
Physical state (e.g. hunger, tiredness)	Being aware of the consequences
Self-esteem and self-confidence	Having a bigger picture about consumer behavior
Social dependences (e.g. peer group pressure)	Responsible for life
Addiction (physical, games, alcohol, sweeties…)	Good self- and time management
Compulsion (strong converted behavior habits)	Being aware of environmental consequences
Intensity of drive (energy)	Reflected money-management
Sexual frustration	Ability to identify quality
Emotional receptiveness	Ability to identify meaning
Striving for a specific or general relief	Can identify genuine needs
Blinded excitement	Efficient life-management
Habits with deep roots (early childhood)	Having a perspective for past-present-future
Conditioned reflexes	Ability to assess the real need or want
Role models	Good self-protection from environmental factors
Impatient character	Carefully balancing the wants
Lack of all-round satisfaction	Being aware of the motives for a purchase
Lack of inner fulfillment	Can set priorities and urgencies
Unconscious copying	Able to identify compensatory needs and wants
Shortsightedness	Have a distinguished education
Stubbornness	Are well informed about the product
Defense reactions	Use in general their mental capacities
Projective dynamic	Calculate time, effort and money
Sheep behavior	Are able to decisively renounce

	something
Naivety and credulity	Are awake in a buy-setting
Reduced thinking capacities	Have a distinguished communication
Magic thinking	Are in general patient
Greed and stupidity	Are able to think in complex networks
Fast-satisfaction syndrome	Can rationally convince themselves
Neurotic dynamic (distorting everything)	Have a moral character
Narcissistic, egoistic need for satisfaction	Can identify human values
Psychotic tendencies (have lost the ground)	Can rationally argue about pros and cons
Megalomania (unlimited self-image)	Can compare with other options
Oral or anal neurosis	Not overloaded with unconscious complexes
Strongly brainwashed by media and marketing	Identify lack of satisfaction and possible solutions
In general very uncritical towards the world	Can think tactically and strategically
Overestimation of one's capacities	Are in general critical and have questions
By trend lazy and lazy-minded	Identify the setting of a decision making
Chaotic and imbalanced in life matters	Give balance and order in life matters

The General Factor of Greed

Let's say: Firstly people need 100 goods and services to live their life. The market offers 500 goods and services. Then they want another 200 goods. If they get some more goods, then they want more goods. The market offers now 1,000 goods. Logically people need more goods now and want much more goods. Finally, one day, the market offers 50,000 goods and services. Now people have become a 'machine of increasingly satisfying needs and wants'. They want 5,000 or even 10,000 of these goods and services depending on the money they have at their disposal, or are able to obtain on credit.

Mankiw gives us the principle: "Markets are usually a good way to organize economic activity." This is an assessment, a normative suggestion. Are there also 'bad ways'? In which way should this be a principle? What is a market and how would we understand the market if greed, stupidity, carelessness, lies, cheat, deceit, distortion, brainwashing and manipulations are the essential factors that organize economic activity? What a stupid principle! It's only pulling the wool over people's (student's) eyes.

The madness never ends because the more goods and services people can afford, the more they lose their genuine humanity and become nothing more than a consuming robot, daily bombarded with direct and indirect manipulations and stimulations. The inner deficit has reached explosive levels. People can't control their decision-making process anymore. They are dehumanized. Rationality is reduced to the level of infantilism. This is the beginning of the end of humanity. Here again we are now with the accredited economic theories and the 'sacred' reputations of Harvard, Oxford and other elite educational institutions.

Conclusion

→ Successful businesses must consider the irrational factors related to their product or services.
→ Consumers with high irrational decision factors are not aware of their irrational functioning.
→ Irrational consumers don't know (or little) that businesses operate with irrational factors.
→ For all kind of irrational decision-making there are always specific products and services.
→ For all kind of products there are always consumers with irrational (blinded) decision-making.
→ The bigger a consumer population, the more the functioning of the

economy is guaranteed.

➔ Irrational factors together with manipulation from the 'invisible hand'; this list makes them visible!

➔ Intervention of governments can easily destroy their own economy through wrong decisions.

➔ Economics is like archaic religion: they satisfy the inner deficits of people in a distorted way.

3.4. Give Up and Get it

Mankiw & Taylor describe a principle: "The cost of something is what you give up to get it... Making decisions requires comparing the costs and benefits of alternative sources of action." [84] The authors introduce in this context another term: "The opportunity cost of an item is what you give up to get that item." [85] Do people really make their decisions comparing the costs and benefits of alternatives? In important matters this is probable for a selected population; in matters of low value most probably not.

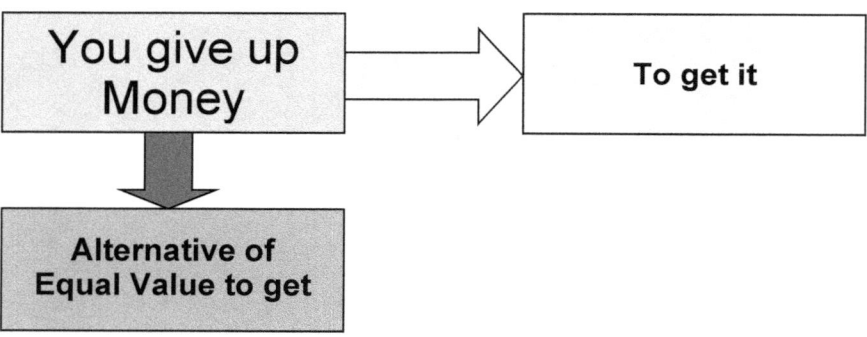

"Give up to get it" is the opportunity cost. The thesis is: "The real cost of something is what you must give up to get it." Krugman says: "The concept of opportunity cost is crucial to understanding individual choice because, in the end, all costs are opportunity costs." And the author specifies: "The opportunity cost of a choice is what you forgo by not choosing your next best alternative." [86]

---

[84] Mankiw (et al.), p. 5
[85] Mankiw (et al.), p. 6
[86] Krugman (et al.), p. 7

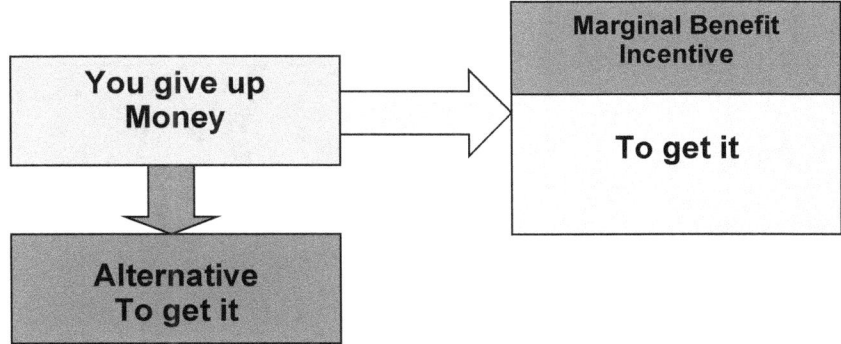

Do (all, most, a majority of) people really think on "what they forgo by not choosing…" during a process of choosing and purchase? This principle is a sandpit game, far away from reality. The principle "give up to get it" may be applicable for specific products. First of all, in a purchase people give up (give away) some money to get it (a product). And sometimes people are not sure if they really should buy this or that, simply because then the money is gone.

The other option is: If I buy this chicken I give up buying a pack of 4 sausages. And such a 'mechanism' is a principle? It's a trivial fact. The motive to buy a chicken or to choose the four sausages can depend on the weather (if it's nice weather the buyer wants to make a barbeque and if it's raining he prefers a chicken to put in the oven. There are many other motives. We could conclude: the purchase of a product depends on 100 different factors that have got nothing to do with a 'give up'. Such a phenomenon the economic experts call a 'principle'! It's not a principle! Where do they have their mind?

Another principle of Krugman is the "decision at the margin". It's about an "either-or" choice. "How much" is a decision made at the margin, the author explains. "Decision involves a trade-off, a comparison of costs and benefits." It's about "a little bit more of an activity" or "a little bit less". [87]

---

[87] Krugman (et al.), p. 7

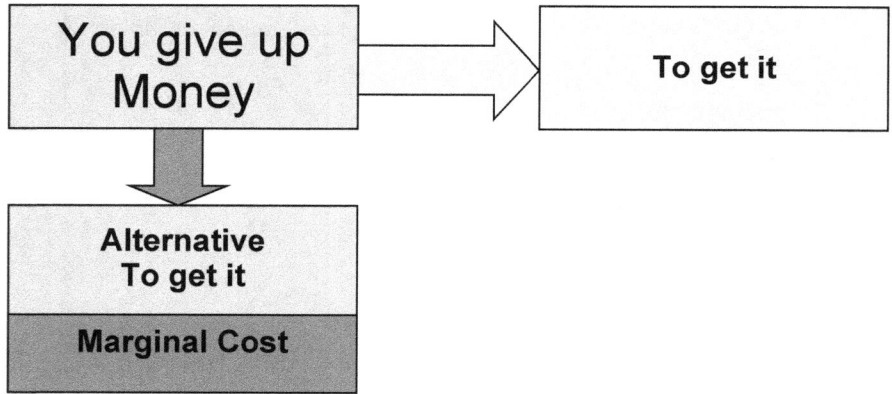

This principle is about a characteristic of a purchase behavior in the moment of choosing a product, e.g. in the supermarket and in front of 500 (let's say) different wine bottles. There are a hundred red wine bottles with a different origin and a price of 3.45 Euros (dollars) plus/minus maximum 30 cents. We assume a comparison of costs and benefits cannot occur here. And there are countless products where such a comparison does not occur. The factor of a choice is simply a meaningless reflex or an uncontrollable variable in people's mind. We must conclude that this thesis cannot be a principle, in the best case a thesis for certain circumstances. The 'How much?' principle is at its best a question?

Another principle of Krugman: "When people are offered opportunities to make themselves better off, they normally take them." And the author clarifies: "The principle that people will exploit opportunities to make themselves better off is the basis of all predictions by economists about individual behavior." [88]

There are two obscure words in this principle-statement: 'better off' and 'normally'. What is better or worse has in people's mind a million variations depending also on the product. And 'normal' can be a statistic figure (i.e. average) or it is in contrast to 'abnormal'. Apart from that, the word 'opportunity' has become boring: many people are tired of this marketing

---

[88] Krugman (et al.), p. 8

trick. They know: the product is old, from last year; freshness nearly expired, style of the product ugly; and the product was not a runner on the market (means a failure). This statement about opportunities is never a scientific approach. Such use of terms cannot be the core element of a principle. Everything is possible, including countless deviances.

"An incentive is anything that offers rewards to people who change their behavior." [89]

The financial potential may have a decisive impact in such considerations. People with low income have a small range of interests. Most wants are faded out. With an average wage for example in Spain of 1,200€ for 80% of the population, an average rent of 500€, average car costs of 250€ per month, the bill for electricity, gas, oil, water, and food and beverage, additionally some other little indispensable needs, the decision making occurs in a very small frame of 100-150€ per month at the individual's disposal. There is not much to get and give up within this financial frame. They alternate every month their 'get it' and 'give up'. 'Give up' could also mean: 'Get it later' or 'Get it now and pay later'; but this is not discussed by the authors.

People with a considerable income over 3,000€ per month (e.g. in Spain) have a better home, a bigger car, more expensive clothes and shoes, some more appliances; and in the end also only a small frame of 300-400€ per month at their disposal. There is not much to get and give up within this financial frame. They alternate every month their 'get it' and 'give up'.

People with a significant income of over 6,000-8,000€ per month (e.g. in Spain) have a much better home, a much bigger car, much more expensive clothes and shoes, some more appliances; and in the end maybe a frame of 1,000-2,000€ per month at their disposal. There is much to get and little to give up within this financial frame. They don't need to alternate every month their 'get it' and 'give up', maybe every six months. During a period of 5 years they can afford many goods and services and don't need to give up something seen in such a time perspective. Once their home is full of goods they needed and wanted and now have, they need a bigger home with more space for more goods. It never ends! These consumers are the ideal clienteles for the market.

Where does this principle of "Give up and get it" lead? What is the economic interest of such a principle? Fact is, a private loan helps 'to get it' without 'giving up' and without having to work for it. This is how people have

---

[89] Krugman (et al.), p. 9

managed their finances for the last 25-30 years: living on credit; the infectious pest imported from the USA to Europe and the world. Its sources lay in their understanding of economics. Therefore we can conclude: economics (and the economy) shapes humans, their values, their needs and wants, their mind and behavior.

To 'give up' implies that they can have it; or that it is their right to have it. Why should lazy, uneducated people, with a 'difficult' character, with miserable working attitudes and minimum performance quality and quantity have the 'right to get it all'? Why should people whose existence only produces one thing: polluting and contaminating the planet with waste and sewage, and the environment with their poisonous mental energy, have a 'right to get it all'? We are talking here about billions of people.

Conclusion

This principle of "Give up and get it" does not significantly work when taking into account the majority of the world's population. There is no economic relevance in this economic principle, except for educated, intelligent people that use their mind for their 'consumer behavior'; that means for planning their decision making. The topic could be considered for educational purposes about "how to plan and master life and find the necessary satisfaction and personal fulfillment". People must learn: there are limits related to their economic status and there is no natural law and right that everybody can satisfy 'just like that' all possible needs and wants. The economic market in the capitalistic world always tries to break these limits, to suggest with marketing the illusion of "You can get it all! You deserve it all.........NOW!"

Price-Consciousness in our View

- People are somewhat price-conscious within the frame of their financial potential.
- People may consider cheaper prices, but lose control over real and important needs.

→ Significant rational choice by price-consciousness is in many cases not given.
→ Significant rational choice by price-consciousness is not even given by people with very limited finances.
→ Price-consciousness is only one of many factors that influence a purchase.

Price and Quantity

An economic theory focuses on how buyer and seller determine the price and the quantity of goods they purchase.

Making a decision is based on different financial factors:

- People compare prices.
- People want the best goods at the cheapest price.
- People have set financial priorities before making a choice.
- People see and have alternatives for the same amount of money.
- For some people quantity comes before quality; for others the other way round.
- People know that the price of getting something reduces getting other things.

- To spend money for something is compensated by the benefit of having this something.

Thesis: Rational People Think at the Margin

Mankiw & Taylor describe another principle called "Think at the Margin": "... the term 'marginal changes' describes small incremental adjustments to an existing plan of action ... Marginal changes are adjustments around the edge of what you are doing." [90] The authors explain: Thinking at the margin <u>can</u> make decisions better. The marginal benefit should exceed the marginal cost. Incentives have an impact in such decision making processes (which is another principle described by Mankiw & Taylor). A critical element here is the word 'can': in 10%, 50% or 80% of all cases of decision making? If the importance and weight of this 'can' are not proven, what then can we do with this principle? It's meaningless and irrelevant if we don't have the specific pattern of a purchase. Such a statement can never be a pillar of economic theory. Nevertheless, let's continue with a critical analysis of this principle to understand this shopping mechanism.

Also Colander says: "A marginal cost is the additional cost to you over and above the costs you have already incurred... And the marginal benefit is the additional benefit above what you've already derived." [91] From there the author gives advice: do it if the marginal benefits exceed the marginal costs; and don't do it if the marginal costs exceed the marginal benefits. And he gives a hint to the reader (the students): those who fail the courses do not graduate. We interpret: understand and accept the marginal issue or you fail.

For Colander economics is a passion: "Recognizing that everything has a cost is reasonable." [92] Of course: life has a cost, talking has a cost (time and energy), sleeping has a cost (as I must choose between sleeping and doing something), love has a cost, kissing has a cost, manipulating others has a cost, creating poverty has a cost – and a benefit due to the opportunity cost.

The word 'marginal' appears in countless contexts: marginal cost, marginal benefit, marginal value, marginal utility, marginal incentive or marginal financial value or marginal human value, and marginal returns. Sometimes it means this, sometimes that, sometimes the other way round, and sometimes nothing or nonsense. It's all a deliberate confusion. Whatever you understand with 'margin' it is wrong and right at the same time, depending on the view

---

[90] Mankiw (et al.), p. 7
[91] Colander (et al.), p. 7
[92] Colander (et al.), p. 8

and interpretation. That's the economic science in its core! From a psychoanalytical perspective I would say: what you feel when reading it, is the true meaning of it: confusing, worrying, typically neurotic, perverse, psychotic, compulsive, irrational, stupid, etc.

It seems that the thinking in 'margins' is not only referred to financial calculations. It is a process of interpretation to balance and weigh reasons, secondary benefits and comparisons in other contexts. Pros and cons are balanced in a wider field of interest.

Same Marginal Benefit (Incentives)

- More quantity
- Sale opportunity
- Additional sample
- Nice color of packaging
- Discount
- A time benefit
- A money benefit
- A free trial
- A pleasure
- Brand value
- Friend likes it
- Attraction
- The 'WOW!' factor
- Glamorous bag
- Near to a café (for posterior relaxation)
- Increase of self-image
- Positive projection
- Tactile (touching) effect

Marginal Cost

- Travel expenses
- Parking costs
- Less quantity
- Criticism from a friend
- No brand
- Boring presentation
- No 'WOW!' factor
- Not nice color (packaging)
- Expensive café (No posterior relaxation)

- Decrease of self-image
- Negative projection
- No tactile (touching) qualities

Diagram: Decision Making Process

Decision
And
Purchase

Start:
External
Internal
Stimulus

Thinking
Emotional
Reaction
At the
Margin

There are also:

- Habits
- Cultural Norms
- Social Pressure
- Role Models
- Self-Confidence
- Decision Ability
- Physical State
- Emotional State
- Frustration
- Inner Deficit and Pain
- Compensation Value
- Boredom, Laziness
- Stupidity, Naivety
- Thoughtlessness
- Time Frame
- Sheep Behavior
- Preoccupations
- Stress Factors
- Sales Environment
- Sales Communication
- Sales Presentation

Need
Want
Identified

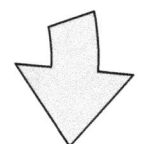

Perception
Good
Service

Opportunity
Cost
Packaging
Incentive

Research
Meaning
Adjusting

Creation of
Libido
Attachment

Theses

→ The wheel rotates endlessly during life – mostly without learning much.
→ Obviously the marketing and selling processes should consider such factors.
→ These factors are active in dependence to the person and the good or service.
→ A neurotic person is influenced in his decisions by the neurotic dynamic.

'Incentive' is a word than can be used for many kinds of stimulus. The principle of incentive argues that a stimulus influences at the margin the consumer behavior in favor of a purchase. But we must state the thesis that a stimulus is often only a factor that spontaneously attracts attention. In other words: once a consumer's attention is achieved (through an incentive at the margin), he or she buys without identifying a special benefit. People do not spend unlimited time in searching for what they want and which of two or more (similar) products they want to buy. Incentives are often only a manipulating factor. There is no guarantee that a stimulus operates only as a motivation factor for a purchase. Therefore the principle of incentive is a mere assertion; and as a scientific term and thesis not explored precisely enough.

- In human life there is rarely a 100% decision based on weighing pros and cons.
- People ponder with all kind of rational and irrational factors when taking a decision.
- People identify elements of benefits for a decision.
- People identify alternatives of spending money they can easily abdicate.
- Comparing costs and benefit with loss of alternatives can change behavior.
- People adjust with marginal benefits and costs to take a decision.
- The marginal benefit of an action exceeds the marginal higher or lower costs.
- People tend to respond to incentives when taking a decision.
- The effect of price on decision is not always crucial for buyer and seller.
- The effect of benefit together with the options to abdicate can be crucial.

Conclusion

→ Rational decision making requires trading-off one good against another good.
→ Most people do not take their decisions rationally by secondary needs or wants.

➔ Unconscious influences have an immense impact in the purchase of many products/services.

➔ The bigger and stronger the unconscious impact, the less the price-level becomes relevant.

➔ People in general cannot weigh one good against all other options, including human values.

➔ As there are not a lot of people that take their decisions rationally, the factor 'rational' is secondary in the world of selling.

Marginal Analysis: Comparing Benefits and Costs

Marginal analysis means: "Comparisons of marginal benefits and marginal costs … 'marginal' means: extra, additional, or 'change in'." [93] And the author explains: "…the decision to obtain the marginal benefit associated with some specific option always includes the marginal cost of forgoing something else." [94] And later he says in continuation: "An opportunity cost – the value of the next best thing forgone – is always present whenever a choice is made." Do people really in a majority of cases consider the value of the next best thing forgone? That's ridiculous! This would make people compulsive, nasty, stubborn, inflexible, intolerant, avaricious, enslaved and programmed robots!

We can interpret: An 'extra' and an 'additional' is always important when making a choice. This smells of greed: "I want a marginal benefit or I don't take it", or: "I always must examine that there is not a tiny marginal cost." We can also interpret: Give me as much as possible and I pay as little as possible. 'Always' also means: 'normal', 'good', 'right', 'naturally legitimated', 'everybody does it', 'it's natural', and with that: 'it's a must for everybody; and therefore those who do not act like 'everybody' are not 'natural', not 'normal', are dissenters, and dangerous for society. With this 'always' the author has lost the ground and has become psychotic. A psychosis is a much higher grade of mental disorder than a compulsion or a neurosis. It becomes dangerous for the collective if the tools at the disposal of such a person can reach the collective world.

It also ignores the fact that such marginal analysis is really not always of relevance when people make a choice. But it is always relevant when a compulsive disposition is given. The word 'always' is simply wrong and again expresses a compulsive character of a person. We are talking here about the people, normal people with 'normal' budget and normal 'wants'. And they absolutely do not always make a choice that considers a possibly given

[93] McConnell (et al.), p. 5
[94] McConnell (et al.), p. 5

margin. We are not talking here about decisions on a level of millions or billions of dollars!

The absurdity we have already discovered in every corner of economics leads us to the question: who does it serve? The logical orientation is: the application of such terms and principles within the world of big corporations and / or a frame of millions and billions of dollars must end in astronomic profit and in the control of governments and the entire humanity. This is a hypothesis to be verified, respectively falsified.

More Variations of a Decision Making Process

☑ A Spanish family doesn't go to Chinese restaurants because they fear this unknown world of China.

☑ An Argentinean man doesn't buy British cheese because he can't stand their warmongering.

☑ German person B doesn't buy Spanish wine because he lived in France and buys only French wine.

☑ A Spanish man only buys a Toyota, would not want a German car because he doesn't like the Germans.

☑ A mother goes shopping with a list of 20 items; she comes home with 5 items and can't understand it.

☑ Another person will never buy a BMW because he is a typical Volkswagen man like his grand father.

☑ A family on holidays had lunch in Puerto Banus, paid a lot for cheap food; so they never go back to Spain.

☑ A 40 year old CEO went to a 5* Hotel in Madrid; there were mostly old ladies so he left after one night.

☑ A Swiss woman lives and works in Barcelona and buys only Swiss shoes because she is often homesick.

☑ There is a bakery close to John's home; but he takes the car to go to another bakery as he is too lazy to walk.

☑ Perfumes are offered: 'get 3 for one', but the young man chooses another similar one for the same price.

☑ A 35 year old man never buys and reads a book because his parents never had a book in their hands.

☑ John gets offered a bottle of wine for $1.80; he buys a bottle for $2.20 because he thinks this one is better.

☑ Mary went to a store and bought 50 items; she only wanted to buy a few things; she can't understand it.

☑ There is a clearance sale; a lady goes there and finds what she wanted very cheap; she doesn't buy anything.

☑ There are 20 different sausages on a shelf; some people always buy the

same one and never try the others.
- ☑ A man went to 10 sofa shops and found what he wanted, negotiated a good price, but left without buying.
- ☑ Lucy buys a toy for her son; there are a lot; she walks up and down counting, stops and takes the 12th toy.
- ☑ Four bottles of water are offered for half price, €2 in total; but 80% of the buyers take only one bottle.
- ☑ An Italian man opens a Pizzeria next to another one, offers the best pizza for half price, but nobody comes.
- ☑ A French man has examined five different German cars within his price range; finally he buys a French car.
- ☑ A man never buys sea fruit, not even with an offered discount, even though everybody buys sea fruit.
- ☑ A teenager buys 10 shirts offered at half price, goes home and realizes that she also wanted to buy shoes.
- ☑ There are a hundred different cheeses on the shelf; a 50 year old man always buys the same Dutch one.

There are many more examples ...

Conclusion

The models of decision-making we find in classical economics are not only greatly reduced and distorted, but also absolutely don't cover the reality of the decision making processes of consumers. The "rational thinking at the margin" is an artificial construction that does not even explain one percent of the real mechanisms behind the purchasing behavior of people. It is indeed unbelievable how superficial and incompetent the scientific knowledge of these experts and highly reputed professors is. Certainly, for the students it is strenuous and hard to go through such ridiculous constructions. But they must go through them for their exams, their grades, and their graduation. It must be true because they are professors of accredited universities. Besides, these students have no time and no skills to reveal all the lies and distortion.

3.5. Decision and Trade Off

Purposeful Behavior

McConnell explains the 'purposeful behavior': "Economics assumes that human behavior reflects 'rational self-interest' … They allocate their time, energy, and satisfaction … Consumers are purposeful in deciding what goods and services to buy…'Purposeful behavior' does not assume that people and institutions are immune from faulty logic and therefore are perfect decision makers. They sometimes make mistakes. Nor does it mean that people's decisions are unaffected by emotion or the decisions of those around them … economists acknowledge that people are sometimes impulsive or emulative. 'Purposeful behavior' simply means that people make decisions with some desired out-come in mind." [95]

Economics assumes: Science doesn't assume; people assume. 'Assume' can mean a hypothesis, a probability, an interpretation, a speculation, a presumption or guesswork, and sometimes a premise. This is a very vague statement!

Purposeful in deciding: The explanation includes the attribute 'sometimes': not perfect decisions, also faulty logic, also mistaken decisions, decisions affected by emotions, influenced by others, impulsive decisions, and emulative decisions. The word 'sometimes' reveals the meaning: low probability, low frequency, not often, less than 50% (or 30%, or 10%).

This is a very vague statement! It also says: "Humans are not perfect", which is a lapidary statement with an undertone of excuse used as a mechanism for self-protection from critics: "Economics is not perfect and economists are not perfect". Absolutely stupid, even infantile! Perfect social science doesn't exist! But everybody expects that the statements are extensively clear, transparent, determined, and proven within a frame of probability and specific reality.

The author reduces his statement: People make decisions with some desired out-come in mind. Again we identify a very vague word: 'some'. This means

---

[95] McConnell (et al.), p. 4

that people have 'some' idea about the decision in their mind. Such a statement is always true; even with a 'drunken' state of mind. In the end with such additional explanations the 'purposeful behavior' becomes the frame of 'can be or can not be'. What is the value of such a statement if most of the decisions people make are not rational decisions, nor in their 'self-interest', maybe partly rational and partly in self-interest? This is blabber, not science! It is incomprehensible how such a statement (thesis) can or should ever be a premise or a principle, or even a rock-solid proven presumption in the foundation of economic science.

Such a generalization of a statement is misleading, worrying, confusing, distorting, simplifying, and a reduction to a meaning that is always correct, sometimes true, but sometimes not. People do science; people develop science; and, the results of science are made by people. Seen like this: These authors are misleading, worrying, confusing, distorting, and simplifying; working with a lot of fog, or pulling the wool over students' eyes. Doing so is a pattern of heavy neurosis or momentous evil doing with very critical effects in the real life of society. A neurosis always contains compulsive elements of dynamic and behavior. A neurosis also has an oral orientation (greed, satisfaction; 'comes in'); or an anal orientation (e.g. relief, control, suppressed anger or rage; 'goes out').

Goals of Decisions

"Making decisions requires trading off one goal against another." [96] Some considerations can help us to understand the context of this thesis in real life. The core question is: What is meant by 'goal'? We explore some examples:

- Buying food to be nourished
- Renting an apartment to have a home (small, simple, luxury, big, etc.)
- Paying for electricity to have light and energy for home appliances
- Buying a car for going to work and having more time for leisure or whatever
- Buying a lot of alcoholic beverages and having a more relaxed feeling
- Buying a Ferrari to get attention from other people
- Buying a porn magazine to increase sexual excitement
- Spending time on Facebook to avoid real social encounter or to satisfy narcissism
- Buying electrical tools to work with, for more efficiency or convenience
- Becoming a member of a club with daily activities to avoid spending time with the children
- Having an internet connection to reduce spending time with the partner
- Going to the gym to increase health or to be more fit
- Going to a spa for relaxation
- Spending money in clubs to have fun and entertainment (or alcohol, cocaine, ecstasy)
- Paying a psychologist to get help for resolving difficult problems
- Paying a doctor for a therapy to recover health
- Paying a disproportionately high price for a car with leasing to boost personality or importance
- Spending a lot of money on holidays and as a consequence ignoring educational needs
- Buying prepared food and having more time to watch television
- Buying an expensive mobile phone and therefore getting attention from others

Do people know what goods and services are good for them, e.g. for wellness and health or fulfillment of life? Another question is: Do people really rationally consider the trade off of one goal against another, especially an emotional goal? Most probably there is a 'third force' in action: The stronger the drive for a good or its secondary effect (as a goal), the more these people are ready to pay for it, even if the price is high and blows their budget. In

---

[96] Mankiw (et al.), p. 4

other words: if an emotional deficit or problem comes into play, the drive is a preponderant decision maker! Clumsy examples of emotional receptiveness are: sexual stimulation, narcissistic stimulation, belief confirmation, self-pity consoler, etc.

The 'Invisible Hand'

Mankiw & Taylor introduce based on Adam Smith an "invisible hand (that) directs economic activity." [97] This invisible hand "leads (households and firms) to desirable market outcomes" and has "the ability to coordinate the millions of households and firms that make up the economy.[98] This sounds like the hand of God or of an evil ghost. This hand is seen as 'irrational' and 'unknown'. Mankiw & Taylor explain that governmental interventions in the market, especially in planned market economies (communism) and taxes distort and hinder the invisible hand to act properly. Such a thing like the 'invisible hand' is introduced when people don't know what's going on and can't explain it, or don't want to reveal the real truth.

Maybe we could say that the law of the chaos theory balances all economic interests of a society. But the reality around the globe shows us that such a law (if it exists) doesn't work properly. Let's explore more and hopefully find out what this 'invisible hand' really is.

➔ Our thesis is: There is no 'invisible hand'!

Colander has a clear understanding of the 'invisible hand': "When goods are scarce, those goods must be rationed ... Economic forces are such mechanisms ... Market forces ration by changing prices ... The invisible hand is the price mechanism, the rise and fall of prices that guides our actions in a market." [99] At the same time the author says that social, cultural, and political forces play a major role in deciding whether to let market forces operate. These forces, sometimes together with legal or historical forces, work together against the invisible hand. Nothing is clear with such statements. The invisible hand as the price mechanism must have to do with humans, as a mechanism itself does not change or determine any price whatsoever.

Therefore, behind the invisible hand are humans. Humans decide about prices and interventions in the prices of a market.

---

[97] Mankiw (et al.), p. 10
[98] Mankiw (et al.), p. 10
[99] Colander, p. 10-11

We will start exploring these mechanisms:

If a good is too expensive for the majority of consumers, most people don't buy it. If a lot of people want a specific good, the prices rise if the amount of this good is limited. The higher the amount available of a good and the lower the amount of people wanting this good, the cheaper the price.

Does this really simply work like that in the market? A seller of a good can also increase the price if fewer people buy it. Or the other way around is also a fact in the real market. So, the invisible hand has its own mood or interests. An example:

An event is planned, once every year. Normally the organizer calculates with 1,000 visitors. A ticket costs €10. So he expects to earn €10,000 from this event. He calculates with an increase of 10€ and 300 less visitors due to the higher price. He expects to make 14,000€. Where is the problem?

Factors of Trading Off

- Importance
- Urgency
- Necessity
- Indispensability
- Entertainment factor
- Fun factor
- Emotional factor
- Brand factor
- Social attention
- Drive relatedness
- Interests
- Receptiveness
- Emotional factor
- Self-Identity factor
- Self-confirmation factor
- Compensation effect
- Satisfaction effect
- Happiness effect
- Reputation factor
- Curiosity
- Mood improvement
- Need to relax
- Inner suffering

- Inner deficit
- Subjective preferences
- Comfort
- Repression dynamics
- Habits
- Occasional stimulation
- Recommendation

Conclusion

Trading off one goal against another has apart from the value of money very often got a value that does not refer to a direct financial value. People spend money for a value that has an emotional importance and not a value of a real (physical) good.

Emotional goals have a different value between people. One good or service may have an enormous (non-financial) value for an individual; but for other people it has no value.

The culture of selling (e.g. marketing, presentation, sale communication) very often considers the non-financial value of a good or service, even if it is completely irrational or illusionary. This can be or is mostly considered in the ways of packaging (presentation) and pricing or verbal and visual messages.

The decision of a trade off is not simply based on the real financial value of the good or service needed or wanted. Therefore a trade off with another good or service for a personal (psychological, spiritual) benefit includes more dimensions than the disdainful money.

Importance of Human Values

Most people do not invest in education and social human values: Giving a present to the partner and children every month, or buying a book every month or occasionally participating in a program for personal development or health improvement, participating in a course for vocational further education, buying reports (DVDs) about the state of the world, buying educational quality toys for the children, going to museums, exploring local and regional culture, learning to play a musical instrument, acquiring tools and materials for creative art work, saving money for a period of 'bad times', celebrating a candlelight dinner with the partner, or regularly buying flowers for the home, etc. Such humane goals are the losers in the battle of needs and wants.

Cheapest Price

Let's explore a bit the above mentioned thesis "People want the best goods at the cheapest price".

- Do people really want the best goods?
- What do people understand by 'best'?
- What do people see as 'cheapest'?
- The extreme case: people want everything for free.
- People want more for less.
- People do not want to give adequate value for a good (or service).
- People do not respect the work, time and production or service invested in a good.
- 'Best' and 'cheapest' are relative to the economic, cultural and educational state of people.

Conclusion

→ The attitude of the masses is greed and disrespect: You give me more and I give you less. Or: I am too lazy to learn, to perform and to work to get the 'best goods'.

→ Maximum earnings for minimum work mantra.

→ The people's attitude for 'best goods at cheapest price' forces the producers to offer 'best shape' or 'best packaging' or 'best presentation' with unidentifiably low or lowest quality.

→ The more unnecessary products on the market, the more people feel a need or want for more and more; and obviously at cheapest price whatever it is.

→ The manifoldness of products without human values makes people confused and irrational in taking decisions. Unsettled in human values they run for the cheap goods.

→ People do not make rational choices in the context of their personal life quality and valuable enrichment as this requires reading books, personal further education, and thinking (contemplating) a lot.

→ Marketing and the media shape the unconscious decision making processes of consumers. They know how the unconscious mind works; people don't know.

→ The inner state of people since prenatal time is the 'battle field' of manipulative forces. As a consequence people are now pre-programmed for the consumer market.

→ The concept of 'rational decision' is a delusion, a Fata Morgana, a cheat, a lie, and an ideology.

Rational decision by price-consciousness requires a corresponding education and a balanced inner life that is highly developed, psychologically and spiritually. Collectively such a condition is not given.

3.6. The Cost-Benefit-Analysis

The cost-benefit-analysis is about: marginal, increments, costs, and benefits. "Choice involves compromise between competing interests." The cost-benefit-analysis resolves this problem. Cost-benefit-analysis requires "ways to measure the relevant costs and benefits." [100]

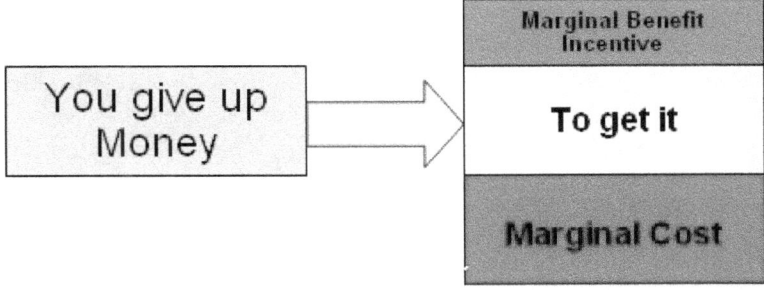

And this is another cost-benefit analysis to challenge:

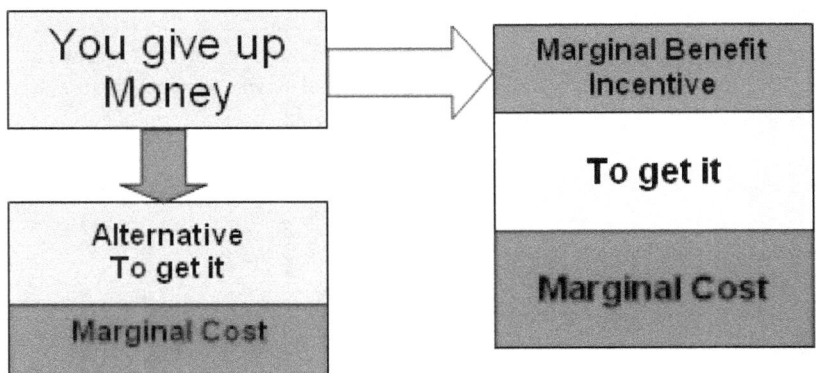

The cost-benefit model of how people make decisions is very powerful, in that it appears to correctly describe how most decisions are made." [101] The

---

[100] McDowell (et al.), p. 4-5

concept is called **marginal utility** and it focuses also on 'how much' somebody will consume. The author explains that people have a limited budget and therefore they can consume to maximize their total utility. The other way round is also a topic, but not mentioned: To find out how to take the consumer's money away in the shortest possible time with a minimum of cost and maximum profit. Sometimes what the authors are not saying is more important than that what they are describing.

Is the cost-benefit-model really always 'very powerful'? What is 'powerful' here? All reasonable limits are broken here, if we interpret that people take 'always powerful decisions'. Exaggerations often serve as a deviating function. 'Powerful' suggests something real and having high importance and relevance. For whom are the people's decision powerful? Is this model really that powerful? For whose benefit or profit? Are the decisions people make really in a majority of cases 'powerful'? How does the author 'powerful' as a variable observe and measure? What is powerful on the side of the producers (and sellers? And this statement is very vague: "<u>it seems</u> to describe correctly"; does it only 'seem like' or is it definitely? It looks like that, but it is not? O.K., sounds interesting: how much people eat, how many coffees they take, how much beer they drink, etc.

Economic surplus: "… is the benefit of taking that action minus its cost." And the author explains: "The opportunity cost of an activity is the value of the next best alternative that must be forgone in order to undertake the activity." [102]

McDonnell says that opportunity costs are a sacrifice: Sacrifice is the opportunity cost of the choice." [103] To make it clear: Opportunity cost is not a real cost; it is the value of the forgone (not chosen) second best choice! Now let's take a visual look at the opportunity costs:

---

[101] Antonioni, p. 31
[102] McDowell (et al.), p. 7
[103] McConnel (et al.), p. 4

Diagram: The Opportunity Costs

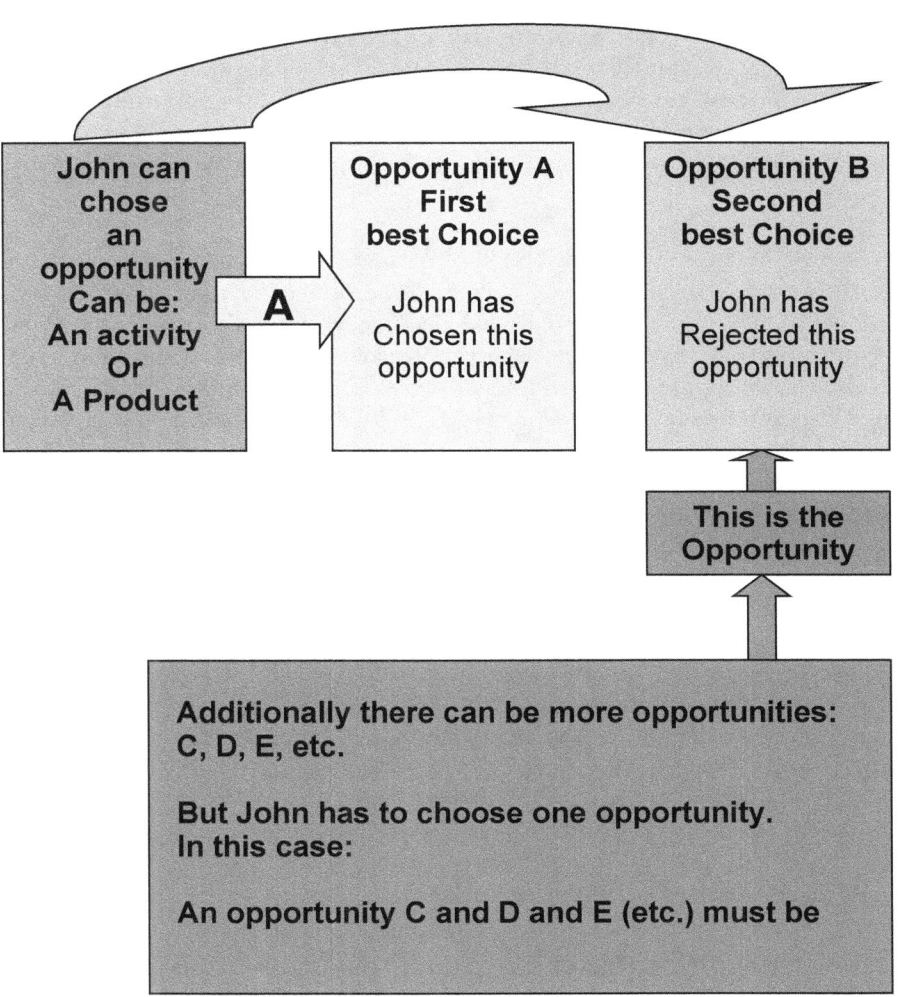

| John can chose an opportunity Can be: An activity Or A Product | Opportunity A First best Choice

John has Chosen this opportunity | Opportunity B Second best Choice

John has Rejected this opportunity |

A

This is the Opportunity

Additionally there can be more opportunities: C, D, E, etc.

But John has to choose one opportunity. In this case:

An opportunity C and D and E (etc.) must be

Critical Approach – We identify here:

a) Abuse of the word 'opportunity': An opportunity is something that one can get during a limited period of time for a reduced price; or a special something that one can only get on a specific date or at a given moment. In general here and there, there are always 'opportunities'. An opportunity is something special, beyond the 'normal' market. People run for opportunities! An opportunity promises a reduced price, a unique good or possibility. This is not mentioned in the statement of the authors; therefore irrelevant in the thesis.

b) Abuse of the word 'cost': The core message is: what you don't use is the cost! It sounds absurd to state, that the good or activity somebody does not choose is a cost. In the mentioned decision pattern, the real costs of an opportunity have no importance and are irrelevant. The use of the word 'cost' is used inappropriately, doesn't make sense; but promises something related to a relevant money factor (value) which can't be.

c) Abuse of the extension to uncountable opportunity options: An opportunity does per se not refer to innumerable options one can choose at any time. Opportunities are meant to be limited in the amount and time frame.

d) Abuse of reality: The word 'opportunity' in the real world refers to clear characteristics which are not meant in the statement of the authors about this topic. The effect is: it confuses, it is not logical, and produces worry: 'How can I understand this strange use of the word? Why do we have to speak about 'costs' although there is no real cost? The 'opportunity cost' concept is neurotic: everything is displaced, distorted and does not reflect the truth of a reality. Logically it produces unnecessary stress: "I must understand this important concept given by the authority; in order to pass the exam and to graduate".

Example 1: 'Opportunity cost'

If there are two opportunities and one chooses one of both possibilities, then the opportunity costs include the value of both opportunities. John has two opportunities for lunch: a steak or fish. The steak costs 20€ and the fish 10€. If John chooses the fish, then the opportunity cost is 20€, as John would get 2 fishes for the 20€ that the steak costs. That must be added to the costs of the first opportunity (the 20€ for the steak); means total opportunity cost: 40€. Such a calculation means: what you decide to do has a cost, and what you forego to do at the same time (the second opportunity that could be taken for the 20€ are the two fishes) as an alternative is also a cost to be added, rejected now and / or used later. – Only a very perverse mind can develop such strange ideas. This calculation is not real and it doesn't make sense.

Imagine: you want to buy a car for 50,000€. You have two 'opportunities', both at the same price. You buy the blue one and not the red one. The opportunity costs are 100,000€. You can buy it immediately; if you wait 6 months to buy the car, you must add the time of 6 months to the opportunity costs. But if you wait for 6 months then you have lost the time of owning the car during those 6 months and this is a cost. Do you get that? Partly it makes sense; partly it's absurd to make such calculations.

Example 2: 'Opportunity cost'

John wants to buy a business. He has two opportunities. Both opportunities have the same purchase price. Business A allows him to make a profit in the range of 1 million Euros per year. Business B allows him only 500,000€ profit p.a. Business A is in a city with immense contamination. Business B's location is in an idyllic landscape close to a small town. John decides to buy Business B. Therefore based on the economic use of the term, the 'opportunity costs' are the one million Euros he foregoes. --- But what is the point or purpose of such a calculation?

The very strange description of this term from several authors may allow one to determine the parameter 'opportunity cost' with the difference between profit A and profit B, which means: 500,000€ difference (that what business B would bring in; in other words that is the loss of profit because he decides to buy business B and not business A. If in general, as said in some definitions of this term, also immaterial values are considered as 'cost' or 'benefit', we have on the one hand the financial differences and on the other hand the immaterial values: business A with 'contamination' (unhealthy environment) and business B with 'healthy and peaceful environment' that includes most probably a longer life (and many more years of happiness and maybe profit; meanwhile the business A would bring him a lot of additional health care costs and in the long run much less profit as he would often be ill and ultimately die at a younger age).

We can construct this example the other way round: John takes the opportunity of business A and pays 1 million Euros. He says that he doesn't need to live in the city (there are wonderful areas outside the city) and the contamination is anyway an exaggeration by people with a deformed mind. Therefore the opportunity cost in this example is 500,000€ (what he would have to pay for the business B. The business A also brings much more profit per year. This is a positive result. From this point of view John is the big winner in three ways: much less opportunity costs (saved 500,000€), no problem with contamination, and a much higher profit per year. From an economic point it doesn't make sense to buy business B. – Here we are now in the middle of capitalistic thinking; distortion of human values in the interest of highest possible profit.

In a certain way it implies and justifies greed from its origin: In the example 1 you could have both opportunities! Or you have opportunity one and secretly you would want both opportunities. The missed opportunity follows you (in the mind) with a sense of frustration. Obviously people can't always have the two or more opportunities, either opportunity A or opportunity B. A clever human now can think: there must be a way I can get both (or all opportunities); and he searches for a mathematical strategy to get both! Long term profit of opportunities is an essential part of the decision making process for people with rational thinking.

If we multiply this absurd greed, envy, and jealousy of global dimension, then we come to the hidden 'want': "I want to possess and dominate the entire world with every vivid and non-vivid thing (Genesis I, verse 28) and I also want to be everything in one – or I get frustrated and angry, and then I destroy the world and everything to get the supreme victory over every human and even over God that hinders me to get it all: the best opportunity, the highest profit, all resources, humanity as a whole, the entire planet, and finally being God in the other world".

Again a psychoanalytical dimension: Some people in the world of economics indeed want to be God. With that we discover the genuine and inerasable humane inferiority. Such humans can't accept to be unimportant in the context of the whole, weak and incomplete as a human being, never able to possess all existing opportunities in this world and in the other world, with a small penis and very limited power (potency, virility). Ad infinitum and incessantly they claim: "I want to posses the entire world and global power!" In essence it becomes a titanic fight against God. This is the capitalistic economics with their economic and religious string pullers behind the curtains, today on the pathway with full power ahead towards the goal of domination.

e) The authors mention that the 'cost' can also be seen as immaterial costs: anything of value, including time, reputation, happiness, pleasure, etc. John has two opportunities of an activity. He can't do both at the same time. Therefore the time for the first activity must be added to the time of the second activity as he does the second one later or not (which is unimportant; in either way both opportunities are calculated).

At first sight to add these immaterial costs to the material costs does not make sense. But it is very meaningful: "I want love, care, happiness, attention, reputation, satisfaction, trust, inner peace, justice, fun, pleasure, orgasms, tenderness, joy of life, completeness, totality, wisdom, all human values, and finally the highest psychical-spiritual fulfillment including all highest archetypal processes completed in my soul." On the unlimited capitalistic pathway it is not possible to get these archetypal and humane values; especially not without having worked (practically, psychologically and spiritually) for it. Therefore the frustration and anger is immense and must be compensated with terrestrial megalomaniac 'wants' beyond imagination.

f) The entire use of the mentioned terms is irrational, absurd, illogical and very confusing. And this is the effect: if you don't understand, then you are the problem and eventually you will fail the exam. One must believe that it is correct what is written there. This is the aim for all intents and purposes. It doesn't make sense, but it's the statement of an authority. Believe it or leave the college / university!

g) It is obvious that the same mechanisms of use of words we find in religion: you believe and accept, first you believe and then you will know, or you will be punished (you can't enter into the paradise).

h) Who cares about the cost of something that one has not decided to get? Nobody!

Example: John has two girlfriends. He wants to marry one of them. He chooses one and calculates some costs as she is very demanding. The other woman is less demanding, but more sexy and this gives the promise of more sex per week. Therefore John has to calculate the costs for the first woman (the one he wants to marry) and he has to add the values of having more sex with the other woman. Finally John doesn't chose to marry and will not have sex with her in the future. – Sounds really funny and it has something real! But it would not be advisable to proceed like this in such a case. The end of the marriage could follow rapidly and the sexual dreams could later anyway dissolve into an illusion.

In general, after analyzing several descriptions about this opportunity cost theorem' we identified differences in the use of the concept in a way, that it can be applied for any absurd composition of opportunities and any kind of costs. We impute that this is an intention for at the moment unidentified purposes. Who can be so sick in the mind to construct such an absurdity?

Now we can explore this use of words for economics in a psycho-analytical way: The concept of 'opportunity cost' has some similar structures to a compulsion. The first characteristic is the distortion of meaning and a charade. The second characteristic is the magic effect. And the third characteristic logically is that there must be something hidden. It is also a perversion of meaning. Therefore an important meaning is perverted and it must have to do with sexual drive, embarrassment, and guilt. The defense works with rational re-grouping of meanings up to the irrational and absurd extreme.

If this is true here, what can be so shameful and so burdened with guilt that starting from this the economics authors develop a very complicated and inscrutable economics? It must be something immense, much more than a suppressed sexual desire. The entire system of economics is, apart from religion, developed to extend such charades, so, this 'something' must be horrifying and worse than guilt. At the beginning (at its roots) lies a murder, a father being murdered; but finally it must be even more and that can only be deicide.

Later on I will prove that deicide is the true source and aim of the capitalistic economy. It is not of Arab source. It is not of genuine Christian source. It is not simply a perversion, or a compulsion, or a neurotic psycho-dynamic. It is of the worst devilish dimension that humanity has ever seen up to today, but its roots lie back more than two thousand years.

The authors add: "Economists use the cost-benefit principle as an abstract model of how idealized rational individuals would chose among competing alternatives." And the Author continues: "... a rational decision is one that is explicitly or implicitly based on a weighing of costs and benefits." And a bit later the authors reinforce: "Knowing that rational people tend to compare costs and benefits..." [104]

A specific problem of rational decisions is explored with many examples: Rational decisions also have pitfalls. The cost-benefit-analysis resolves this problem. [105]

The problem with the cost-benefit 'principles' in McDowell's explanations: [106]

---

[104] McDowell (et al.), p. 9
[105] McDowell (et al.), p. 9-21
[106] McDowell (et al.), preface xviii-xix

2. The Cost-Benefit-Principle: Take no action unless its marginal benefit is at least as great as its marginal cost.

First of all it shows a correlation between three variables: action + marginal benefit + marginal costs. It also includes advice that cannot be understood as a principle. This is not even a scientific statement. If people would only take action when they calculate the marginal benefit, they would need to do this calculation at every occasion of a purchase. This is unreal and the interrelation is not even elaborated for a scientific research. This statement is never a principle.

3. The incentive Principle: "Cost-benefit comparisons are relevant not only for identifying the decisions that rational people should make, also for predicting the actual decisions they do make."

We have already developed a new model about decision-making and explained why the given models do not work. Most decisions people take are in the best case partly rational. This can be understood as a correlation or a weighing of relevance. But 'relevance' is not a measurable variable. Maybe the meaning is: Cost-benefit analysis is only feasible in the context of rational decisions.

Here a prediction is in the air: It is not proven that if people take a rational decision (in a situation) that they take in the next (equal or similar) situation also a rational decision. In case such a statement can be taken with a certain low probability. But the statement is not even a scientific statement. This statement is never a principle.

4. The principle of comparative advantage: Everyone does best when each concentrates on the activity for which he or she is relatively most productive."

What is meant with 'to do best'? How can 'best' be measured? Is there a 'good', 'better', 'very good', and 'nearly best'? 'To concentrate' and 'the activity' is not specified. 'Relatively most productive' is vague: What does 'relatively' mean? How can this 'productive' and 'relatively' be measured? This principle is not even a scientific statement. There is nothing that could express a 'principle' in this interrelation between 'best' + 'concentrate' + 'activity' + 'relatively most productive'. Apart from that the market today does not allow for most people such 'optimization of productivity'. This statement is never a principle.

5. The principle of increasing opportunity cost: Use the resources with the lowest opportunity cost before turning to those with higher opportunity

costs.

Choosing the next-best alternative that has a benefit is the opportunity cost – a must for rational people. Economics "lead people to view questions in a cost-benefit frame work". [107]

This is an advice and not a scientific statement. There is no reason or argument that allows for such an advice to always be recommendable. The word 'resources' and the word 'use' are not clarified; does it mean raw resources and 'abuse'? Or does it mean "'products' and with that the advice would be: Buy your resources only with the lowest opportunity cost? Or does it mean: The resources you need for production you should buy at the lowest possible price. Such an advice would allow 'exploitation of resources' at any humane and environmental costs (externalities) and with lowest possible wages for the laborers. This statement is never a principle, but certainly a dirty capitalistic attitude.

---

[107] Colander, p. 9

3.7. Efficiency

In the section about 'decision making' we mentioned what efficiency means according to Mankiw & Taylor: "The society is getting the most it can from its scarce resource." There is some analytical work that needs to be done here: we must clarify first the use of terms and their implications.

We interpret: 'Efficient' means 'when getting the most'. 'The most' is not specified. The way how the most can be gotten is neither clarified. We associate here: the highest, the biggest, the best amount; as much as possible. And we extend: any means can be discussed (or used?) to get the 'most'. Natural resources are limited (scarce). 'Resource' in this understanding can be understood as raw resources. But there are also other resources such as labor, money, etc. The other option is the country must import resources (goods). And this costs money. Or there are ways to cultivate resources (e.g. agriculture) which means: land and work.

The line is thoroughly the same: exploitation at the highest possible level (getting the most). In this context there is no balance in the understanding of 'efficiency'. With the industrial tools (machines) and their efficiency today, the resources of an average sized country can be plundered within decades. Above that the necessary money resources for getting the most can be solved with public debt. The greed smells to the heaven! And the collateral damages are ignored; never balanced in the understanding of 'efficiency'.

The **Efficiency** Principle: "Efficiency is an important goal because when the economic 'pie' grows larger, everyone can have a larger slice." [108]

Efficiency is defined: "… all the opportunities to make some people better off without making other people worse off …" [109]

Another thesis (principle) from Krugman: "Resources should be used as efficiently as possible to achieve society's goals." And the author explains: "Money is only a means to other ends. The measure that economists really care about is not money but people's happiness or welfare." And: "An

---

[108] McDowell (et al.), preface xix
[109] Krugman (et al.), p. 14

economy's resources are used efficiently when they are used in a way that has fully exploited all opportunities to make everyone better off." He explains more: "…efficient is if it takes all opportunities to make some people better off without making other people worse off." [110]

It seems here: We are allowed to make the planet worse off; or at least this criticality is irrelevant in the context of efficiency. This is a clear example – paradigm of economics – how naïve and selective or evil the economic science operates (and how these 'scientists' are thinking).

Another principle from Krugman: "When markets don't achieve efficiency, government intervention can improve society's welfare." Further explanations to this principle are: "This happens when markets go wrong." Therefore economics also have to explore what and why something goes wrong. [111]

Colander: "Efficiency means achieving a goal as cheaply as possible." [112] This is the invisible hand theorem, the invisible price mechanism that tends to allocate resources efficiently. Continuing he comments that if you don't know the assumption, you don't know the theory. In another context he interprets productive efficiency: "…achieving as much output as possible from a given amount of inputs on resources." [113]

The efficiency principle is not a principle. The statement is rather a deceit, or a distortion or a lie: It is not proven that when the economic 'pie' grows larger, everyone can have a larger slice. What is this 'pie'? Is it the profit or the amount of goods? The profit in general does not go to the work force (labor), not even in a half-appropriate way. The infinite production of goods is heating up the market with more and more goods without questioning if this is 'efficient' for the individual life, for the society, and for the planet (the people living in 100-200 years will also want a benefit from the planet's resources). The message of this 'principle' is: buy, buy, and buy more, as much as you can.

The statement "government intervention can improve society's welfare" is not a principle. It simply says that the government can do something for improvement of society's welfare. There are many others (people, institutions) that can do a lot for the improvement of society's welfare. This perspective is ignored. Mankiw's principle "Governments can sometimes improve market outcomes" shows the same negligence in formulating principles. And the

---

[110] Krugman (et al.), p. 13
[111] Krugman (et al.), p. 14-15
[112] Colancer, p. 13, 31
[113] Colander, p. 29

principle from Krugman that says "Government policies can change spending" is also a hollow statement that focuses on a possibility; but this is never a principle. Again and again we identify that (some) top-experts of economics deal with words and 'principles' in a very sloppy way.

The **Equilibrium** Principle: "A market in equilibrium leaves no unexploited opportunities for individuals but may not exploit all gains achievable through collective action." [114]

Krugman explains this principle: "An economic situation is in equilibrium when no individual would be better off doing something different." [115] And the author continues: "… at any time there is a chance, the situation will move to an equilibrium." [116]

Krugman's principle says clearly: "Markets move toward equilibrium." [117]

The economic history teaches us: Western countries periodically experience inflation, recession, and depression. And this is not 'equilibrium'. It shows that markets also move towards complete disequilibrium. The principle is falsified, a lie and useless.

Another principle says (Mankiw): "Society faces a short-run trade-off between inflation and unemployment." It says that there is a direct correlation between inflation and unemployment. Does this correlation really reflect the real mechanisms? Or are there many other intervening factors between both variables? There are! And therefore this is a false statement and not a principle, or it is a misleading thesis that avoids telling (seeing) the real truth about inflation and unemployment.

If we look around the globe, then we can't identify any equilibrium. Nothing is balanced in societies. As a scientific statement the implicit thesis is not provable. This statement doesn't make sense: "A market in equilibrium leaves no unexploited opportunities." Who says and how can it be proven that this should be something valuable or that this really exists in the market? The idea behind it is: all opportunities for the market must be exploited. Such an ideal is in the best case a capitalistic normative. The motto is: Exploit as much as you can! In the statement "no individual would be better off doing something different" is a hidden advice. How can a science identify and measure the 'be better off'? This is all capitalistic hot air! This statement is never a principle.

---

[114] McDowell (et al.), p. preface xix
[115] Krugman (et al.), p. 12
[116] Krugman (et al.), p. 13
[117] Krugman (et al.), p. 11

"Equity means that everyone gets his or her fair share. Since people can disagree about what's 'fair', equity isn't as well defined a concept of efficiency." The author makes it clear: "People also care about issues of <u>fairness, or equity</u>... there is typically a trade-off between equity and efficiency." [118]

How should the equity-principle be a scientific statement or a 'principle', if it is not a well defined concept? The word 'fair' is also very vague and not measurable in quantity and quality or moral. The global reality shows us: an estimated 6 billion people don't get their fair share. "People care about fairness": this is more like a joke. More and more people know perfectly well that there is no fairness on the market and in human life in general.

➔ Efficiency and 'the most it can' means: accumulation, quantity, illimitableness – and not quality!

In this economic concept we identify another principle. Principle of all production and services is:

➔ Minimum cost + minimum time + maximum performance = for maximum profit

We can not identify this statement as a principle. It is simply a calculation that aims to maximize profit. Enlarging the 'profit pie' by using as little labor as possible, working as long as possible for as low a wage as possible and replacing labor with machines that can achieve and grow the 'profit pie'. The 'profit-pie' however does not go to the people! And the 'maximum possible profit' hides the externalities with immense costs and irreversible damages that the following generations will have to pay for. This 'principle' is really evil and has got nothing to do with science. The concept 'efficiency' is very short-sighted and blinds out the negative costs of such a concept of efficiency.

Critical Development of Equilibrium

"One person's spending is another person's income." And more about this: "Because one person's spending is another person's income, a chain reaction of changes in spending behavior tends to have repercussions that spread through the economy." [119]

---

[118] Krugman (et al.), p. 13
[119] Krugman (et al.), p. 16

154

The statement is not a principle. It describes a short movement from a person A to a person or entity B: The money goes away from A and goes to B. We could also say: If a person leaves the home; he is not at home anymore. Is such a statement a principle? Sounds trivial and is indeed a platitude, not a principle. It sounds like the gravity law and it's logical without the need of a scientific test. But the gravity law is related to environmental conditions (e.g. air, or on earth or on the moon). And the statement "money goes away from A and goes to B" is related to nothing else than the good and an entity A and an entity B. A and B can be a person or a firm or any kind of entity on the market. As money has a value, the value moves from A to the use of B. We can give frames: the place B is a worker in Asia getting a wage of 30€ per month. Or it goes to a corporation that produces weapons. Or it goes to another country where corruption is the law of the market.

Therefore: What is the value (meaning, importance, efficiency, or axiom) of this statement? What scientific construction could be built up on such a statement? Are there conditions where this 'law' doesn't work? But the statement gives groundbreaking stimulations: A wants that 50-65% of the money in Europe (or in the United States) flows to his bank account. He invents the mega-corporations with a mega-allocation-network and mega amounts of products. All people go shopping there. And the money flows to his bank account with astronomic profit. This makes sense. The statement converts into an instruction about how to get as much money (profit) as possible. The 'invisible hand' helps through the sheer power, size and reach of the corporation.

"Overall spending sometimes gets out of line with the economy's productive capacity." [120] The author explains: The consequence is a **depression**. "If overall spending is too high, the economy experiences inflation." And: "This rise in prices occurs because when the amount that people want to buy outstrips the supply, producers can raise their prices and still find willing customers." The author continues his explanations: "Government policies can change spending." "Government spending, taxes, and control of money are the tools of macroeconomics policy … trying to steer it between the perils of **recession** and **inflation**. [121]

Components of Efficiency

- Time factor

---

[120] Krugman (et al.), p. 16
[121] Krugman (et al.), p. 17

- Energy factor
- Collateral effects
- Externalities
- Sustainability
- Skills
- Decisiveness
- Self-Confidence
- Abilities
- Knowledge
- Strategies
- Tools
- Costs (the price)
- Money disposable for investment
- Performance
- Experiences
- Perseverance
- Planning
- Organization
- Manpower
- Human factors
- Environmental factors
- Quantity of the resource
- Quality of the resource
- Importance
- Communications
- Transport
- Geography

Diagram: Concept of Efficiency in Economics

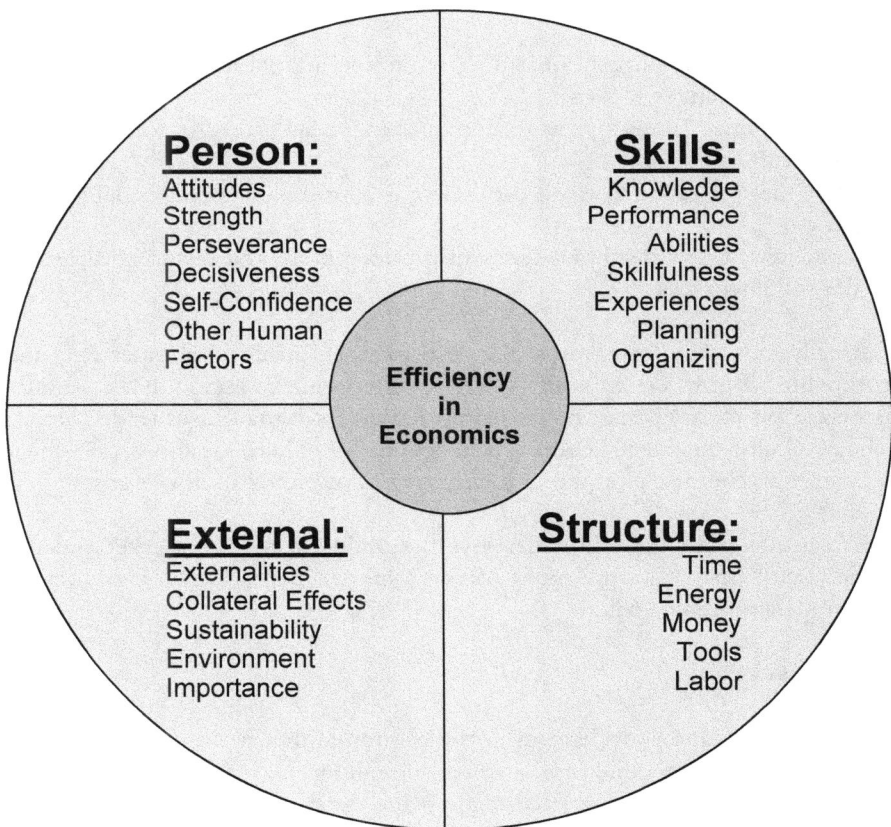

Person:
Attitudes
Strength
Perseverance
Decisiveness
Self-Confidence
Other Human
Factors

Skills:
Knowledge
Performance
Abilities
Skillfulness
Experiences
Planning
Organizing

**Efficiency
in
Economics**

External:
Externalities
Collateral Effects
Sustainability
Environment
Importance

Structure:
Time
Energy
Money
Tools
Labor

The Trap of the Lowest Cost

If everybody searches for the lowest cost of what they want, then they provoke a war between the competing producers (sellers). Competitors are then forced to reduce their costs to sell the good even cheaper than the other competitor. If we develop this dynamic further, then there arises a moment where nobody can produce the product cheaper. This would be a dead end of the competition concept. But clever economists will then find new ways to make their products cheaper, for example:

- They mix farina with paper or wood or stone powder.
- The buy slaves and put them in a cave where they live and work.
- They find a way to put very small air bubbles in the product to make it bigger.
- They hire children to do the work, 12 hours per day.
- They transform human and animal excrements into sterile substances to make hamburgers.
- They produce milk that consists of water and add laboratory minerals and chemical additives.
- They produce laboratory vegetables and meat, and add the corresponding taste with chemicals.
- They hire prisoners to work for them for 10 cents per hour, and 12 hours per day.
- They invent new machines that can produce more and faster; so they can fire more workers.

Certainly, they will do the most they can to make products cheaper than the competitor. But where will this end? Why can't humans accept that a product is here a bit cheaper than there, or more expensive than in other locations? The source of this lunacy comes from economics. There the top-experts heat up: cheaper, cheaper, cheaper … lower costs…lower costs…lower costs …

This is so sick! In the end it destroys the middle class, the market and the society, and first of all the mind of every human being, which is without a doubt their supreme goal.

'The most I can'

There is a regulation mechanism in the economic theory decision processes: getting something requires renouncing something; and obviously there is a 'price' (money, time, energy) for 'getting the most possible'. Regulation can balance the factor 'efficiency' and 'the most possible'. But do such regulative mechanisms in the decision making process work in real life to aim for and get a balance? Doubt arises!

→ The component 'the most it can' is a normative-operational term. It includes a demand, an option, an aim, and a value. Such a term is in the context of its use normative and not descriptive.

→ In the context of efficiency, 'the most it can', and the regulative mechanisms is no criterion that refers to quality (human values) for human's life and fulfillment nor a guarantee considering such humane dimensions! Such factors simply do not exist in the above mentioned definition.

→ One must think about such a use of terms and definitions beyond the visible, towards the utmost end and multiply it by millions or billions; and then we see where such terms and their implicit concepts lead to and what such terms and definitions are worth.

But the aim of 'getting the most' (of resources) includes that all components of the efficiency must be optimized to the most possible extreme. It also includes: getting the most possible goods for society. Who says that this is necessary, healthy and indispensable for wellbeing or living standard? Within decades such proceedings in a country would lead to extreme high public debt and its own resources can be plundered down to extinction. Such an extension simply doesn't make sense. The end is foreseeable: the society destroys its resources and in the end itself.

The Profit-Principle ignores a Series of Human Factors

There are professions for goods and services that require patience, intuition, empathy, understanding, creativity, and the use of the unconscious mind, especially irrational perception (6th sense) or the spiritual intelligence (e.g. visualization, experiencing meaning). Operating here with the time-factor and with the minimum effort factor makes such businesses a complete failure.

General examples are: Psychotherapy, psychological counseling, psychoanalysis, general medicine, music, arts and craft (e.g. painting), philosophy, education, nursing, architects, designers, authors, scientific explorations and research, politics, planning, animal keeping (e.g. zoo), mediators, conflict resolution, etc. If a profession could be or should be an expression of inner potentials or talents, then such quality can never be developed and performed under the required time factor for efficiency.

Other examples are: This time factor reduces an animal in industrial cattle breeding to a mere product. The time factor reduces agricultural land to a mere circumstance for agriculture ignoring the world of species living in the soil and contributing to a natural balance. The time factor is also minimized in all kind of dealing with nature: deforestation, mining, pesticide, antibiotics, and other chemical products must increase the result in the shortest possible time with the least technical tools; and in the end we have pollution and contamination, and products of very low quality.

Last, but not least we must also consider the time factor related to labor, the workers: they must perform as much as possible in as little time as possible (minimizing performance costs). The consequences are well known in the capitalistic world: stress, psycho-somatic reactions, depressions, anxiety, sleeping disorder, alcoholism, unhappiness, frustration, anger, aggression, feeling of being exploited, mentally enslaved, and in 80% of all workers a loss of inner dedication (commitment). Secondary effects are: all kind of accidents (work, traffic, leisure, sports, and home), divorce, lack of communication within a family (partner, children), emotional atrophy, dehumanization, etc. The humane chain reactions are even greater and end in the dehumanization and self-destruction of human beings.

In general, we observe in the principle "minimum time + minimum costs + maximum performance for highest possible profit" a complete lack of human values, meaning for life, and respect for nature and species as well as for the natural resources in general. This principle destroys humanity and the planet. It also especially destroys the psychical-spiritual evolution of humanity. Such an economic principle operates as a devilish self-destructive requirement. In this principle the lemon is squeezed until the last drop, and then one can throw the fruit skin away forever: humans, nature, the soil, water resources, all kind of raw resources, the world of animals, and finally humanity as a whole. It will not take 50 years to come to this breaking point! And then there is no need or want anymore for any economy, any economists, or economics as a science.

Efficiency: 'The most it can'

Where does such understanding of efficiency lead to? Here a first insight into the consequences:

Optimizing efficiency: 'The most it can'	
Time	Minimal time at any risk due to stress and collateral effects (external damages)
Costs	Minimal costs, exploitation of manpower, throwing 80% of humans into poverty
Performance	Highest possible performance of manpower and rational intelligence
Profit	Maximum profit at the costs of low wages, un- and underemployment
Humans	Consequences for health, mind, social life, inner fulfillment are irrelevant
Human's Potentials	Inner sources such as creativity, cultural talents, spiritual intelligence are ignored
Resources	Exploitation as much as possible at any price of nature and

	species
Environment	Destruction, contamination, pollution: irrelevant as much as laws and controls allow
Quality	Standardized at cheap and unhealthy quality for 90% of the population
Tools	The most efficient technical appliances and machines must reduce work places
Education	In the interest of industrial efficiency avoiding topics for mastering life
Human Values	Irrelevant as they hinder the capitalistic understanding of efficiency (profit)

The Result of 'The most it can'

- Stress, psycho-somatic reactions, psychical disorder, and behavior disorder will enormously increase.
- Poverty and misery in developing countries as well as in the Western world will increase dramatically.
- The distribution of wealth will take on new extremes: 0.5% super-rich, 9.5% well off and 90% brutal poverty.
- Unemployment and underemployment will reach 1.5-2 billion people; this is the systemic destruction of mankind.
- Physical illnesses and deformed human beings will increase due to the all-embracing cocktail of contamination.
- Mental diseases from stupidity to naivety, narcissism to neuroticism and psychosis will dehumanize society.
- Human rights, democracy, ethics and human values are already a basket case, abused to destroy countries, folks, and to justify wars in the interest of economic power.
- Contamination increasing exponentially: Chemicals, pharmaceuticals, fine dust in the air, soil, water, and food chain.
- Unimaginable mountains of waste and sewage from 7 billion and later 10-12-14 billion people will destroy all human life and the planet.
- Increasing climate change will produce unimaginable disasters: drought, desertification, tornados, and floods, and migrations of hundreds of millions people, etc.
- Rising sea levels will steadily eliminate beaches, islands, land, immense deltas, and hundreds of big cities; also followed by migrations.
- All eco-systems are damaged and will be irreparably damaged and destroy all food chains and water reservoirs.
- Nature around the globe is already damaged, increasingly destroyed and polluted to the point of no return.
- Natural resources are increasingly exploited, unrecoverable; most in less

than 30 years poised to extinction.

- A huge number of species are disappearing and with that the complex balance of natural life will be destroyed.
- Natural catastrophes will become bigger and more frequent; and destroy huge areas, urbanizations and life.
- Inhumane living environments will suffocate most of mankind transforming them into dehumanized creatures.
- Tourism will vanish due to financial collapses; leisure will mean hanging around, and crime will be the new sport.
- Decreasing agricultural land, poisoned by chemicals; food will be 95% industrialized for degraded humans.
- Transport and car traffic will absorb enormous resources; contaminating every vivid being and the entire planet.
- Energy demand will enormously increase and its production and use will increasingly generate toxic emissions.
- The production of goods requires huge resources and produces unbelievable amounts of collateral toxic damages.
- Financial institutions and large corporations operating mad business models with brutally disastrous consequences.
- Political systems will revert to fascism, dictatorships, and police states with absolutely inhumane management.
- Politicians and all kind of leaders will be the enslaved protagonists controlled, managed, and paid for by the elite.
- Certain leaders, driven by religious psychosis, are ready to eliminate their own followers and billions more.
- State administrations will operate with a 100% control of their citizens 24/7 and with extremely rigid regulations and constant monitoring.
- Central banks and rating agencies are already the main tools of the elite to destroy entire countries and folks.
- Certain private banks are responsible for wars, hunger, misfortune and the dire misery of billions of people.
- The astronomic levels of debt cannot even be paid back in 200 years and will choke any efforts for change.
- Global lifestyles have fully lost their genuine culture; merely expressing compensation, lunacy or a fight for survival.
- Wars: Militarism and immense wars will explode around the globe and produce frightening suffering everywhere.
- Law (national, international) will serve the elite, the governments, and the corporations in order to rule humanity.
- Crimes and prisons: crimes will be a daily practice with prisons and the police managed by corporations for profit.
- Trouble spots around the globe will dramatically increase and produce

irremediable suffering and hate.

- Public education in the service of the economy excludes most human realities and requirements to master life.
- The media in the hands of a few elite thoroughly brainwashes, manipulates, and dehumanizes billions of humans.

'The most it can' is also a matter of the production side: Practicing obsolescence, a widely used practice, leads to the concept: higher demand and therefore higher profit. Interesting is how in not one index of the three classical books of economics (discussed here) is this "demand and production drive factor" mentioned. And there are more mechanisms to stimulate (or force) a demand:

And all this will continue to grow because the earth population will reach 10 billion people in the years around 2050 and 12-14 billion at the end of the century; but there will not be enough energy, food and water. This is also a result of the ideological economics, called 'capitalism'.

Conclusion

This economics (science) and the global practicing economies of countries based on this science is a complete failure; it is suicidal – in the long term also for the super rich and the elites.

3.8. Equity

'Equity' according to Mankiw & Taylor means that the benefits of those resources are distributed fairly among society's members. Mankiw & Taylor say that equity refers to how the sum of the goods is divided. We have three terms to clarify: Equity, fairly, and divided. [122]

The meaning of '**Equity**' in the context of distribution: Equality, egality, balance of interest, just, allover, evenly spread (distributed), etc. What are the criteria for such an assessment? Equity is de facto not always possible. Equity must include in its definition a determined level of equity (e.g. which level of living standard for all people?). It is not simply a fact of action; it is mainly directed by the amount of a local demand. The term has a normative-operational value that does not determine the distribution or the level of limitedness.

The meaning of '**Fairly**': fair, decent, orderly, properly, etc. The term has a normative-operational value. Who can say what or when something is done fairly, decently and orderly? What are the criteria for such an assessment? The term has a normative-operational value that does not determine the distribution and it does not reflect economic realities.

The meaning of '**divided**': To divide is a duty of the economy of any country. To divide is also indispensable to sell goods and services. From a purely logical point a division can cover area-wide or with a certain area-concentration. In reality it is not reasonable to establish a business with 10,000 products for sale in every corner of the world where people live. The disposable volume must reflect the amount of people and their financial potential living in such an area appropriate for selling 10,000 products and services.

There are de facto a higher concentration of goods and services for sale in big towns, cities, and especially in mega-cities. As a consequence equity is linked with accessibility, amount of people and their financial power. Division is related to the amount of population in an area.

---

[122] Mankiw (et al.), p. 5

Real equity = fairness + distribution + accessibility + population + financial means

The bigger the distance from the living location of a human, the lower is the probability that he goes to a significantly distant area with 10,000 goods and services. Time and costs for travelling to such a location has a serious impact in decision-making. Such is the human experience of scarcity although the goods and services are given. Equity is not given in such a case (and in many other cases) and is impossible to realize.

Conclusion

→ Equity and fairness have got absolutely nothing to do with the distribution of goods. A fair distribution (allocation) among all members of a society is an illusion and as a theory a delusion. Distribution is not a question of fairness and equity; it's a question of the amount of consumers with the level of financial potential on an accessible location (for all people).

→ We have here again an ideological blandishing in the economic market theory and reality. Economic prosperity for all members of a society can't be guaranteed with fairness, equity and distribution.

→ The life standard of the Western world, especially Europe and the United States is not simply the result of hard work and intelligence of people; it is still today founded on robbery, murdering, thievery, stealing land, genocide, wars – all in the name of democracy and the Christian God – and in the economic destruction of countries (through the UN, IMF, World Bank, Central banks, many more private banks, and other financial institutions).

→ There is no equity in the economics (theory) or economies around the globe. The big corporations have destroyed all human values and abused everything and all human achievements around the globe. There is nothing 'fair, decent, orderly, or proper' in the economics or the economy of the countries around the globe. This is a fairy tale to cheat the economic experts, the students of economics, and the folks. 'Equity' is a magic lie on the same level as the dogmas of the Christian religion.

3.9. Normative-operational Realities

Mankiw & Taylor use normative-operational words in several contexts where they describe their 10 economic principles. [123] We observe the same normative-operational words in the 7 principles from McDowell. [124] Let's take a closer look:

Careful, orderly, efficient, skillful management
The realities show us: Such qualities are indispensable principles for efficiency. But the problem is the aim of management, the humane costs, and the abuse of grey-zones in laws and (lack of) regulations.

Avoiding collateral damages (no externalities)
The realities show us: There are immense collateral damages around the world: nature, species, agriculture land, contamination, pollution, destruction of environment, etc.

Economizing costs
The realities show us: The bigger a business, the more they spend on megalomaniac self-presentation. Costs are economized by reducing wages and working contract conditions.

Optimizing profit
The realities show us: Optimizing profit goes at a cost to the environment, labor, and the service or product quality. Profit goes mostly to the management and investors.

Avoiding waste of time and effort
The realities show us: Avoiding waste of time and effort goes at a cost of increasing stress, restless sale strategies, ignoring biorhythm of humans and animals.

Sparing and restrained use of (i.e. resources)
The realities show us: On the one hand the price is: lower quality. And on the other hand the greed for endless more exploitation of resources destroys

[123] Mankiw (et al.)
[124] McDowell (et al.)

nature and the environment.

Achieving maximum effect with minimum effort
The realities show us: The main tool is industrial mass production and dehumanized business interaction. Both attributes are related to quantity and not to quality, at costs to labor.

Equilibrium in a micro- or a macro-system
The realities show us: In the majority of countries around the globe there is practically no economic equilibrium. Many countries show a maximum (extreme) disequilibrium.

Determining how scarce resources are allocated
The realities show us: Scarcity is per definition unlimited and in a majority of fields stimulated by marketing and the inner state of humans (inner deficits, compensation drive).

Saving money by spending less
The realities show us: The usefulness of spending less depends on where to spend less. The other critical question is: What for is the saved money used and who gets this saved money?

Free-market or planned market
The realities show us: There is neither a free market in the capitalistic world nor a complete planned market in the so called communist world of today. There is a chaos of regulations, abuse, blind decisions, shortsighted views, etc.

Conclusion

A house is not simply a house, a physical construction of determined dimensions. A house has a deeper meaning: it's for humans to live in, have a private sphere and a protection.

A household does not simply mean the management of goods and services for the people living in a house. It must include also the people's management of needs and wants.

The management of needs and wants requires understanding these needs and wants. And the process of understanding requires practical, psychological and spiritual knowledge.

Humans need education to enable them to master life; and mastering life requires a lot of knowledge and skills, including psychological and spiritual ones.

The fewer humans are appropriately educated, the more chaotic and irrational are their needs and wants and the management of their needs and wants.

→ Economics as a science excludes most of the knowledge about psychological needs and wants.
→ Economics as a science is based on the chaotic management of needs and wants of people.
→ Some of these requirements suggest an immanent positive connotation, even responsibility.
→ Not one of these normative-operational requirements is achieved in the real world.
→ All corresponding norms are ideological and ignore the inherent collateral effects.
→ Complete ignorance towards the fact that humans are working and the result is for humans.
→ All humans are much more than manpower and have daily humane needs beyond economics.
→ The benefit of these requirements always goes to the top-manager, elites, and investors.
→ Most requirements at best, serve the optimization of profit at any humane and natural cost.
→ These requirements pose questions: What is meant with 'waste of time'? What is included in 'equilibrium'? What happens with the 'saved money'? What is 'maximum effect'? Etc.

The Evil Moral Cheating of Economics

Most of these normative orientations reveal the capitalistic principle: minimum costs, minimum time, minimum substance, calculated effort and performance for maximum profit in the shortest possible time.

The given normative aspects of an economy are functional and promote exploitation of humans as well as of the planet. There is a complete lack of considerations about genuine human values and meaning of life.

Such an understanding of economics as a science is never sustainable in the future!

3.10. Time and Money

People have to work for money. Work always includes a time factor: the amount of hours people work for their money, including the journey to or from work.

If people work more than the required hours (regulated by law), then they can make more money with a side job. But they have much less time for their personal life.

Some people, especially in the intellectual fields, must work more than people work usually; often up to 60-75 hours per week. Therefore they have much less time for their personal life.

For example the academic professional chooses a life of learning but rarely is rewarded financially, even though he is likely to work just as hard and long as the entrepreneur. One devotes time for contemplation, learning and research which might not see useful benefits for years, whereas the entrepreneur focuses on the generation of short term rewards, one of which is financial benefit.
Both however are in the minority, as the majority, are on set wages for a set number of hours.

The more time people spend working, the less time they have for themselves, for friends, partner, family, social life, fun, entertainment, distraction, going out, travelling, culture and further education.

Higher education and special vocational further education leads to higher income, but also means: no (or less) earning during the education period and costs for education and life.

Money Creates Money

John always has 200€ at home for occasional spending; but he never uses this money. A neighbor tells him that a year ago he also had 200€ at home. He lent it to a friend at 10% interest and got 20€ interest after the first year and therefore in total on his IOU paper he now has 220€. His friend continues working with the 200€ from the neighbor. John is animated now and finally understands that he can't just let 200€ lie around at home. He also lends his 200€ to this friend. But this friend is clever and does not tell John or the neighbor what he does with this money. He does not tell him that 10 other people also gave him 200€ for 20€ interest per year. This clever man does business with this 10x200€ and has had a profit up to today of 1000%; he smiled when he gave the 20€ to the neighbor. In five years this friend will have a huge amount of money and then he will give back the 200€ to all the 10 'friends'. John will then have 500€. And this clever man will have 50,000€. Time makes money if it is placed on the right location without doing anything. Money grows itself! The problem is that this clever man is speculating with food prices (because he knows how to do it from a friend that works in a bank).

This attractive promise of doing nothing (or very little) whilst the money grows is the essence of a speculative mentality: In essence creating something out of nothing in the shortest possible time. Is this 'something out of nothing' artificiality not the foundation of the banking industry and the whole monetary system?

Do you understand now why your bank wants that your wage should go directly into an account? Do you understand now why banks offer for example 50€ starter bonus when you let your wage gets transferred to an account of the bank? You can feel happy because they offer you 2% interest per year. But the bank is clever and does business with your money and earns, let's say 35%. The bank speculates with wheat futures because the wheat prices are rising sky high due to the catastrophes of climate change. Logically 25% of the world population now can't afford to buy enough flour anymore.

Leisure Time of People in the Western World

In the western world (e.g. EU) a week of 7 days has a flexible average pattern of the masses:

a) Monday to Friday:
Hygiene
Breakfast
Going to work
Working
Lunch
Working
Free early evening time: 2 hours
Dinner
Watching TV: 2-4 hours

Hygiene
Going to bed
b) Saturday: Free time (or working and free another day of the week)
Shopping
Cleaning
Washing
Spending the rest of the day in many ways: 3-6 hours
Evening: Going out
Or: Watching TV, visiting friends: 2-4 hours
Hygiene
Going to bed

c) Sunday: Free time
Sleeping up to 10-11 a.m.
Breakfast
Lunch
Spending the day in many ways: 5-7 hours
Dinner
Watching TV: 2-3 hours
Hygiene
Going to bed

Total of free time per week: 14-24 hours

The essential questions are now:

→ How do people spend these daily time-units seen in an average per year?
→ For what kind of activities during these time-units do people spend money (average per year)?

Use of Leisure Time

Internet surfing, writing emails, sending messages (mobile phone), talking on the telephone, driving around, hanging around in bars, clubs, parties, watching TV, going to the Gym, participating in a football match or in other sport events, going to a café and meeting friends for a chat, reading magazines or newspapers, reading a book, going to buy a lottery ticket, going to the hairdresser or beauty salon, having a drink here and there, eating in a restaurant, art work activities, shopping, visiting a psychologist (a doctor, a psychotherapist, a life coach, an esoteric service), participating in a course program for further education, or going to church, etc. Here there are variable costs for a single person and much more variable costs for a family.

For most of these activities people need to have a variety of electronic appliances and other goods (e.g. a car) or to spend money for services and entertainment and traveling.

Observations

- Free time is an essential condition to spend money because spending money costs time.
- Lifestyle has a strong impact in the purchasing of goods and services.
- The more free time people have, the more they spend on services, fun and entertainment.
- If people have to work 9-10 hours per day, they spend much less money during the week.
- People working a lot during the week, tend to relax during the weekend and spend less money.
- The more people are bored, the more they spend time watching TV, surfing the internet, or spending time and money mindlessly in shopping centers.
- People that like cooking and healthy eating buy less prepared food (and the other way round).
- A majority of people want fast satisfaction and tend to spend more money for prepared food.

Conclusion

→ Lifestyle can influence scarcity and price-management of products and services.
→ Scarcity can change lifestyle and with that consumer behavior.
→ To consider all the behavioral options is of high importance for the business' marketing.
→ Lifestyle is concentrated on certain activities, products and services.
→ Fast satisfaction and fun-elements are a decision making factor.
→ If a collective lifestyle changes, then the market (products and services) also change.
→ Educated people tend to read more books, participate more in further education.
→ Psychically and spiritually developed people spend less money on frivolous activities.
→ Factors that produce changes of lifestyle not linked to consumption cause economic problems for the business world.

3.11. Trade-off

Mankiw & Taylor explain another economic principle: Trade <u>can</u> make everybody better-off. "By trading with others, people can buy a greater variety of goods and services at lower cost … Countries as well as families benefit from the ability to trade with one another. Trade allows countries to specialize in what they do best and to enjoy greater variety of goods and services." [125]

The principle the author mentions is called: "People face trade-offs." [126] Is such a statement a principle? It simply describes a fact, one obvious factor of any purchasing process. 'Trade-off' in essence means: exchange, or swap; a process that is the essential characteristic of a purchase; or it is simply another word for 'purchase'. Said in another way: People face purchases (or: processes of purchases). Does it make sense to call such evidence, 7 billion people experience every day, a 'principle'? Not at all! It's nonsense. It's like saying: People face weather conditions.

Trade-offs are certainly a real fact and basically desirable. Interpreting this statement as a 'can' makes it interesting and important to the economy of a country. But it also can mean: 'worse-off', depending on the network of a trade-off process (e.g. externalities; or debt if purchased on credit). Part of this statement is the explanation that each family competes with all other families; and the same dynamic happens between countries trading with each other. Unfortunately the mechanisms that guarantee such success (without critical collateral effects) are not elaborated theoretically.

There are always good examples, but does it work in general as presumed? Why does trading with others lead to an increase of goods and services? Because the need for goods can lead to good ideas (innovation) and that leads to the creation of work opportunities. Is there really a balance between the trade-off of two countries? Usually to provide a lower cost good, one party has to provide something cheaply, mostly because they do not have any other choice. If this is their 'trade-off', then the idea is based on 'I win: You loose' rather than the theoretical 'Win: Win' and that trade can make everybody better off that economists falsely describe. What is the reality of trade-offs

---

[125] Mankiw (et al.), p. 9
[126] Mankiw (et al.), p. 4-15

linked with taxes?

Conclusion: at least it is interesting and desirable for governments that spend too much money for stupid activities such as rearmament, war, prestige constructions, boosted administration, etc. What is the 'trade-off' here austerity for me but comfort and luxury for you (government officials)? I pay (taxes) and you (the government) spend it all as you see fit?

There is another element of this principle to discuss shortly: "people <u>can</u> buy a <u>greater variety </u>of goods and services at <u>lower cost</u>". People can buy, but do they need an endless greater variety of goods? Who says that everything must be at lower cost, and that 'lower cost' is always a good thing? There is an ideological background in such a principle. And it heats up greed and the drive to buy more and more, endlessly. Such a statement can never be a principle. It's only in the interest of more and more profit, and in the end of economic growth. Who says that economic growth is a good thing as it is the main factor of global destruction and dehumanization? Who says that economic growth makes people happy? Who says that economic growth creates wellbeing? It's absurd to say such things! And therefore this principle contains nothing more than an ideological and financial interest – not for the citizens.

Markets Organize Economic Activities

Mankiw & Taylor compare communism (planned market) with capitalism (free market). Communism: "Only the government could organize economic activity in a way that promoted economic well-being for the country as a whole." And: "In a market economy, the decisions of a central planner are replaced by the decisions of millions of firms and households." [127]

We summarize from the description given by Mankiw & Taylor: [128]

1. Millions of firms and households are the decision makers.
2. Households decide which firm to work for and what to buy with their income.
3. Prices and self-interests guide their decision.
4. Trade-off creates and promotes overall economic well-being.
5. Prices are the instrument that directs economic activities.
6. Prices reflect the value of a good and the costs for production.
7. This mechanism (thesis 6) maximizes the welfare of society.

---

[127] Mankiw (et al.), p. 9
[128] Mankiw (et al.), p. 10

8. This is the magic 'invisible hand' that makes it all work.

Mankiw & Taylor add: "When the governments prevent prices from adjusting naturally the supply and demand, it impedes the invisible hand's ability to coordinate the millions of households and firms that make up the economy."[129] And: "We all rely on government-provided police and courts to enforce our rights over the things we produce." [130] The authors also mention two reasons for governmental intervention in the economy to promote efficiency and equity: enlarge the economy and the rules to divide the cake (the goods and services).

Critical Analysis

Thesis 1: Millions of firms and households are the decision makers.

Making a decision happens within a certain frame: time, money, accessibility, personality, behavior skills, social pressure, etc. The rational aspect of decision-making is rooted in countless irrational factors. The millions of firms and households form an uncontrollable stream of needs and wants. And finally the stream becomes decisive in decision-making and not individuals and firms.

Thesis 2: Households decide which firm to work for and what to buy with their income.

Nowadays there are not that many options to choose from. People can be happy if they find any job within a certain radius of their location. On top of that, the firms decide who they want working for them. The smaller the income, the more reduced the flexibility for purchases are. As wages are decreasing (in Europe), the frame of decision making also becomes smaller.

Thesis 3: Prices and self-interests guide their decisions.

We have already explored that the price plays only a relative role. 'Self-interest' is a word that in this context is always in a certain sense right. What people buy is in general what they are interested in, seen in a subjective context. But the complexity of decision processes reveals that many times people don't really buy in their 'self-interest'. Nobody buys in the interest of others, except if they buy a gift. On the other side this statement hides the fact that firms set prices and sell what is in their interest independent from

---

[129] Mankiw (et al.), p. 10
[130] Mankiw (et al.), p. 11

the interests of the buyers. A majority of people consume (buy) on credit. Therefore the available money (without having worked for it) also guides people's decision.

Thesis 4: Trade-off creates and promotes overall economic wellbeing.

That's a joke; or simply not true. 'Well-being' or 'Welfare' is a very subjective and normative word. Most people must fade out the fact that they are neither happy nor do they feel well in the consumer society. People compare their economic status with 'higher' level of lifestyle. In this context they are mostly not happy, and don't feel well. The imbalance in wealth and level of wages makes them frustrated and angry. This statement ignores the realities around the globe, especially that of the 5-6 billion people living in poverty.

Thesis 5: Prices are the instrument that directs economic activities.

What does 'economic activities' mean? Production? Amount of products and services? In another context economists state: "needs and wants direct economic activities"; and primarily not the prices. "The lower the price the higher the economic activities" would suggest that prices must be low to get better (higher) economic activities. But the prices must be low because most people have very low wages. This thesis is in the air, and not really provable. So the idea is: We need higher economic activities (for profit) and therefore the production costs must be low and accessibility everywhere guaranteed. Why do the authors not say: "The quality of products and services directs economic activities"? Other options would be: "Human's genuine needs direct economic activities." Or: "Sustainability and protecting the environment and the planet direct economic activities? They ignore and do not mention such options due to ideological interests, especially concentrated accumulation of capital through the big corporations.

Thesis 6: Prices reflect the value of a good and the costs for production.

How can these authors tell such a lie? In too many cases this is not true! As maximizing profit is today a widespread practice, we must include the calculated profit in this thesis; let's say: much exaggerated profit. There are a lot of products and services on the market that have a very low value, but an inappropriately high price. Sometimes the thesis is true: Many products are indeed not even worth a cent; are only junk and have absolutely no value, but a price.

Tourists that come to Spain may know this problem: The plate costs 12€ and the production cost of the content of the plate costs is at the best 1€. A small bottle of water additionally is charged at 3-4€. What is the value here in relation to the price? Or an 'espresso' costs 1.50€ –2.50€, but the production costs are less than 10-12 cents. It doesn't matter because next year anyway other tourists will come. The price reflects a shameless speculative exploitation of tourists and nothing else. We know that in most cases the owners of business premises are the main causes of such business practices as they demand very high rents (to get a lot of money without working for it, which brings us back to speculation) and thus forcing business owners to price their products and services without relation to the value.

Thesis 7: This mechanism (thesis 6) maximizes the welfare of society.

How should this mechanism maximize welfare? Increase of production itself and prices that do not reflect the value of a good do not automatically increase welfare. Welfare is also a human quality and not only an economic figure (e.g. GDP). The factor 'externality' (damaging environment, exploitation of resources, causing poverty in other countries, etc.) is completely excluded. We would rather say: This mechanism is the tool for collective suicide within 35-40 years.

Thesis 8: This is the magic 'invisible hand' that makes it all work.

Yes, there is a stage where economic activities visibly happen. But behind the curtains of the visible stage is another invisible stage. And there is the invisible hand, a body part of some people there that pull the strings of the visible stage. That's one of two mysteries of the invisible hand. The other hand is in the unconscious mind of people, also directed by the people that pull the strings. Again, this magic 'invisible hand' is the same hand that operates in all religions. Here it is called 'magic mechanism' and there it is called 'belief'.

Economics is not a science like chemistry, physics or biology. Fundamentally the mechanisms and principles that make any economy work are created by and operated by and for humans. Therefore we must always ask: Who and where are the people and what are their motives to operate in this way, and how and for which purpose do they operate?

Diagram: Circular Flow of the Market

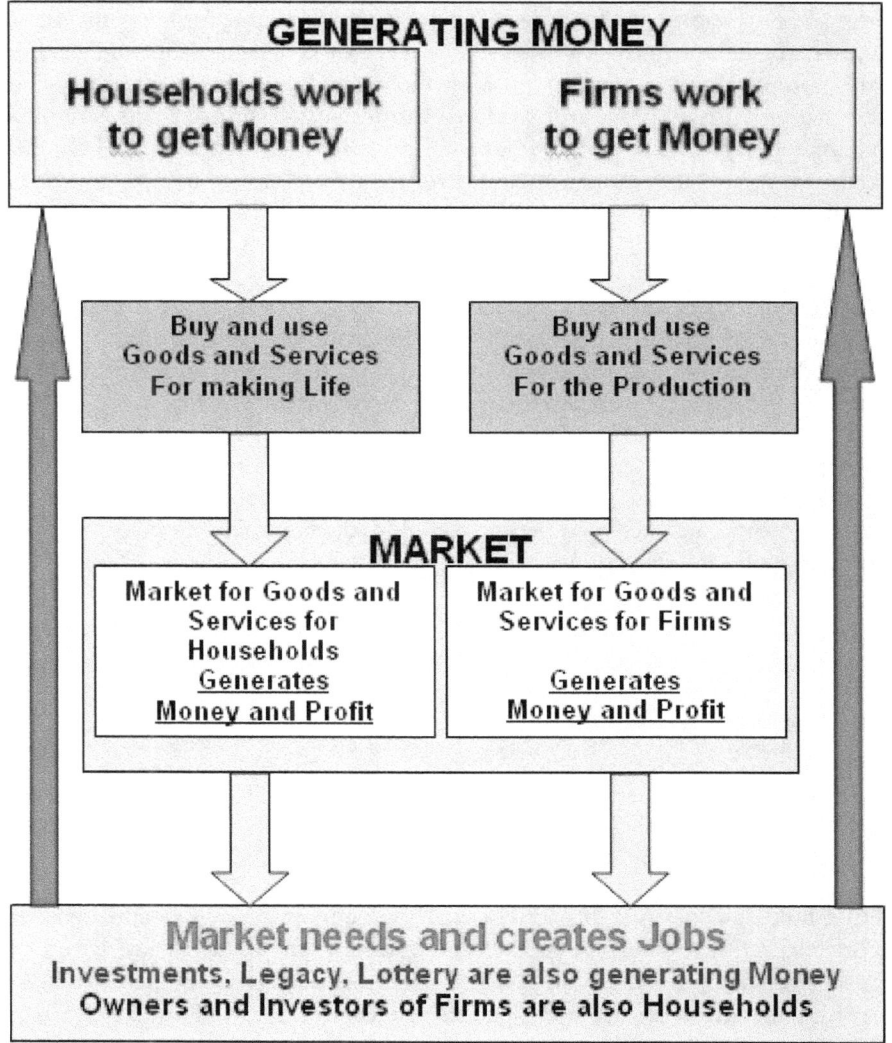

3.12. Economics and Trust

In the first chapter we have extensively shown that the future is inevitably uncertain. Therefore trust is an essential topic of economics. But the classical study books about economics (at least those we discuss here) do not discuss the matter of trust in the real world of economics (businesses and economic parameters). This is a very fundamental omission, as trust is one of the key foundations of the human world, from personal relationships to social, business and political activities. Without trust nothing functions correctly in any society.

Nevertheless there are some sources that elaborate this matter. Dasgupta says: "Trust is the basis of cooperation." [131] Therefore we want to draw a picture about the trust-issue in the real world of economics and we have chosen one small book with a chapter about trust and economics.

"Attitudes toward others and towards one's institutions are significant aspects of a society's culture." Going from there we can conclude: if trust in the business world and between people is of low degree, then the culture of this country is of 'low' Quality. [132]

Trust can be low, medium, or high. Although trust is an attitude, it also can be limited to selected fields of life, institutions, or people.

The Economic Trust Thesis

"Trust is good for economic growth and several other things beside." And the author reinforces: "The degree people have trust in one another goes hand with economic progress." [133]

Trust holds all systems and activities of the economy together and makes it work efficiently. Society in general and economy in particular are based on trust. Everybody trusts in the systems and tools of society. If there wouldn't be trust, the entire society and especially the economy would not work. There are three essential questions:

---

[131] Dasgupta, p. 33
[132] Dasgupta, p. 59
[133] Dasgupta, p. 58

- Can or do people really trust in the concrete systems of society?
- Can people trust in the scientific and practical concepts of economics?
- Do the systems of a society really work efficiently and constructively?

The Term 'Trust'

The term 'trust' is used in many ways in everyday life of human beings: I trust that my car works when I start the car, i.e. for going to work. I trust in my friend or partner. I trust people. I trust the doctor. I trust the clerics. I trust my parents, the church, politics and the politicians. I trust in the value of my money that it will still be the same tomorrow. I trust my house is on a stable foundation. I trust my money in the bank will also be at my disposal tomorrow. I trust the food in the supermarket is healthy. I trust in my business partner. I trust in my teachers (that they teach the truth). I trust the experts. I trust the appliance I bought yesterday will work. I trust the words and information I get from people and books. I trust the other car drivers. I trust the Holy Bible. I trust science. I trust the fulfillment of a contract. Trust essentially means 'confidence'. [134]

"Trust is not merely a basis of words and verbal promises ... Mere promises are not enough." [135] Obviously the author concludes: "One should not trust blindly!" It is a simple fact of life that trust needs to be justified with experiences and observations.

→ In all these cases 'trust' is an emotional and / or rational positive attitude related to reliability.

'Trust' has Different Focuses

People. Institutions. Authorities. Value of money and goods. Security. Functioning of a good. Etc.

Trust has Different Meaning

Trust has to do with reliability, honesty, expectations based on experiences, rules, habits, facts, conditions, etc. Trust can mean 'faith' or 'hope'; but also 'I know' or 'I suppose' or 'I assume'.

---

[134] Dasgupta, p. 31
[135] Dasgupta, p. 31

Trust Creates

Attention, devotion, security, delegation, sense of care, acceptance, naturalness, openness, cooperation, readiness, correctness, appropriateness, order, stability, etc.

Trust can be Created by

Comfort and security, reliability, transparency, emotional attention, mutual enforcement, mutual interests, understanding, care, a brother or friendship kiss, an embrace, expressions of friendship and love, positive experiences, sharing same thoughts (opinions or attitudes), giving gifts, professional clothes, cleric clothes, majestic buildings (expressing authority), long term relationship, character traits, official sources of information (authority), creating a father or mother projection, strong hand shake, etc. Helplessness, low self-esteem or self-confidence very fast put people in a disposition of projective trust or direct distrust.

Trust can be Reinforced by [136]

- Rule of laws
- Governmental authority
- Police, court, punishment – the legal system
- Social norms of behavior
- Disposition of reciprocity
- Disposition to obey norms
- Cultural environment

There are also negative factors that hinder people to break trust; for example: Fear, Guilt, Anger, risk of being caught misbehaving, and (social) punishment.

Distrust can be Created by

Abuse of trust, imbalance, injustice, lies, abuse, empty promises, cheat, exploitation of people, corruption, lack of justice, inefficient law systems (court), brutal policy, scarcity in essential basic needs, wages that do not allow for a basic living, overpriced goods and services, high taxes, unemployment, political failure, corruption, arrogance, cowardice, hypocrisy, warmongering, political oppression, misuse of political competences, exploiting labor, politicians making empty promises or operating with false flags, etc.

---

[136] Dasgupta, p. 43

Theses

- Trust in the functioning of any construction is a matter of correct construction and technical evaluation.
- Trust in people is a matter of real experiences, of reliability, of moral character, of integrity and personality, and often of naivety, credulity and stupidity or unconscious projection.
- Trust in natural phenomena is a matter of natural laws and therefore not really trust, but more about evidence.
- Trust is sometimes a matter of herd behavior with either trust or distrust. "False rumors and propaganda create pathways." [137]

Conclusion

→ Today most societies and economies are on an extremely low level of trust due to institutional failures in politics, religion and economy.

→ Trust is in most cases not simply a rational disposition towards people, institutions, goods, and services. But too many people are blinded, naïve and credulous.

→ Trust can be created through facts and real experiences, but also through lies, manipulation, and fabrication.

→ Trust has in many ways and is mostly an irrational component rooted in deficits of trust in the unconscious mind of people.

→ Trust can be conditioned through marketing that suggests a connotation between a good or a company (or a brand) a meaning (pretension) and functionality of trust.

→ Trust is not only a rational term in the structures, facts, theories and science of economy; it's a manipulating factor in ideology and religion.

→ Today there is de facto not much trust in the economy (the world of business and government) and even less in the science and theories of economics.

→ Considering the state of societies, humanity and the planet, there can't be much trust (or: culture of trust) in the society's economy.

→ The history of the economy shows us: there is never long term reliability in politics or economy and therefore trust can't be constant.

→ In the context of economy, the term 'trust' is a chewing gum that after a while becomes very distasteful. Everywhere there are factors in corporations that produce distrust.

---

[137] Dasgupta, p. 46

Comment

Ignorant and stupid or naïve people that say they are happy with their life and trust in politics and the economy is not a parameter of existing objective and sustainable factors of trust.

Saying a high level of life standard is a factor that rectifies trust in politics and the world of businesses (or the economy as a whole), is a misinterpretation. The Western high level of living standards is mainly due to historic colonialism, imperialism, wars, exploitation of manpower and natural resources, stealing fish resources and agricultural land of other countries, abuse of other countries' labor, destruction of the environment and the irreversible damages of the global eco-systems.

The fact that so many people have a car, a nice home, even their own home (but with high mortgage) can go on holidays to countless resorts, have enough food, some a good wage, have an internet connection and a credit card, and have access to health care, etc. hides another fact, namely that all these folks are in a certain way still slaves, a worse state of enslavement than the slaves in the Roman Empire.

- Economics has destroyed the dignity of humans with effects already starting in early childhood.
- Economics deals with scientific words in a sloppy, grossly negligent and distorted way.
- The cheat begins with words whose content is varied in the substance and meaning.
- Economics has become the government's whore; both are dominated by the dogma of the 'invisible hand'.

Trust is essentially a word that refers to human relations. The economic theory abuses its connotations transferring it to a world that is basically not trustworthy and works for hidden ideological (capitalistic) interests.

3.13. Market Dynamics and Failure

Mankiw & Taylor stress out three market failures: "The market on its own fails to produce an efficient allocation of resources. ... A cause of market failure is an externality (e.g. pollution) ... Another possible cause of market failure is market power ... the ability of an individual person (or small group) to unduly influence market prices." [138]

Certain mechanisms or even the entire economic system can fail: "Public policy is not made by <u>angels,</u> but by a political process that is <u>far from perfect.</u>" [139] In other words: nothing is guaranteed, not the allocation of resources, not the amount of products and services, not food and clothes, and not even the 'invisible hand' that makes the market work.

What have these statements got to do with science? The words 'angels' and 'far from perfect' have a strong emotional connotation and are completely displaced in such a context. Everybody accepts this for anything on earth; sometimes even the Pope although he (or his Church) is declared to be infallible. It's a magic self-excuse, protects all the rubbish of economic terms and theories, and unconsciously opens the door to accept any failing economic theory. Such simplification is not just evil but very unscientific!

Market Dynamics also depend on the Following Factors

- Externalities
- Market power
- Financial power
- Influences of individuals
- Vested interests
- Rental prices on premises
- Taxes
- Profit greed
- Astronomic bonuses
- Corruption
- Getting without having worked for it
- Governmental intervention
- Bank practices

---

[138] Mankiw (et al.), p. 11
[139] Mankiw(et al.), p. 11

- Riots, unrest and wars
- Trade restrictions (with taxes)
- Incompetent politicians
- Economic crimes
- Hidden power entities
- Catastrophes
- Growth of world population

Market Failures

- Externality: uncompensated impact (e.g. contamination)
- Market power: activity to unduly influence market prices
- People are willing to pay high prices for selected interests
- The invisible hand does not exist; it's all about manipulations
- Nothing ensures that everyone has sufficient goods, services
- Public policy does not aim to achieve equitable distribution
- Political self-interests hinder a balanced economy
- Politicians are not well informed or are paid for by vested interests
- The human values and the value of human life is ignored

Leaders in politics and the economy, and the members of the top-elites are very often identified as 'psychopaths', as greedy and reckless humans, as megalomaniacs, or dehumanized individuals. Fact is today: a majority of these peoples has converted from this mad psychical state into a new state, until today a never reached dimension: the evil itself fully behind the aspect of 'human'. In this state, these individuals are not anymore humans; they are monsters of a category never known before until today.

Diagram: Market Dynamics

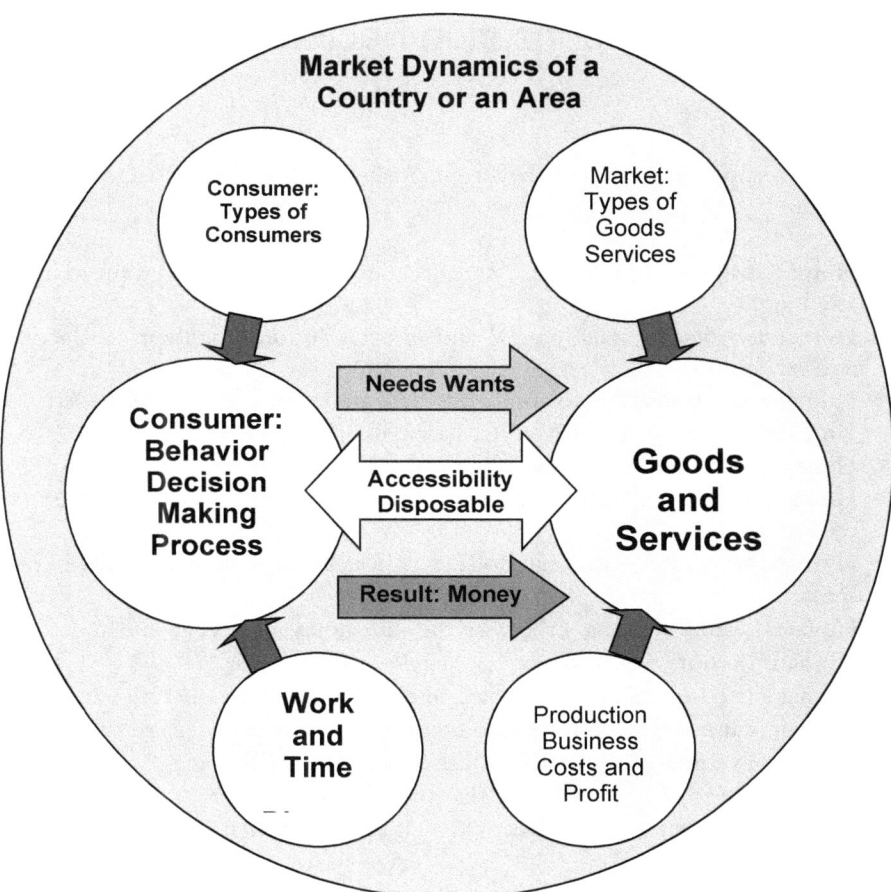

3.14. The Compensation Factors

Behind compensations is a belief: it makes free, gives satisfaction and salvation:

- Humans are lazy, lazy to think, sluggish, superficial and don't want to learn anything.
- Humans want easy, fast, simple and direct solutions for their satisfaction and salvation.
- Humans are submissive to authority, easily deceived and easily enslaved.
- Humans are like sheep, driven herd animals and followers.
- Human are cowardly and fearfully paralyzed by social pressure.
- Humans believe in 'untouchable lies' because they themselves lie, live in a web of lies.
- Humans believe in economic nonsense, because they themselves live nonsense.
- Humans want to belong; otherwise they are alone and feel excluded.
- Humans do not want to take responsibility for the truth.
- Humans need the ideological belief, in order to live their quarrelsomeness.
- Humans cannot give up their ideological belief, because they are stubborn.
- Humans live their sick cantankerousness with their ideologies.
- Humans are scared of the shock that the truth can release.
- Humans have such a small ego, that they refurbish it with belief in the consumption ideology.
- Humans think they are better with their consumer participation, than those who reject it.
- Humans are scared of life and therefore cling to the collective economic stream.
- Humans themselves play a false, deceitful, deceiving game in life.
- Humans are psychically on the stage of development of a small child.
- Humans can live their own, open or concealed arrogance with their consumption behavior.
- Humans choose material illusions over the strong facts of life and humane being.
- Humans hope for the redemption of their unconscious complexes by consuming.
- Humans compensate their human weaknesses with their goods, with

wealth and money.
- Humans have enormous concealed guilt, partly real and partly self suggested.
- Humans increase their extremely low and bad self-value with their consumer goods.
- Humans expect help from economic policies instead of helping themselves.
- Humans compensate their weak, unstable self-confidence with consumption.
- Humans flee from themselves and their own inferiority with their consumption.
- Humans think that consuming can tame their 'unworthy' compulsiveness and lust.
- Humans see their life as unworthy and low; create balance with goods and services.
- Humans cannot live themselves and need the 'mother bank and insurances'.
- Humans have not been loved and hope to receive the love through material goods.
- Humans have experienced suffering and with consumption they experience comfort and relief.
- Humans strengthen with goods their own imperiousness and tyrannical personality.
- Humans don't have a genuine self-identity and find it in their consumer community.
- Humans conceal their extremely low psychical-spiritual development with goods.
- Humans do not have any substantial self-enlightenment and do not want any.
- Humans do not want to see, how their own parents are completely archaic people.
- Humans suppress their hate of their father, mother and life by running for consumption.
- Humans are sickened by themselves, their own body and flee into the material worlds.
- Humans have an increased feeling of triumph, by being in the 'true' possessive world.
- Humans are submissive and masochistically bonded in their drive to any kind of belief.
- Humans are orally unsaved and nurture themselves through fixation on goods.
- Humans do not have any substantial knowledge, to question themselves or

others.

- Humans are scared, to look at themselves in the inner mirror.
- Humans are scared, to recognize the devilish lies of economics and politics.
- Humans fear to recognize themselves, how they are abused by the world of big businesses.
- Humans loose their ground, when they recognize the 'infallible' economic truth as a lie.

Do you understand now the 'body of the invisible hand'?

4. The Parameters of Economics

4.1. The Labyrinth of Economic Definitions

1) Economic Growth

Economic growth means: an increase in the capacity of an economy to produce goods and services to satisfy the wants of goods and services. In short: Increase in the capacity of an economy is good.

The needs and wants are unlimited; the resources of the planet are limited. Stupid, useless, damaging and highly contaminating wants should be considered separately in the economic growth.

2) Recession

A period of economic decline, defined as a decline in the parameter 'GDP' (stock market, housing market, increase in unemployment). Speculations are the engine of stock market and housing market. Increase of greed for highest possible profit and speculations convert at a certain level into a downfall in the economy. The principle of growth as an imperative of economy leads to the assessment that a decline in the rate of growth is bad. Indeed, if there is an astronomic public debt, then the government needs economic growth to pay back the public debt, and first of all the interest on public debt. Excessive public spending, especially military, administration, and general household expenditures, unemployment and pension payment requires a permanent increase of the GDP. High public debt together with high public cost and in the background speculation businesses is a lethal combination.

Therefore the mechanisms leading to recession lie in the world of policy, banks, and investors; and not in the hand of the 'normal' citizens. Either it's a failure of politicians, or it's purposefully geared up by the 'invisible hand'.

The correlation 'recession leads to unemployment' is a highly reduced and falsified interpretation of the picture. There are many factors that in the long term lead to **unemployment**:

- Increase of industrial techniques to produce faster and with higher result leads to less work.
- Regulations that complicate and reduce business activities lead to less work and unemployment.
- Dislocating production to developing countries leads to less work at home

and unemployment.

- Concentration of money beyond the small and medium sized businesses leads to less work.
- Bank's investment practices destroy small, medium sized businesses and therefore work places.
- Profit maximization of big corporations together with immense bonuses lead to less work.
- Ignoring human factors in services' and product's quality leads to dismissals and unemployment.
- Lack of pioneering and vanguard vocational education and projects leads to a market regression.
- Non-productive costs suck up immense financial potential that could be used in other ways.
- Ignoring the genuine and essential human value of 'working' favors technology for production.
- Neglecting 'art and craft' leads to industrialization (mass production) with less self-employed people.
- Ignoring human factors in economics and favoring profit parameters leads to unemployment.
- The principle 'time is money' and calculating every minute of production leads to unemployment.
- War-like competition leads to the destruction of humane businesses, and therefore to unemployment.

If we would change the content of the parameter GDP, then the whole picture about recession would be different. We will discuss this matter later on.

So, o.k., recession is bad. Let's look into it. A decline in GDP means unexpected decline of growth in the economy. There are strategies and tactics with economic implications that pave the way for a recession:

- Owners of some banks want more profit, much more profit because they have a roadmap and some upcoming steps are prepared and must be achieved.
- Billions and trillions of dollars and Euros must flow into the same command and control center. Corporations are the tool. Hail to globalization! Greed for profit is the engine; high wages and bonuses the 'oil'.
- To increase their profit, they must invent terrorism or any kind of enemy in order to increase the business of weapon's manufacturing. Fuelling conflict in far away places is good too! This field promises billions in profits.

- With an invented enemy politicians are occupied and the citizens support them to get rid of such evil beings. The folks finally can project their own evil doing and their aggression onto a constructed enemy.
- Wars must be triggered with false flags and proxy programs. This must secure all kind of resources and the control of the trade routes. Profits from the drug market and needs of the armies become abundant.
- They played on the stock market with speculations, primordially with food and other resources, expecting high profit; then they lost too much money in this game.
- The banks lend a lot of money to construction companies and other investors to increase the construction market; all expecting high profits.
- Banks also lent a lot of consumer money (credit and loans) to increase the production sector; during a first phase the production increases and then the borrower struggles due to excessive consumer spending.
- They built a lot of houses and then the construction companies (better: the investors) asked too high prices in the sale of property; and the demand decreased dramatically.
- Banks offered mortgages at very low interest rates, 2.5-3.5%; later they increased the interest rates, and many owners could not cope with this: they went bankrupt and the banks got the property.
- The construction market collapses and hundreds of thousands of workers, in construction and the supplier fields lost their job. Unemployment explodes. Millions have significantly less money for buying goods and services. Now even more businesses have to close.
- A very high demand for jobs leads to low wages; most workers are happy to get a short-term job with minimum wages. The profit of such companies rises.
- The lower priced market of many corporations increases. They can sell goods on a level of 1-3 Dollars or Euros and make a lot of profit: some cents on every good multiplied by hundreds of millions.
- The governments spend a lot of money for unemployment payments. The tax incomes decline drastically. They need fresh money from central banks or private investors.
- The banks get a lot of money, but at 8-30%. As they urgently need money, they accept any condition. Governments go into billions and trillions of debt. Now the banks are in the hands of the lenders. The lenders dictate the policy of the governments. Democracy becomes a show.
- At the same time 30-50% of the citizens are in fear of losing their job, struggling to pay back their loans, and have no time anymore or space in their mind to understand what's happening.
- Obviously now some restrictions in freedom and consumption are necessary. Wages of public employees get cut at the end of the month.
- To make such a program work protagonists (CEOs, directors, managers,

etc.) are needed because the puppet masters are never on the visible stage. The protagonists get immense wages and bonuses.

- Politicians, CEOs, directors, managers, and other leaders don't understand what's going on. They have mortgages and some even loans, plus excellent reputation; they obey the 'principles of economics'.
- The folks go crazy; social unrest rises, protests expand. The governments give the order to increase the police force, imprisonment, and the total control of all citizens with other projects, e.g. Facebook, Twitter, email and mail intercepts and CCTV surveillance.
- Austerity measures must be increased to get the stupid folk and the naïve politicians under complete control. Everybody must suffer from now on. Everything works fine with the economic principles!
- Now we arrived at the goal: the governments and the citizens are under control of 'the invisible hand'. But this is only the beginning of a new development: the new world order under fascist rules.

3) Depression

An extended period of negative economic activities, measured by GDP - leads to unemployment, credit defaults, decline in production and income, currency devaluation, deflationary economy.

On a certain level of recession, the economy and the entire country (many countries) everything becomes depressing (psychologically). It seems there is no fast solution. Unemployment can't be solved; production has dramatically decreased while the cash register of the wirepuller is more than full of trillions of dollars and Euros. Chaos arises in the world of money, some prices fall in the cellar and other prices explode for those who have a lot of money. The banks have hundreds of thousands of properties in their portfolio. The rules of accounting allow them to manipulate their dire status. It's all for a higher goal. Everybody hopes that this disaster will end soon and the golden age will come back. Depression paralyzes; the mind can't work properly, and fear and distrust everywhere creates a bleak business atmosphere.

Poverty increases, many small businesses must close and the middle class shrinks dramatically. Politicians get weird as they do not understand the principles of economics. They still have a good wage and a guaranteed monthly payment when they have to leave their seat. Democracy is anyway an impotent theatre: first, the candidates must run to get attention; then they are elected and must first learn how the rules work in their office; and then, after 2.5 years they need 50% of their time to prepare for their re-election. This has to do with the economic principles of the hidden rulers. The world is in the hand of the monsters now. It's time to start a big war soon: the next step of the road map. War is after all a great economic stimulus. Everything is working just fine with the economic principles!

In a few words: An extended period of negative economic activities is bad. Yes, it is when it reaches an economic depression! But the depression in 1930-1936 in the United States and today is not really the same game; or maybe it is. One thing is certain: World War II was the next step of that program! Therefore: there was a planned roadmap in the United States and even with the Versailles treaty! Hitler fell into that trap, chained with enormous public debt. And the enemy was very quickly declared. False flags and proxy activities triggered the avalanche. The 'invisible hand' was even operating in the office of Hitler and Co. The same plot as today! Unbelievable! Who rules the world? Money rules the world! Who at that time had and today has the decision power over billions and trillions? The same banking families and institutions.

4) Inflation

Increase of prices of assets, products and services, measured by the Consumer Price Index (value of money decreases).

Examples:

One year ago people got one liter of milk for 1€; now they get only half a liter of milk for 1€. But they do not earn 50% more than last year, sometimes even less than last year. Increase of consumer prices allows for the domination and disciplining of the citizens, and to direct their way of living and thinking. It's an indirect dictatorship.

The interest rate of mortgages is increased. People have to pay more for their mortgage, but there is no increase in the value of the property. Increase of mortgage rates within a contracted period is a shameless exploitation of people.

Businesses want to make more profit. They calculate: even with a decrease of demand due to a higher price, they can make more profit. The economic calculation here is all about the critical line.

Sometimes the increase of prices is the result of improvements of a good (e.g. devices, cars). This is not what is understood with 'inflation'. The higher price goes along with 'more' of the good. The CPI does not distinguish in this case. Therefore the CPI is a deceptive and misleading manipulation.

Speculation on resources (food and non-food) always aims to make high profit. If an important good becomes scarce and there is no equivalent alternative for the consumers (e.g. due to catastrophes, crop failure, real estates speculations), then the prices rise. Speculation businesses on a high level are an evil doing and in the long term destroy human values, society, and entire folks.

Inflation is part of the above detailed road map and game. The increase of prices is not simply a result of high demand, but much more a result of greed and money concentration: Businesses had no other choice than to increase the prices of their products and services as the landlords of premises and the banks don't want to reduce the rental prices respectively the interest rates on mortgages or loans. Greed dominates the period of inflation. Landlords and banks hinder a balanced development or survival of businesses. Everything is according to plan, the roadmap is working just fine.

5) Deflation

A decrease of prices of assets, products and services due to a lack of money or credit. Deflation can also be a healthy process due to an overpriced market. Deflation is also a result of businesses dropping prices in a desperate attempt to get people to buy their products. Measured by the Consumer Price Index (CPI).

People have little money and are directed (forced) to buy 'cheap stuff'. That's good for some industrial corporations. Some other parts of the production sector collapses; and the business world (small and medium sized businesses) is forced to reduce their prices in an attempt to survive.

Lack of money paralyzes the business world. Lack of money paralyzes governments. Lack of money produces a lot of fights everywhere. Lack of money paralyzes pioneering and vanguard business projects. Lack of money, paralyzes freethinking and stifles the inner potentials of humans. Lack of money puts people in a state of depression and fear. There we are: the people are enslaved within themselves. Divide the people and you can conquer. That's a way to manage and control the masses of people and distort reality in particular.

Who is the authority that decides to print fresh money? They regulate the amount of money and with that the entire economy of a country. Is there an aim to let the economy of a state collapse? Destroy the enemy by dividing the rich from the poor, the politicians from the citizens. If you reach this, then you have the power over a nation.

Price reduction due to a lack of money paralyzes a government as a decrease of prices leads to a dramatic decrease of tax income. This leads again to higher public debt. And public debt leads to the control through external financial institutions (e.g. IMF, World Bank, central banks, and 'investors').

Therefore deflation is a tool used to destroy a nation. You don't need an army, you don't need political power; all that you need is the power over the money sources and the control over money channels. The CPI is totally irrelevant; the criticalities of deflation happen within another frame.

Who are the investors? Who rules the IMF behind the curtains of the visible stage? We need to know the people by name and especially their religion, as already Goethe said: "Tell me your religion and I know your motives!"

Wasn't it the same game with the Roman Empire? The Roman Empire collapsed due to economic factors and not due to a bellicose enemy. Who were the winners? Who had the significant benefit from these developments? We are still describing economic principles and we have a lot more economic questions, especially about the body of the 'invisible hand' and its ulterior motives.

6) GDP – Gross Domestic Product

The total market value of all final goods and services produced in a country in a given year, equal to total consumer, investment and government spending, plus the value of exports, minus the value of imports.

In a few words: The total market value of all final goods and services produced is good if it is high. Who says that the GDP should include the total market value of all final goods and services? Governments decide about the basket of goods. The picture is disfigured and contains cancer viruses.

Explorations

What does it mean 'good' and 'bad' in the economic realities? And why does or can something that is good suddenly become bad? Why is 'increase' always good in the opinion of economists? We observe that 'good' and 'bad' is related to figures of parameters. Therefore an economic parameter itself is an indicator of 'good' and 'bad". But 'good' and 'bad' is de facto in the end always related to humans. But these indicators do not relate to the genuine 'good' human life and they do not consider all humans of the entire community of a country or an area.

a) The Basic Goods for Humans

- Everybody can get work (after education and above age 18)
- Every working person has at least a minimum wage to realize their life
- A father has a minimum wage that allows him to support the entire family
- A single working mother additionally has money that allows her to pay for the child (children)
- Everybody has at least a basically furnished home, a safe shelter
- Everybody has enough healthy food and water to be satisfied
- Everybody has at least the necessary clothes and shoes for living
- Everybody can pay the minimum of electricity, water, detergents, and toiletry items
- Everybody has at least a little bit of pocket money for extras
- Free access to health care is guaranteed for those who can't pay
- Free public education (primary and secondary) for mastering life
- Free vocational education for everybody
- Performance is paid according to education and level of performance
- Healthy air and environment for everybody (lowest possible contamination)
- An efficient network of public transport all-area covering (for work, shopping)
- A well functioning and increasing social mobility with countless small/medium businesses
- A society where human values have highest importance

There is more to say about this later on.

b) Bad for Humans

- Lowest level of poverty (inability to pay for life with a minimum wage)
- Unemployment for more than 4-6 months
- Unhealthy food and dirty water
- Brainwashing (marketing, media, religion, economics, politics)
- Not paid accordingly to education and performance
- No access to health care for those who can't pay for it
- Not enough education for mastering life
- The domination by big corporations, including banks
- Contamination and pollution
- Destruction of the environment and eco-systems
- Trade mechanisms that destroy or block development of other countries and societies
- A monetary system that exploits people and countries

- Exploiting manpower and limited natural resources
- Crimes in the environment (corruption, mafia, drugs…)
- A society where human values are treated like shit

There is more to say about this later on.

Conclusion

Therefore new economic parameters must be determined that measure the indicators that show the level of satisfaction of what is basically needed for the citizens to realize their life.

Economic parameters should enable politicians to take the correct efficient measures to balance the economy in the interest of establishing everything that is necessary and good for basically all people/citizens.

The free market is not in danger if governments take measures to guarantee what is good for the people to realize their life. However, an unlimited free market is anyway an illusion, not given today and was never given in the past due to the invisible hand behind the curtains on the invisible stage.

A balance between free market and planned governmental intervention is indispensable in the future aiming for 'what is good for people'.

4.2. Economic Growth

Mankiw & Taylor mention more principles we want to have a closer look at:

1) "An economy's standard of living depends on its ability to produce goods and services." [140]

2) "Citizens of high-income countries have better nutrition, better health care and longer life expectancy than citizens of low-income countries, as well as more TV sets, more DVD players and more cars." [141]

3) "In nations where workers can produce a large quantity of goods, and services per unit of time, most people enjoy a high standard of living; in nations where workers are less productive, most people must endure a more meager existence." [142]

4) "To boost living standards, policy makers need to raise productivity by ensuring that workers are well educated, have the tools needed to produce goods and services, and have access to the best available technology." [143]

The corresponding terms are generally described with:

Economic Growth (EG)

The increase in the amount of goods and services in an economy over a period of time. Economic growth is related to employment and unemployment. Economic growth leads to higher employment (over a certain level).

Standard of Living

Certainly, a standard of living that satisfies the basic genuine needs is desirable in a country. It is also desirable and a reasonable goal that a country has a market for wants from cheap to luxurious. But the term 'living standard' should not only be seen under economic factors. Living standard does not

---

[140] Mankiw (et al.), p. 12
[141] Mankiw (et al.), p. 12
[142] Mankiw (et al.), p. 12
[143] Mankiw (et al.), p. 13

guarantee happiness and not even wellbeing. "Surveys have found that income doesn't contribute to happiness among people who have a good deal more than the basic necessities of life." [144]

Happiness and wellbeing are psychological and spiritual categories that are in the essence of the meaning independent from goods and services. Consumer ideology is a manipulative society, abusing the libido of a desire making believe that consumer goods will satisfy subconscious desires. They call this kind of satisfaction 'happiness'. To be happy there must also be a spiritual dimension and a balance between mind, human values and body.

Globally genuine human values are rotten to the core. And the collateral effects due to a largely Western lifestyle (life standard) have caused irreversible damage to the planet. This we have shown extensively in the first chapter. These damages will backfire in the coming decenniums up to the doom as the machines run on for more exploitation, more goods and more profit.

Under such a perspective, the glorified living standard in economics is perverse. It reveals the inhumane science of economics that ignores all essential human values as (anthropological) premises and basic principles. Why should the "ability to produce goods and services" be generally linked with living standard? The principle that says "An economy's standard of living depends on its ability to produce goods and services" must be linked with humane factors. And in general it is not simply about 'goods and services'. It is also about peace, justice, balance, healthy environment, living potentials and talents, the truth about everything, etc. Therefore the principle is not only shortsighted and a hidden ideology of glorifying greed, it is also very dangerous for a country and for humanity as a whole.

From a certain level on, the economy's standard of living converts into a very destructive concept and reality. The simple fact that everything is limited on earth must also be considered in the world of the production of goods and services. It is a normative principle to state: "Resources should be used as efficiently as possible to achieve society's goals." [145] 'Should be' is normative and the 'goals' are also normative. Therefore we must first clarify and find a common understanding of the right economic goals. Economics as a science doesn't make sense without considering the people. And people are humans with a mind and an inner life, and not simply human biomass. Humans are defined by their psychical-spiritual being, and not only by their physical body,

---

[144] Dasgupta, p. 63
[145] Krugman (et al.), p. 13

consumer behavior and statistics.

Considerations

The word 'growth' suggests that "'growth is good': increase of goods and services in an economy (over a certain period of time) is desirable, if not necessary. Another implicit understanding is: The more goods and services, the less unemployment (or seen the other way round: the more employment). The negative correlation would be: a decrease of goods leads to a decrease of employment and implicitly to an increase of unemployment. – This is simply a lie! We confront this assumption with the following theses:

- The more machines in the production process or in services, the more it reduces labor.
- Displacing work to Asia makes the labor costs cheaper; but at home it produces unemployment.
- If the investment in machines is cheaper than in labor, then to choose machines seems favorable.
- Growth is related to the amount of (cheap) goods and not to the quality of (more expensive) goods.
- An increase of sales of goods and services requires cheap prices, avoidable for the masses.
- The lower the wages of the masses, the cheaper the products and services have to be.
- If 1 rich person buys goods for €100,000 and the mass human for €5,000, growth disfigures reality.
- If 35% of all goods are totally unnecessary junk, then 'growth' attains a critical meaning.
- If the collateral damages of growth goes into billions and damages humans, then EG is absurd.
- If growth is paid with public debt that can't be paid back in 200 years, then it's amoral and criminal.
- If growth is achieved by stealing resources, even with wars, then economics and politics are evil.
- If growth is achieved by the destruction of the planet, then economics becomes a basket case.

→ Increase in growth has itself absolutely no useful meaning; but it suggests a positive value.
→ There is no substantial argument that rectifies growth as something indispensable for society.
→ We have here again an ideological term with a hidden agenda that nobody should identify.

Explorations for a New Understanding of Growth

The term 'growth' suggests that growth is good and right. Economic growth is good for humans. The question remains in which sense is it 'good' and 'right' for humans. What is actually relevant to be identified as 'growth' is also a question that arises; e.g. is more or less good for people. However, we must pose the question: Who assesses what is 'good and right' for humans? Furthermore the question is given: How is the human (his needs) and the human life determined in the sense of 'good and right'?

The term 'economic growth' suggests that endless economic growth is 'good and right'. Starting from this, that growth has limits (or that limits must be determined), and that an unlimited growth is never possible (or that this could be 'bad and wrong'), another question arises: What follows if the determined (healthy) limit of an economic growth of a country is reached? Additionally there is also the negative growth; meaning a decrease of growth. Who can claim with which arguments that a negative growth is 'bad and wrong' and causes damages? Is it simply the word 'negative'? 'Negative' suggests that here is something bad. A smiling imp crept in here!

It is stupid, ignorant, incompetent, amoral and criminal to claim: "Economic growth is always good and unlimited."

→ 'Growth' itself does not say anything about 'good' or 'bad'; but indeed a growing cancer is certainly not good.

Economic Result of Growth

The data below are estimated figures, taken from several sources. With an increasing world population these figures and names will change rapidly. Please, consider these as a raw draft with the sole intention of provoking questions.

- 1.3 billion people earn less than $1 per day.
- 3 billion people struggle to survive on $ 2 per day.
- 1.4 billion people dispose of less that $1.25 per day.
- 3.5 billion people live from less than $2.50 per day.
- 5.6 billion people live from less than $10 per day.
- 1-1.2 billion people live in reasonable or good economic conditions.

- 10 million people dispose of a wealth of more than $1 million.
- One of 100 of these millionaires disposes of more than 30 million.

- The richest 20% cover 76.6% of the worldwide private consumption.
- The poorest 35% cover 1.5% of the consumption volume.
- 3.4 billion people dispose of 1% of the world's wealth.

- The richest 10% (700 million) cover 59% of all consumption.
- The rest of 90% (6.3 billion) cover 41% of all consumption.

- 2010 there were approximately 10.9 million super rich around the globe.
- 1029 billionaires dispose of an estimated wealth of $74 trillion.
- The global financial elite dispose of $42.7 trillion.
- The world's richest 1% owns 40% of all the wealth.
- The world's richest in 2011 held a total of $92 trillion.
- By 2020 the world's richest will possess $202 trillion.
- 13 million people own more than 50% of the world's wealth.

- The poorest population, 2.8 billion, disposes of 5% of the global income.
- The richest population, 1.4 billion, disposes of 75% of the global income.

With a yearly salary of $84.3 million the boss of Viacom (MTV, Paramount, Nickelodeon), Philippe Dauman, led the way. Software producer Oracle's Larry Ellison, came at second place with $68.6 million. Third place was granted to TV mogul Leslie Moonves, from CBS with $53.9 million.

The media bosses came at the top of the ranking. Other big earners included Ford CEO Alan Mulally ($25.8 million), IBM boss Samuel Palmisano ($24.1 million) and oil corporation ExxonMobil's, Rex Tillerson with $21.0 million. The best earning German was the former Siemens CEO and today's CEO of the Aluminum producer Alcoa, Klaus Kleinfeld, with $12.2 million. [146]

146

http://article.wn.com/view/2010/02/20/Alcoa_CEO_Klaus_Kleinfeld_earned_112_million_in_2009_as_alum/

Diagram: Result of Economic Growth

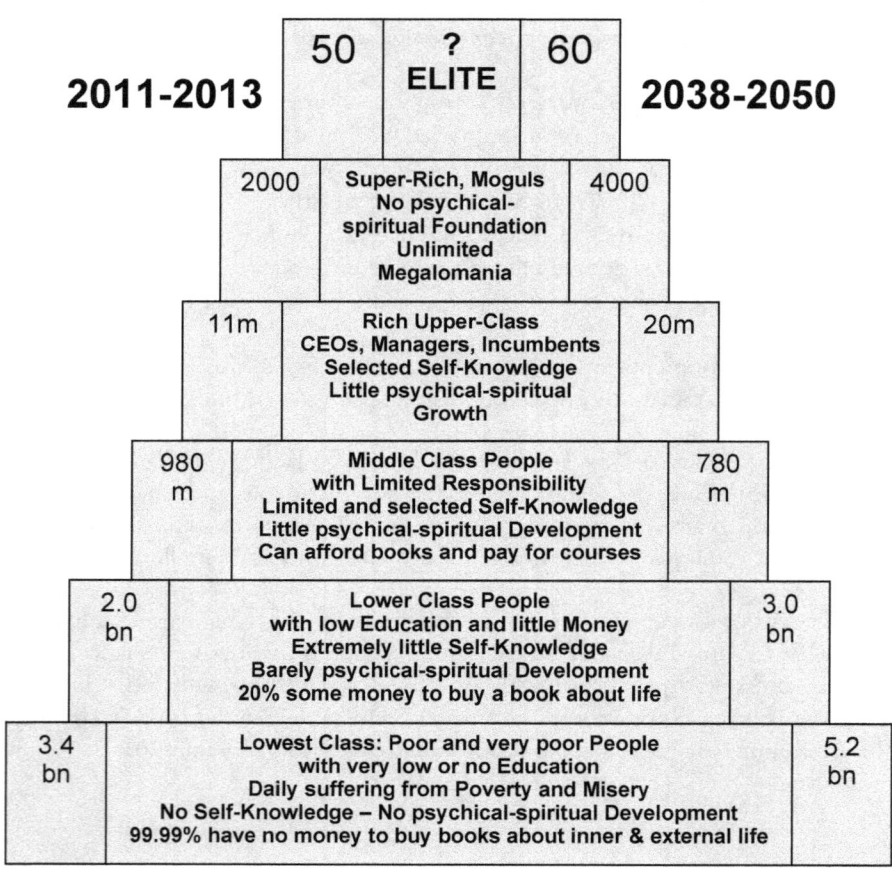

2011-2013	50	? ELITE	60	2038-2050
	2000	Super-Rich, Moguls No psychical-spiritual Foundation Unlimited Megalomania	4000	
	11m	Rich Upper-Class CEOs, Managers, Incumbents Selected Self-Knowledge Little psychical-spiritual Growth	20m	
	980 m	Middle Class People with Limited Responsibility Limited and selected Self-Knowledge Little psychical-spiritual Development Can afford books and pay for courses	780 m	
2.0 bn		Lower Class People with low Education and little Money Extremely little Self-Knowledge Barely psychical-spiritual Development 20% some money to buy a book about life		3.0 bn
3.4 bn		Lowest Class: Poor and very poor People with very low or no Education Daily suffering from Poverty and Misery No Self-Knowledge – No psychical-spiritual Development 99.99% have no money to buy books about inner & external life		5.2 bn

➔ Class definitions are based on income not values.

➔ That being the case, all forecasts predict that globally the 'Middle Class' will increase mainly due to Brazil, India and China.

➔ Changing the data does not alter the impact or point of the chart; in fact it serves to highlight how the adoption of the Western model is unsustainable

Conclusion

The term 'economic growth' is a theoretical construction and suggests a positive value, which in that way does not exist and hides the negative value that is charged on a great number of people with dramatic consequences. In a certain way economic growth is like religion: it declares something as true, right and important for humans which in that way does not exist and the matter however can't be theoretically true, right and important. The term 'economic growth' pulls the wool over people's eyes! In essence we have here a human problem.

The first human problem is that politicians, economists and other economic experts have a human knowledge on a base of maximum 5-10%. The second human problem is that they have a self-knowledge on a level of maximum 2-3%. Thirdly also their psychical-spiritual development is nearly thoroughly on lowest level, referred to as 'archaic'. Hence the fourth question results: How can these politicians, top-managers and experts know what is really 'good and right' for the people? They don't know! They have a massively reduced, disfigured and dehumanized understanding of humans and the 'good and right' life of humans, including of the humane evolution as a whole.

The future belongs to the evolutionary psychical-spiritual human. This kind of personhood in its complete being and destination must become the beginning and aim of politics and economy. Archaic politicians, economists and experts of economy pull down humanity and the planet into the abyss! Therefore a completely new understanding of society, politics, the economy, and with that economic growth is indispensable. Beyond this there is no solution for the big problems of nations and humanity.

Amplitude, quality, efficiency and sustainability of self-sufficiency based on a holistic quality of life of a country must be understood with evolutionary dimensions and must be put in relation to the concept of economic growth.

Diagram: Growth versus Quality of Life

▪ Provision of food and water (reservoirs of drinking water)
▪ Volume of used farm land of all kind
▪ Manifoldness of goods, appropriate for a good life
▪ Provision of electricity and its toxic-free production
▪ Network and efficiency of sanitation and sewage plants
▪ Quality of living estates and premises
▪ Quality of buildings and of the living environment
▪ Amplitude and quality of the street networks
▪ Area covering networks of efficient public transport
▪ Amplitude and quality of public and private education
▪ Natural resources without contamination
▪ Balanced relation: lower-, middle-, and upper class
▪ Absence of corruption, mafia, crimes, lobbyism, scams
▪ Knowledge, skills and morale in the business world
▪ Active, stimulating and recovering leisure areas
▪ Free space for pioneering, vanguard developments
▪ Humans living in active psychical-spiritual development
▪ Authenticity of democracy and transparency of politics
▪ Health and amplitude of nature and the world of species
▪ Existing working places in relation to the demand
▪ Quality of marital life and family life
▪ Living areas for children, the youth and elderly people
▪ Realized genuine human values
▪ Network and efficiency of Health Care
▪ Efficiency and sensibleness of state administration
▪ Absence of contamination and pollution
▪ Self-support through work and wages
▪ Understanding, social peace and justice
▪ Balance of the economy (wealth, income)
▪ Absence of insane ideology, religion and spirituality
▪ Creative, authentic culture with 'soul and Spirit'
▪ Healthy rhythm of life and work
▪ Balance of the cash flow in municipalities and regions
▪ Debt-free objects, goods, land, institutions, companies

4.3. Gross Domestic Product per Capita

The market value of all final goods and services produced within a country in a given period of time divided by the population of a country to give a per capita figure. GDP includes the amount of goods and services that can be purchased by the population of a country; usually measured by the inflation-adjusted (real) income per head of the population.

GDP is a standard indicator of economic activity, of economic growth over a specific time and of economic well-being. There can be a negative growth, a decrease of the market value. GDP is measured by objective figures. The GDP does not provide information about income inequality. The types of goods that are produced, the accessibility to resources or the freedom of market are not separately accounted.

→ GDP does not reflect the entire economic activity of a nation.

The term 'economic growth' is in itself nothing other than a static term that encompasses economic growth measured by GDP. Economic growth is calculated based on a basket of goods, of final goods and services. The basket of goods includes all kind of products and services: production of weapons, construction of cruise liners and super high speed trains, construction of nuclear power stations and plastic toys, production of infinitely luxurious cars, production of mobile phones and computers, etc.

Who says that the production of all these goods are really in general 'good and right' for (all) people? Who decides which services must be in the basket of goods, the calculations of the economic growth? Which services are 'good and right' for the economic growth (e.g. speculation businesses, mortgages, loans) of banks? Which services are 'good and right' or 'bad and wrong' for the people?

Some goods are not included in this definition: Sales of existing houses, education, and road construction, health care and intermediate goods used for production, building your own house, growing your own food, exchanging goods and services within a community, volunteer work, house-keeping, taking care of children, elderly care by the family, and products and services that are not exchanged in the market.

Excluded are also environmental damages, pollution and contamination and its impact on health, decrease of nature and species, damages due to catastrophes, over-exploitation of resources, and other damages.

Let's explore another problem of the GDP: The criterion that allows including: Goods and services that can be purchased by the population of a country.

What does the GDP with such criterion serve? The extension is determined by "can be purchased by the population". The figure is an indicator of living standard. GDP expresses economic wellbeing and with that the 'good standard of living'. We will have to explore this understanding as follows.

Two other questions remain:

1) Why are some products and services excluded from the GDP calculation?

2) What is the function of excluding some specific goods and services?

Why do economists compare the GDP of different countries although the content of the basket of goods is different and the price level of goods as well?

In a majority of cases production also has damaging collateral effects: destruction of the environment and nature, damage to all ecosystems, pollution, contamination, exploitation of resources, accidents at work, poverty, corruption, exploitation of manpower, unemployment (also through the automation of working processes), human made catastrophes, abuse of medicine, devaluation of humans, loss of human values, psychical disorders, etc.

→ Thesis: The higher the GDP is the higher are also all kind of damages.

Basically the critical collateral consequences of production and services must also be considered. These consequences always have high costs, which must be included in the calculations of economic growth. Hence it always results in a negative economic growth. It is most probable that the critical costs in absolute figures are always higher than any calculated economic growth.

Above that economic growth creates profit or must create profit and serve the increase of money.

The question arises:

→ Who profits from an economic growth?

→ Who loses what with a negative economic growth?

4.4. Standard of Living

GDP per person is positively correlated to economic well-being and with that to a good standard of living.

Questions about GDP

If 35% of all goods and services that can be purchased by the population of a country is 'junk', useless and irrelevant for a basic level of living standard, why then are such junk-goods part of the calculation?

If most of the junk-goods are purchased by the lower and lowest class, why does it make sense to have them unidentified in the basket together with high quality and expensive goods?

If 20% of all the goods in the basket are expensive, not achievable for 95% of the population, and purchased by the 5% rich and super rich people, why are they in the basket?

If 20-35% of all these goods are purchased with consumer credit or loans, then the GDP says absolutely nothing about the real result of working people. The living standard is significantly on tick and not on performance.

If most of the important goods are imported from Asia and Africa, then the living standard related to these goods is a result of exploitation of manpower and destruction of the local environment there.

➜ GDP does not reflect any qualitative element of economic realities. GDP does not allow the politics and the economic institutions to take constructive measures, e.g. to direct the money flow into sustainability, quality, and meaningfulness.
➜ GDP does not reflect a real average and picture of living standard.

But what is meant by 'good standard of living'? The lowest standard of living in Europe and the United States, excluded here extreme poverty, is for many developing countries a 'high standard'.

A 'good standard' can be measured by basic, lower, medium, higher, and very high. A good economic standard does not guarantee emotional and healthy well-being. The word 'good' in the economic context can be used already for 'basic' standard of living in the capitalistic world.

Basic standard means people can satisfy the genuine basic needs: a shelter (means: home), food and water, clothes and shoes, basic devices, toiletry items and detergents, basic stationery, a furnished kitchen and a bathroom, a television and a telephone or a music device at home, basic furniture and dishes, some printed media for information and entertainment, and some stuff for creative arts and table games. Generously we can add some alcoholic beverage, tobacco, and sweeties, maybe a bicycle, some money for the use of public transport for travel to work or shopping, and some small pocket-money for whatsoever. Access to paid TV-channels, a mobile phone, computer and internet-connection are really not needed for a basic life.

The people living on a basic standard simply need a modest but sufficient wage to live such a life. What more is indispensable for making a modest life? Even such a simple life can give enough well-being and satisfaction. People living on a basic standard can live love, can be happy, can enjoy life, can live a healthy life, can feel protected, can have a social life, can care for the partner and the children they have, can be peaceful, they can build up self-esteem and self-confidence, they can be proud about their life and performances, and can also form wisdom and find inner fulfillment.

What is a 'sufficient wage'? It depends on the region; it is related to the local economy. Here and there in a low-level economic area 800€/$ may be enough for a person, 1,200€/$ for a couple, and 1,500€/$ for a family with two children. It makes sense that people in the age of 30-50 earn more than the young people of 18-25. It is also appropriate that those workers who have excellent working attitudes, some additional responsibility, useful professional experiences or even some further education are better paid than those who simply do their job.

The failure lies first in the sick and arrogant public education that does not prepare people for understanding themselves, for dealing with problems in life, or for mastering life and managing money in general. And the other main factor is the marketing bombardments through the media that brainwashes every human bring with perverse tactics 'from cradle to grave' creating more and more and more needs and more wants. Unlimited and never reachable! An essential problem is the collective car-psychosis started in Western societies and spreading globally that most people with lower income would prefer to eat 'junk' in order to afford a car although they don't really need a car.

There is another problem with this GDP:

Example 1:

A country of 7 billion people; 100 billionaires, 25,000 millionaires, 200,000 people earning between 0.5-0.99 million; and 15% poor people, included are 7% unemployed; 65% lower class people, and the rest middle and upper class people. What does the GDP of this country say about such a population, the distribution and financial accessibility of valuable goods and the real quality of life standard and wellbeing of all people?

Example 2:

A country of 7 billion people; 3 billionaires, 1,000 millionaires, 20,000 people earning between 0.5-0.99 million; and 65% poor people, including 30% unemployed; 30% lower class people, and the rest middle and upper class people. What does the GDP of this country say about such a population, the distribution and financial accessibility of valuable goods and the real quality of life standard and wellbeing of all people?

The 'invisible hand' makes it all work miraculously, and just as in religion 'believe in all the miracles and do not question' is the dictum.

Does is make sense to compare these two countries based on their GDP? Not at all! We assume that it costs a lot to calculate the GDP of a country. Does it make sense to even spend this money?

In between the years 1970-1980, society taught that higher education and / or special vocational performances lead to a significant higher living standard. Today this principle may work a little bit for lower levels of living standard, including the lower field of the middle class. For higher living standard a young person must wait and work hard during 25-30 years – without any guarantee of a significant higher living standard.

Productivity

The quantity of goods and services produced from each hour of a worker's time.

We have here again a term that refers to 'quantity' and not to quality and sustainability of goods and services. The interest of the productivity-factor is related to the hours of work of a person.

Productivity measured by figures is of economic interest. It expresses again the greed: more and more is better and better. This is absurd, a meaningless figure, if sustainability, usefulness, quality, weight of human values (of the products and services), sustainability, and the collateral damage (material, natural, psychological, spiritual) are not measured. It reflects an ideology with a sick religious dimension devoid of human values and human's evolution. But the economy is made from humans and shall serve all humans of a society. "Fair distribution of goods and services" is required according to Mankiw & Taylor.

→ Ignoring qualitative human factors and the collateral effects of productivity converts economics into a horrible scam!
→ The more we explore the foundations of economics, the more we get the impression of a very mad neurosis behind the terminology of this 'science'.
→ Neurosis is contagious. Neurotic people tend to get other people into their neurotic thinking and behavior. Neurotic people tend to relate to other neurotic people. And neurotic people created such an economic foundation in theory and practice.
→ Some characteristics of neurosis are: distorting, suppressing, mixing, displacing, hiding, making everything weird and confused, declaring the neurosis as the healthy state of mind. The source lies in sexual frustration, lack of love and care during childhood, strong punishments, and a mad religion.

Most people have the idea that psychology has nothing to do with economics and neither with the management of money. But psychological factors have economic implications of the highest importance. Some examples may clarify the economic components:

- Stress leads to psychosomatic reactions, mental disease, behavior disorder, obesity: Immense costs for recovery and loss of manpower, also loss of quality performance. Across the EU some 600 million working days are lost collectively per year, which simply means that 4 days are lost every year for every single worker due to stress.

- Professional frustration and high preoccupations lead to accidents at work, at home, in leisure and sport: Immense costs for recovery and loss of manpower, also loss of quality performance.

- Critical emotional state due to economic problems reduces concentration and inner engagement: recovery and loss of manpower, also loss of quality performance. Immense costs.

- Unemployment in general costs immense money; including secondary economic effects due to psychical and psychosomatic reactions, also divorce. Immense costs.

- The level of alcohol consumed in a country and also the extension of violence reflects the psychical state of humans due to critical living standard. Immense costs.

- The long list of damages on human's health and of environment, nature, species, the planet, the natural resources, catastrophes, unrest, riots, and wars (and much more) will be a never ending burden for the following generations during centuries – if there is any future.

And all this happens because the classical economics presents itself as a royal science for well-being of society as a whole; but its concepts and theories are like a mad religion and both are never a sustainable tool and guidance for the future of humanity.

Diagram: People Need Goods

An understanding must be formed in each society and country for the satisfaction of the basic needs of humans. There is a difference between needs and want. Essential human values of needs are:

Needs	Human values (give key words)
Home or room to stay, to sleep	
Bathroom or shared	
Kitchen or shared	
Electricity	
Energy for cooking, heating	
Healthy balanced food	
Healthy drinking water	
Home furniture, equipment	
Clothes, shoes	
Toiletry items	
Cleaning equipment, detergents	
Stationery items	
Radio	

Health care access	
Elderly home care	
Homeless people care	

Public transport	

Sanitation	
Safe environment	
Healthy environment	
Work: earning for living	

Some decoration	
Books	
Telephone	
Mobile phone	
Television	
Calculator (solar energy)	
Internet	
Bicycle or scooter	
A car	

Local, regional, national holidays	
Part-time work versus retirement	
Saving money for unemployment	
Cultural events instead of parties	
Going out for lunch or dinner	
Gym, being in touch with nature	
Traveling for inspirations	

More luxurious goods (need?)	
Payment for work incapacity	

4.5. Inflation

Mankiw & Taylor state: "Prices rise when the government prints too much money. Inflation means an increase in the overall level of prices in the economy." [147] The authors comment that the growth in the quantity of money is the main cause of inflation. But is this true? Is there a direct correlation between inflation and too much printed new money on the market? Or is it simply the greed of people?

Printed money doesn't go from the central bank directly to the consumers. The banks get this money for a minimal interest. And the banks sell this money with a higher interest. With such a business banks make profit: the higher the interest, the higher the profit.

People get money from the banks, mortgages and loans with a certain interest. With this money people buy goods and services. People get goods and services without having first worked for them. The interest is something like a punishment: "You didn't want to work before you got your want. Therefore you pay not only for our administration, but also for your greedy need and want."

Now a lot of people have more money and spend more for goods and services. The GDP increases again. The world of business realizes: the demand increases and therefore we also increase the amount of goods and especially the prices to make more profit. Businesses also want and get loans for investments aiming for a higher production, an expansion of the business in the interest of more profit. Businesses boost their marketing with the invisible hand luring and seducing with decent strategies and touching the consumer's unconscious painful deficits and at their embarrassing ego-greed. Now people run for consumption.

This phenomenon contaminates the entire nation. Consumption increases. The banks, as they are also a business, calculate with immense profit, become riskier and blindly throw mortgages and loans out the window for everybody to grab. Banks make a fortune. The owners of the banks (the significant investors), the CEOs and the members of the board get fat wages and

---

[147] Mankiw (et al.), p. 14-15

bonuses. The God-like living standard is achieved. Thanks to economics!

But the day will come, sooner or later, when the people have spent the money they got from the bank and must still pay back the loan or mortgage; at this time the interest rate has significantly increased – the punishment becomes harder. The businesses must reduce their production and can offer less working places. Unemployment increases. People get depressed and the economic depression arises from the bottom of the ocean to punish everybody!

After a certain period of several years, a scarcity of money at the disposal of the consumers is putting in danger the wellbeing of society. The game starts again with printing more money although the previously printed money is still not paid back.

As the Western governments today have astronomic public debt, they need immense money from taxes to pay interest and to amortize the capital. They must re-stimulate the market with the central bank putting again new printed money on the market. The spiral will never end until the resources for production are destroyed and the humans are completely dehumanized.

People are blinded: they buy a home with mortgages, a car and many other products i.e. furniture or devices on consumer credit (loans). They all think: "Now it's my home, my car, my furniture, and my device." But this is never the case: the bank owns the good until the credit is fully paid.

Inflation and Unemployment

Mankiw & Taylor posit: "Society faces a short-run trade-off between inflation and unemployment." [148] The authors explain that when a government increases the amount of money in the economy, then in the short run unemployment rises and can last up to 7 years. This is called the '**Phillips Curve**'. It describes the irregular and largely unpredictable fluctuations in economic activity, as measured by the number of employed people or the production of goods and services, as the authors say. Politics influence these phenomena by changing its expenses, its taxes, and the money they print.

Explanations

To illustrate a case in point let us use the United Kingdom, birthplace of most economic theory.

---

[148] Mankiw (et al.), p. 15

Inflation is calculated in two different ways: Consumer Price Inflation (CPI) and Retail Price Inflation (RPI). CPI is the measure the government prefers. The CPI measure this year now includes trades union membership and vehicle excise duty, or road tax - neither of which was measured before, despite being part of the RPI calculation.

The ONS explains it like this: [149] A convenient way of thinking about both the CPI and RPI is to imagine a 'shopping basket' containing those goods and services on which people typically spend their money. As the prices of the various items in the basket change over time, so does the total cost of the basket. Movements in the CPI and RPI represent the changing cost of this representative shopping basket

How do they compile the data? Around 180,000 separate price quotations are used every month in compiling the indices, covering around 700 items collected in around 150 areas throughout the UK.

Everything is weighted - so some things get more importance in calculating the inflation figure than others. For example, even though there are 23 food and beverage items in the CPI basket, transport is given more weight as it's such an expensive part of people's daily lives. [150]

---

[149]   http://www.guardian.co.uk/news/datablog/2012/mar/13/inflation-basket-goods-2012-full-list
[150]   http://www.guardian.co.uk/news/datablog/2012/mar/13/inflation-basket-goods-2012-full-list

4.6. PPI - Producer Price Index:

The wholesale price level in an economy. Relative measure of average change in price of a basket of representative goods and services sold by manufacturers and producers.

Comment: The PPI could be limited to sustainable fundamental assets, products and services. There is no cosmic law that says everything, including absolutely useless and damaging products and services should be part of the PPI.

BOG - Basket of goods

The basket of goods contains essentially and among others (example UK):

Allocation of items to CPI divisions in 2012 [151]

	CPI weight (per cent)	Observed variation in price changes	Representative items (per cent of total)
1 Food & non-alcoholic beverages	11.2	High	23
2 Alcohol & tobacco	4.2	Low	4
3 Clothing & footwear	6.5	Medium	11
4 Housing & household services	14.4	High	5
5 Furniture & household goods	6.1	Medium	10
6 Health	2.4	Low	3
7 Transport	16.2	High	6
8 Communication	2.7	High	1
9 Recreation & culture	13.4	High	17
10 Education	1.9	Medium	1
11 Restaurants & hotels	11.4	Low	8
12 Miscellaneous goods & services	9.6	High	11

---

[151]   www.ons.gov.uk/ons/rel/cpi/cpi-rpi-basket/2012/cpi-and-rpi-basket-of-goods-and-services---2012.pdf

Examples CPI Basket of goods USA [152]

The CPI represents all goods and services purchased for consumption by the reference population (U or W) BLS has classified all expenditure items into more than 200 categories, arranged into eight major groups. Major groups and examples of categories in each are as follows:

- FOOD AND BEVERAGES (breakfast cereal, milk, coffee, chicken, wine, full service meals, snacks)

- HOUSING (rent of primary residence, owners' equivalent rent, fuel oil, bedroom furniture)

- APPAREL (men's shirts and sweaters, women's dresses, jewelry)

- TRANSPORTATION (new vehicles, airline fares, gasoline, motor vehicle insurance)

- MEDICAL CARE (prescription drugs and medical supplies, physicians' services, eyeglasses and eye care, hospital services)

- RECREATION (televisions, toys, pets and pet products, sports equipment, admissions);

- EDUCATION AND COMMUNICATION (college tuition, postage, telephone services, computer software and accessories);

- OTHER GOODS AND SERVICES (tobacco and smoking products, haircuts and other personal services, funeral expenses).

Also included within these major groups are various government-charged user fees, such as water and sewage charges, auto registration fees, and vehicle tolls.

In addition, the CPI includes taxes (such as sales and excise taxes) that are directly associated with the prices of specific goods and services.

However, the CPI excludes taxes (such as income and Social Security taxes) not directly associated with the purchase of consumer goods and services.

[152] http://www.bls.gov/cpi/cpifaq.htm

The CPI does not include investment items, such as stocks, bonds, real estate, and life insurance. (These items relate to savings and not to day-to-day consumption expenses.).

Inflation basket: what's out and what's in

In or out?	Item	Notes	CPI Class	RPI Section
In	Hot oat cereal	New item. Introduced to improve coverage of bread and cereals which has been identified as an under-represented area of the basket and represents a distinct market not currently covered.	01.1.1 Bread and Cereals	2102 Cereals
In	Soft continental cheese	New item. Introduced to improve coverage of milk, cheese and eggs which has been identified as an under-represented area of the basket. Previously in the basket as brie, removed in 2006.	01.1.4 Milk, Cheese and Eggs	2115 Cheese
In	Pineapple	New item. Fruit prices vary greatly so it is beneficial to collect across as broad a range as possible.	1.1.6 Fruit	2127 Fresh Fruit
In	Bag of branded chocolate sweets	Replaces candy coated chocolate which was becoming increasingly difficult to collect.	1.1.8 Sugar, Jam, Syrups, Chocolate and Confectionery	2122 Sweets and Chocolates
In	Bag of sweets not chocolate	Replaces bag of boiled/jellied sweets, to allow representation of foam sweets which have taken an increasing share of the market.	1.1.8 Sugar, Jam, Syrups, Chocolate and Confectionery	2122 Sweets and Chocolates
In	Stout 4 cans	New item. Introduced to improve coverage in this area of the basket and diversify the range of beers collected.	2.1.3 Beer	3102 Beer 'Off' Sales
In	Walking/hiking boot	Replaces outdoor adventure boot to better represent the sector as footwear fashions change.	3.2.0 Footwear including Repairs	5105 Footwear
In	Vehicle excise duty	New item. Already included in the RPI and now added to the CPI as a result of user need including Europe.	7.2.4 Other Services in Respect of Transport Equipment	6104 Vehicle Tax and Insurance
In	Bundled communication services	New item. Telephone charges, internet access and television subscriptions are already included in the basket but the addition of the bundled package reflects the	8.2/3 Telephone and Telefax Equipment and Services	4404 Telephone Charges

[153] http://www.guardian.co.uk/news/datablog/2012/mar/13/inflation-basket-goods-2012-full-list

Inflation basket: what's out and what's in

In or out?	Item	Notes	CPI Class	RPI Section
		way in which people are buying these services.		
In	Tablet computers	New item. Introduced to represent a significant and growing market. Also improves coverage in an under-represented area of the basket.	9.1.3 Data Processing Equipment	6301 Audio-Visual Equipment
In	Television licence	New item. Already included in the RPI and now added to the CPI as a result of user need including Europe.	9.4.2 Cultural Services	6401 Television Licences and Rentals
In	Book, teenage fiction	New item. Introduced to improve the coverage of books. Books for teenagers were previously represented by adults' and children's books but spending justifies their inclusion.	9.5.1 Books	6304 Books and Newspapers
In	Chicken and chips, take-away	New item. Introduced to improve coverage of catering which has been identified as an under-represented area of the basket.	11.1.1 Restaurants and Cafes	2203 Take-Aways and Snacks
In	Baby wipes	New item. Introduced to represent 'cleansers on the go'.	12.1.2/3 Appliances and Products for Personal Care	5202 Chemists' Goods
In	Trade union and professional organisation subscriptions	New item. Already included in the RPI and now added to the CPI as a result of user need including Europe.	12.7.0 Other Services (not elsewhere classified)	4402 Fees & Subscriptions
Out	Candy coated chocolate	Replaced by bag of branded chocolate sweets. Candy coated chocolate has become more difficult to collect over recent years.	1.1.8 Sugar, Jam, Syrups, Chocolate and Confectionery	2122 Sweets and Chocolates
Out	Bag of boiled/jellied sweets	Replaced by bag of sweets not chocolate. Allows representation of foam sweets which have become increasingly popular over recent years.	1.1.8 Sugar, Jam, Syrups, Chocolate and Confectionery	2122 Sweets and Chocolates
Out	Outdoor adventure boot	Replaced by walking/hiking boot to better represent the sector as footwear fashions change.	3.2.0 Footwear including Repairs	5105 Footwear
Out	Glass ovenware casserole dish	Removed. This is an over-covered area of the basket and expenditure on this item is dropping.	5.4. Glassware, Tableware and Household Utensils	4304 Other Household Equipment
Out	Step ladder	Removed. A relatively low weighted item in an over covered	5.5.0 Tools and Equipment	4106 DIY Materials

Inflation basket: what's out and what's in

In or out?	Item	Notes	CPI Class	RPI Section
		area of the basket.	House and Garden	
Out	Annual leisure centre membership	Removed. A low weighted item in a section which is over-represented. Leisure centre activities continue to be covered in the basket by, for example, leisure centre exercise classes.	9.4.1 Recreational and Sporting Services	6402 Entertainment and Other Recreation
Out	Develop & print 135/24 color film	Removed. This item has a low and decreasing weight due to the increasing popularity of digital cameras.	9.4.2 Cultural Services	6303 Toys, Photographic and Sports Goods
Out	Subscription cable TV	Replaced by bundled communication services reflecting a change in the way in which this service is purchased.	9.4.2 Cultural Services	6401 TV Licences and Rentals

The original: ONS (2011) 'Consumer Price Indices – a Brief Guide'. [154]

Comment

The basket of goods includes subjective judgments about what should be part of it. A strong focus on the real basic needs of 80% of the population would give another content of the basket of goods. Products on luxurious level do not need to be included. The question is: What do the masses need for a basically healthy life, for their psychical-spiritual development, and for their happiness and fulfillment?

Another view: How much money does a person need per month to live a decent life, including healthy life, psychical-spiritual development, happiness and fulfillment?

CPI excludes

Not included in all these definitions and lists of goods, services, and prices or costs are:

- Costs for pollution and contamination
- Costs for human made illnesses and accidents
- Costs for climate change with its consequences
- Costs for repair or prevention of natural catastrophes

---

[154] http://www.ons.gov.uk/

- Costs for crimes and prison maintenance
- Costs for abuse of unemployment payment
- Costs for political and religion's failure
- Costs for abuse of resources
- Costs for public education failure
- Costs for failure in making life
- Costs for sick understanding of freedom and emancipation
- Costs for environmental destruction
- Costs for the damages of the eco-systems
- Costs for lack of education for mastering life
- Costs for inefficient state administration
- Costs for rearmament and wars
- Costs for dehumanizing humanity
- Collateral costs of the traffic systems
- Costs of collateral damages of the industry

General Conclusion

A basket of goods does not reflect the entire amount of products and services an economy offers. It does not reflect the prices of goods and services.

The same basket of goods people in Germany buy during a year may cost 6,000-9,000€ for the lower class. In some developing countries a similar basket of goods may have a local value during a year of 600-900€ or 1,200-1,800€ depending on the area where these people live (e.g. rural or city).

More interesting would be a composition of goods and services that people really need to live a basic life without any special extras (e.g. rural or city). A basket of goods does not say anything about who gets what and how much of these goods. Another option: The basket of goods could also be limited to those goods people really need for living their life; at least not luxurious goods and junk goods.

The usual social class categories of economics (lower, middle, and upper class) should be re-made with at least 10 classes. And a statistical composition of the basket of goods for each of the 10 classes would give a much more informative picture.

The matrix of the economy is a faulty design and a distorted theory that does not allow anyone to find the solutions to its failure.

Quiz: What is in the basket of goods in Cameroon, Afghanistan, Romania, Yemen, Cote d'Ivoire, and other developing countries?

5. Money Flow in a System

5.1. Money Flows Everywhere

Thesis: Money is the key provider for organisms and agents.

Definition

- An organism is a business: small (including self-employment), medium size, or large (companies).
- An organism consists in organs and functions through its agents (humans).
- A super-organism consists in varied organisms forming together an entity (corporate groups).
- All organisms form together the institutional structure of the mega-organism; called the state.
- Humans are the agents in the mega-organism with all the (super-) organisms and organs.

Money flow

- Part of the money in an organism is stored in an external organism or in an own internal organ.
- Money flows within the organism to its organs.
- Money flows between the organs of an organism.
- Money from an organism moves to other organisms.
- Money also flows between mega-organisms.
- Money flows to the agents of the organs within an organism.
- Agents move money to external organisms and organs.
- Agents move money to other humans (partner, own children, parents, etc).
- Depending on the organism, its agents can also move money into another organ of its organism.

The purpose

- All kind of organisms and organs serve the agents: the humans.
- The mega-organism serves the different organisms and the agents: humans.
- The agents as consumers serve the organisms and the mega-organism.
- A mega-organism and its different organisms have no meaning (life) without its agents.
- Money is a key-energy (provider) to make the organisms work.

- Money is a key-energy (provider) for agents to make them function.

Money goes out of an organism

Money goes out of an organism for work, goods, infrastructure, services, loans, investments for other organisms; money goes out also through tourism and visitors (tourists/visitors spending money in other organisms), from people sending money to family, friends, and social or religious or political institutions, by paying interest on received foreign capital, through capital flight, also through speculation businesses, etc.

Money comes into an organism

Money comes in through work, goods, services, loans, investments given from other organisms or agents; money comes in also through tourism and visitors (tourists/visitors come and spend money), for people getting money for family, friends, and social or religious or political institutions, also by getting interest on given capital to other organisms and agents, also through speculation businesses, etc.

Diagram: Money Flow between Organisms and Agents

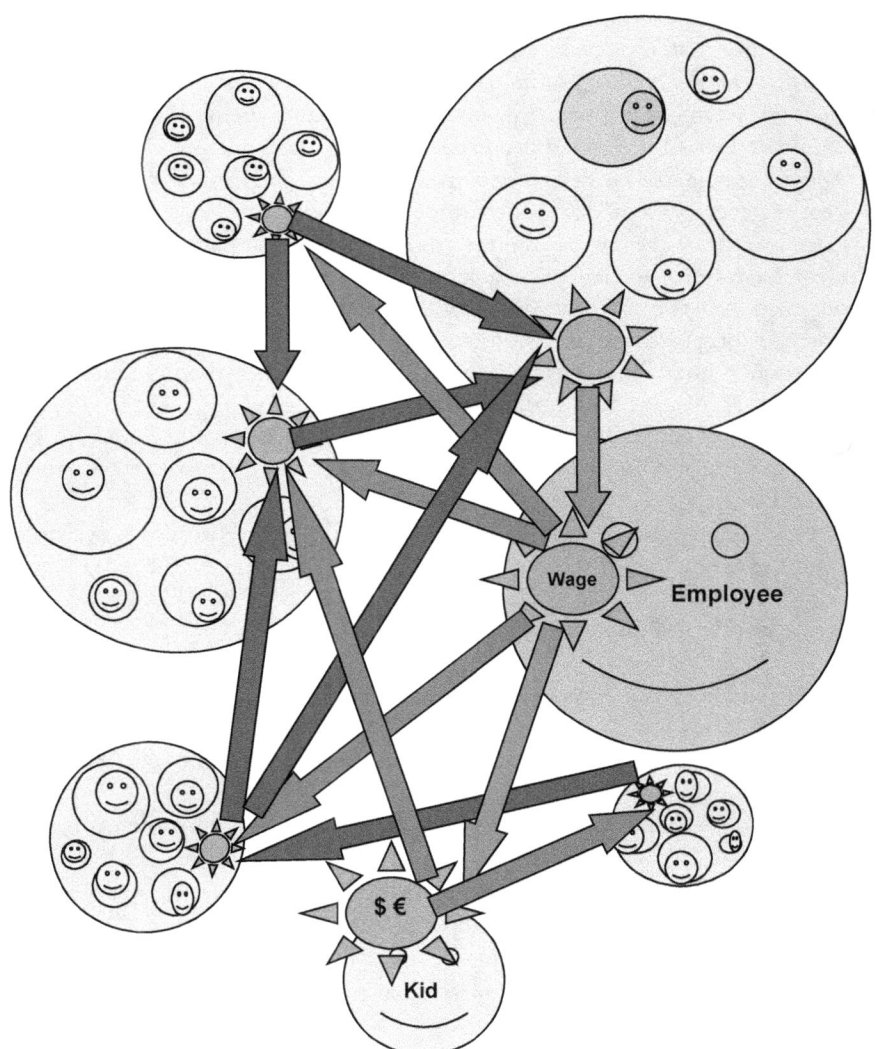

→ Trillions of money movements throughout (e.g.) Europe per year!

Amount of Money

- Organisms generate and accumulate money through work (sale of products and services).
- Generating and accumulating money depends on agents (consumers), buying the products and services.
- The amount of money in an organism can also be increased by printing and distributing (selling) money to the organisms and agents.
- Agents: Payment from received wages means: behind the money is completed work, a realized performance.
- Agents: Loans used for payments means: behind the money is no work; the loan receiver works for it in the future.
- Loans to the organisms require the receivers to pay interest for the received money and to pay back the received money in the future. The organism must work for it in the future.
- Loans, mortgages: Behind the interest is no real work (except for printing the money and administrating the loan and its repayments). Increase or decrease of interest does not represent real work.
- Money can endlessly be traded with a certain profit (interest, gain participation, etc.) and therefore can move from an organism to another organism.
- Interest, gain participation and speculation do not represent a real work from the agents (lenders, investors).

Balance and Imbalance

- Profit (and received capital: loan, investment) allows an organism to grow and expand.
- If the agents get more money, they can spend more money (to give to other organisms).
- Not enough money in an organism or organ causes problems for the organism.
- Absence of money eliminates organs or the organisms.
- The more money flows to selected organisms, the more other organisms are in danger of existence.
- If too little money or no money arrives to the agents, the human's existence is in danger.
- If huge amounts of agents receive too little money, the entire mega-organism is in danger.
- Too little money or absence of money in essential big organisms can destroy the mega-organism.
- The amount of money flow in an organism determines its existence.
- An organism needs a certain amount of money to function, act and

survive.

- Organisms can be created and disappear and this is normal part of the dynamics in a mega-organism.
- If too many organisms disappear, the entire mega-organism gets into serious problems.
- If the creation of organisms is not possible or hampered, the mega-organism gets into problems.
- Concentration of money in some single organisms destroys the economic potential of other organisms.
- An organism can increase its amount of money to get a balance (on a higher level).
- An organism can get a balance on a lower level of financial dispositions and fields of activities.
- Money that represents completed real work is sustainable for organisms and agents.
- Money that does not represent completed real work is not sustainable for organisms and agents.
- Interest, gain participation and speculation create insecurity and imbalance.
- Lack of sustainability of an organism produces with guarantee future imbalance.

Conclusions

- Money is in the end only an instrument for all humans to make and fulfill their life.
- The organisms and the agents have motives to be part of the mega-organism.
- The existence of the (mega-) organism(s) is justified through the interest of human's life and fulfillment.
- The economy must be founded in a sustainable philosophical, spiritual, and psychological anthropology.
- Governments are responsible for protecting and supporting the balance of the organisms.
- Rules alone will never be enough to create balance in and between the organisms and for the agents.
- Holistic education (psychological, spiritual, and vocational) is indispensable for sustainable balance.

Diagram Organism: Money comes in

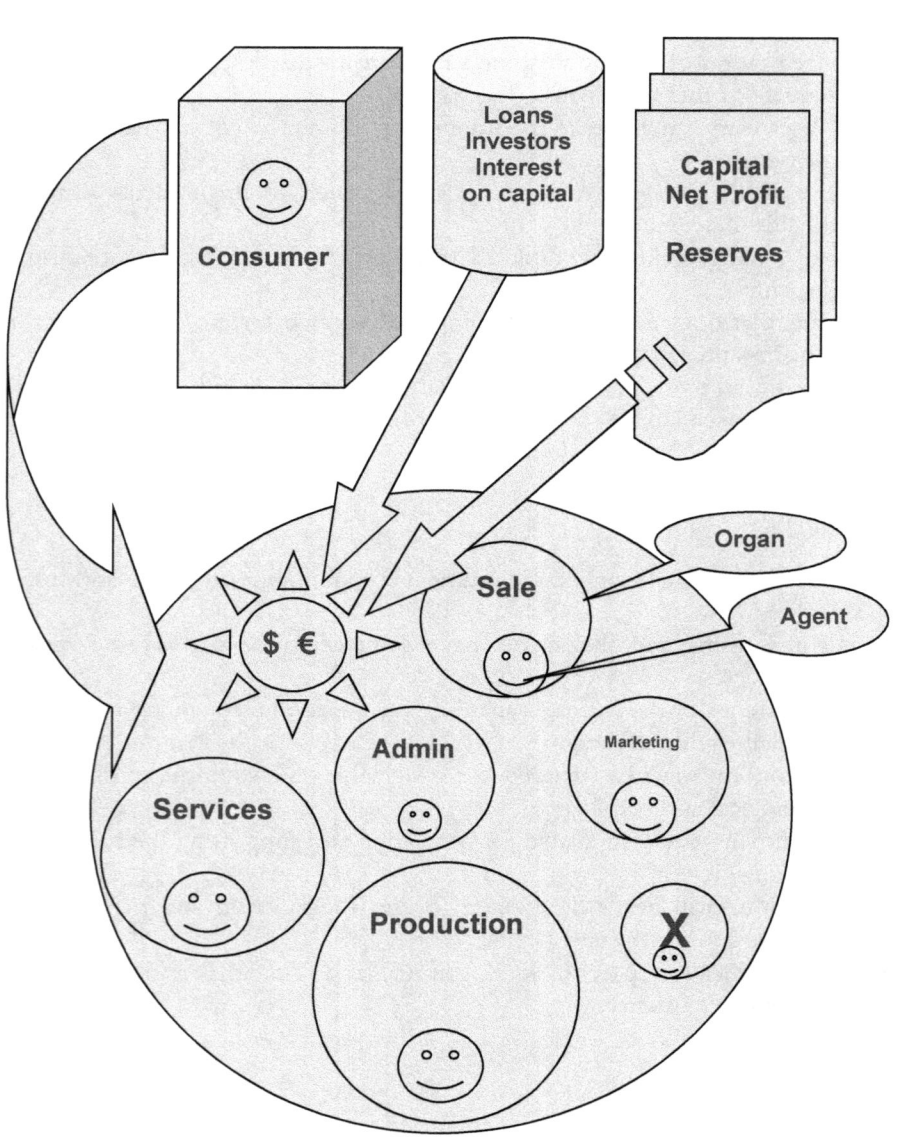

5.2. Money Management

In a system (monetary union) there is a specific amount of money, stored in different places or flowing around from A to B, etc.

In the monetary union live a certain number of people. People need a specific minimal amount of money to pay for the basket of goods.

The prices of what's in the basket of goods form together the minimum income needed to exist.

People must work to get a minimum income needed to exist. Or: they steal the money, speculate, cheat, receive it for free (from friends, family, social institutions), or from the system (state: unemployment payment, additional support from the state) or they get parts of the basket of goods for free (e.g. food banks).

There is a minimum of total money needed in a monetary union if we calculate based on: all people need / have / get the minimum income needed to exist.

- If the population of a monetary union grows, more money is needed within the system so that all people get the minimum amount of total money needed.

- If the population of a monetary union decreases, less money is needed within the system so that all people get the minimum amount of total money needed.

- If parts of a population earn more money than the minimum amount of money needed, more money must be at the disposal of and flow in the system.

Hours, work infrastructure, working risks, quality and efficiency of work, based on education and other components, leads to higher wages and these people get more money to get a (better and bigger) basket of goods.

- If the quality of the goods in the basket of goods increases, the prices for the goods and the sum of the higher prices for the basket of goods increases as well.

- If the minimum wages do not increase in line with the costs for the basket of goods (with higher quality), people have to buy goods of the basket of goods with lower quality.

The more money people earn the more goods of the basket of goods with high and higher quality they can afford. Or they can store money for future expenses.

There are also possibilities for people with abundant money to buy goods (and services) that are not in the basket of goods.

People can work a minimum of 36 hours to get the minimum wage; or 40-45 or even 60 and more hours per week and they get either the same wage or accordingly more money.

Increase of the population, hours of work, work infrastructure, working risks, quality and efficiency of work, and the quality of the goods in the basket of goods requires more money in the system flowing around.

Money goes out of the system into other systems: less money remains in the system. And: Foreign money comes into the system to buy goods and services from other systems.

→ Work has a value and determines (together with other factors) the value of the products and services (basket of goods and other goods or services).

→ Work generates money to buy the products and services (of the basket of goods and other goods and services) or to store it for future expenses.

→ Money can be generated without working for production and services: printing money, getting loans, receiving interest on loans, speculation, crimes, corruption, cheat, prizes, lottery, gifts, donations, etc.

→ Values of goods and products can be influenced by: scarcity, (super-) abundance, demand, speculation, crimes, corruption, cheat, and manipulation of availability or prices of goods and services, etc.

Money and Interest – The Ideology

- Money must generate money (increase) through interest.
- Money must generate money (increase) through speculation.
- To stimulate the market people must get loans, credit and mortgages.

- Capital growth is the engine of a society and therefore indispensable.

Printing Money

Central banks can print money and bring it into the system, mainly via banks. Banks have to pay an interest to the central bank.

The interest banks have to pay to the central bank for new printed money does not reflect the production and administrative costs of this new money.

Banks have not worked and do not work accordingly (production, services) for the new money they got from the central bank. The amount of money does not reflect any value related to production or services.

Organisms and agents can get from the banks new printed money with loans and paying interest (more than the banks have to pay to the central bank).

The interest to pay is not only based on the administrative work of a bank plus the interest that banks have to pay to the central bank, but also depends on risks of repayments of loans and excessive profit they aspire.

The loans received from the bank have to be paid back within a certain period. With that the banks have again at their disposal (in pieces) the new printed money they got from the central bank.

If banks give back to the central bank the money they got for giving loans to organisms and agents when they got it back from the receivers, the money is taken away from the amount of money within the system.

If banks keep hold of the money (they got from the central bank for giving loans to organisms and agents) when they get it back from the receivers, they can earn more money by again giving loans to organisms and agents.

➔ The banks operate for their own benefit with a product (new printed money) that they have not worked for.

Loans must be safeguarded

a) Individuals
Working contract (long term)
Property
Values
Assets

Resources
Insurance

b) Businesses
Resources
Insurance
Properties
Equipments
Values
Assets
Inventories of unsold goods
Bills for goods sold and awaiting payment
Ongoing income

c) Government
Taxes (ongoing income)
Properties
Values
Assets

Risks

→ Loans create economic slaves
→ Loans involve the risk to lose the value given as guarantee
→ Loans means: to possess money, but not having worked for it; therefore to work for it later
→ Lack of future work puts the loan and its guarantee at risk
→ The value of given guarantees decrease due to the market development
→ Variability of the foreign exchange rate
→ Shrinking economy
→ Asset-price inflation
→ Mortgage default
→ Interest-rate arbitrage
→ Bank default

Misuse of Money and Loans

→ The value of given guarantees was manipulated to best advantage
→ The business is a speculation business
→ Accounts are falsified
→ Toxic papers, junk mortgages
→ Stock-market manipulation
→ Hedge funds

→ Pyramid schemes
→ Inflated asset prices
→ Intractable bonds
→ Loans with unsustainable interest rates
→ Monopoly
→ Derivate speculation business

Crimes and Scams

Confidence trick: A con game, Ponzi scheme, scam, grift, hustle, bunko, bunco, swindle, flimflam, gaffle, or bamboozle.

Confidence tricks exploit typical human characteristics such as greed, dishonesty, vanity, honesty, compassion, credulity, irresponsibility, desperation and naïveté.

The common factor is that the victim relies on the good faith of the con artist.

In the case of banks the responsibility has to always lie with lender to lend responsibly, as after all they are not lending their money, but yours and mine.

Diagram Organism: Money moves out

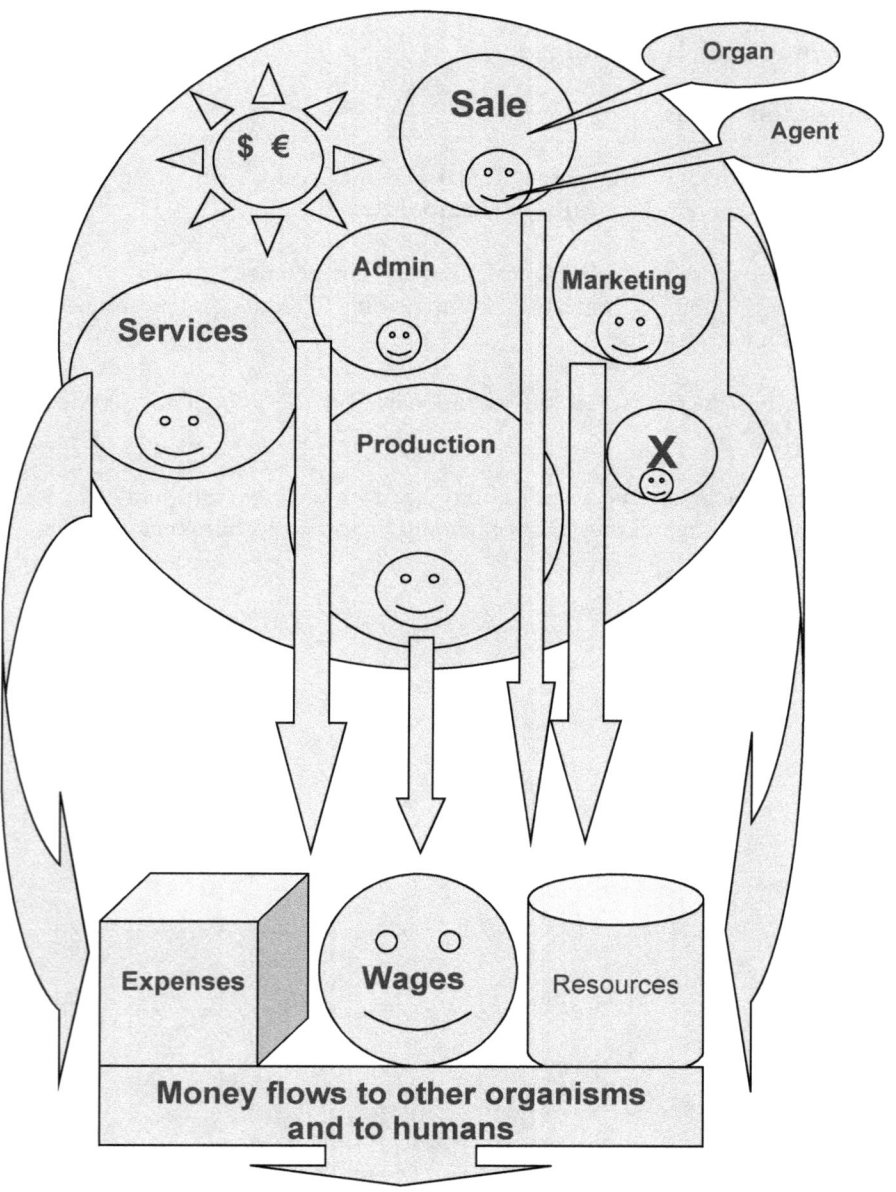

5.3. The Value of Work and Products

Work and Value

- Working (production, services) provides money for making a living.
- Working places allow people to earn money and make their living.
- The lower the wages, the higher the probability to fall into poverty.
- Low wages produce economically impotent consumers (low purchasing power).
- Low purchasing power destroys working places and entire businesses (organisms).
- Exporting working places to other systems (countries) eliminates working places at home.
- Lack of demand for products and services eliminates working places.
- High automation destroys working places.
- Lack of working places put people into poverty with highly reduced ability to consume.
- An organism needs to work to provide for its existence.
- The production and services can be useful, useless, meaningless or destructive for all agencies.
- Production and services can produce collateral damages others have to pay for.
- There are ways of making or getting money without production and services. Some are destructive.
- Unaccountable collateral damages destroy the money resources of the future agencies.
- Destructive ways of making or getting money are not sustainable for the organisms.
- An organism inherits its past and passes it onto the future agencies.

The Value of Products and Services

- The value of products and services are expressed in a certain amount of money.
- If the value increases, the agencies (organs) need more money to get it or must disclaim.
- If the value decreases, the agencies can purchase more of these products

and services.

- If the value remains stable, the agencies can operate with stable balance and eventually expand.
- Stable values allow for stable future planning and give security to all agencies in managing money.
- Unstable values do not allow for stable future planning and don't give security in managing money.
- The less money the agencies earn, the less they can afford (to buy) products and services.

Prices for the Value of Products

- Prices are calculated by costs + profit.
- Mass production tends to decrease the price.
- Low demand tends to decrease the price.
- Lowered economic potential of buyers decreases the price.
- Urgency to sell specific products tends to decrease the price.
- High demand of limited product units tends to increase the price.
- No urgent need for selling tends to hold the price high.
- Greed tends to fix prices high or to hold the prices high.
- The price of a product is reduced, but the quality is impaired.
- High economic potential of buyers increases the price.
- Glamour packaging tends to increase the price.

Prices for the Value of Services

- Prices are calculated by costs + profit.
- Oversupply tends to decrease the price.
- Low demand tends to decrease the price.
- Lowered economic potential of buyers decreases the price.
- High demand by limited supply tends to increase the price.
- Insufficient supply tends to increase the price.
- Greed tends to fix prices high or to hold prices high.
- The price for a service is reduced, but the quality is impaired.
- High economic potential of buyers increases the price.
- Oppressive business environment tends to increase the price.

Non-productive Private Expenses

- Accidents: traffic, working, sports, home, leisure
- Mental health: depression, fear, suicide, social neglect, violence
- Packaging: exaggerated packaging especially at commercial centers

- Internet: extensive use due to boredom and stupid curiosity or virtual relations
- Mobile phone: extensive use due to boredom and unable to be alone for hours
- Television: watching every stupidity to be brainwashed and due to boredom
- Electricity: ignorant and uncontrolled use of electricity
- Water: exaggerated (futile) use of water (home, garden)
- Detergents: ignorant and uncontrolled use of all kind of detergents
- Family: inconsiderate marriage and creating a baby; not prepared for it
- Debt: excessive use of credit cards and loans for cars and consumer goods
- Holidays: traveling to far reaching areas (airplane, long distances with car)
- Car: buying a new car every few years without a serious reason
- Driving: using the car just for fun or even for a few hundred meters
- Food: buying regularly prepared food (e.g. pizzas, pre-cooked menus)
- Newspaper, magazines: daily buying, mainly due to curiosity and boredom

Conclusions

- A system needs a certain amount of money to sustain itself as a complex organism of organs.
- The lower the sum of money in a system, the bigger the social and human problems.
- Making money is indispensable to make the entire system work in a balanced way.
- Imbalance of money power produces enormous human problems, misery and social conflicts.
- Monstrous organs (e.g. corporate groups) create imbalance and destroy the entire system.
- Lack of money in the production and service organs (and sub-organs) destroys working places.
- The system must create mechanisms to hold onto a relative internal economic balance.
- The bigger the lack of working places, the bigger the human and social problems.
- High public debt, corporate group debt, and consumer debt absorb huge amounts of money.
- Collateral damages create enormous economic burdens for the future generations.
- Huge non-productive costs suffocate, weaken, paralyze, and destroy the entire system.
- Non-productive costs hinder the entire system to be sustainable and

predictable in the long-run.

- Excessive export of working places in low-wage-systems destroys the entire system at home.
- Excessive automation destroys work places and the buying power of the lower and middle class.
- Excessive greed for highest amounts of money destroys the (relative) balance of the entire system.

5.4. Network and Spiral of Money

The Bigger Network

- A system is one of approximately 200 systems on this planet: countries with 7 billion people.
- All systems depend on the resources of the planet and the quality of the environment.
- Many systems are economically interrelated between organs, sub-organs, sub-sub-organs.
- The more imbalanced the interrelations work, the more single systems can break down.
- One big imbalanced system can weaken, and damage or destroy the unity of other systems.
- Some big imbalanced systems can break down the entire global organism of systems.
- The bigger the collateral damages and the effects on other systems, the more war is likely.
- The more some big systems are on the brink of collapse, the more humanity is affected.
- Unemployment, low buyer potential, high debt, austerity, and high rate of poverty lead to unrest.
- Austerity measures can not solve the economical imbalance in a system and between systems.
- The economical collapse of interrelated systems puts the guilt on others between the systems.
- To be on the verge of economical collapse provokes survival activities and leads to wars.

Network and Spiral of Economic Factors

- The more people on earth, the more the industry must produce and can make profit
- The more money concentrated in corporations, the more the prime-owners get profit
- The more profit in corporations, the more the prime-owners have financial power
- The more money is in corporations, the more the protagonists get wages and bonuses

- The more people on earth, the more people consume and the governments get taxes
- The more taxes governments get, the more they can increase rearmaments
- The more taxes governments get, the more they can increase their own wages
- The more public debt, the more governments need income to pay interest and capital back
- The more public debt, the more the economic elites dominate the governments
- The more people pay with credit cards, the more the financial institutions make profit
- The more people get consumer loans, the more the financial institutions make profit
- The more people get mortgages, the more they depend on the banks during their entire life
- The more people have mortgages or loans, the more they can be destroyed by banks
- The more money flows through the banks, the more they can speculate for more profit
- The higher the interest rates, the more people and governments are suffocated
- The bigger the banks, the more they control entire politics, societies and businesses
- The bigger the banks, the more they can destroy and dominate institutions and countries
- The bigger the corporations, the more they can influence lawmakers for their interests
- The more public education excludes human factors, the more people remain naïve and credulous
- The more people are poor and suffer, the more they are preoccupied and politically impotent
- The more people suffer and are preoccupied, the more they compensate as consumers
- The more people are stupid, the more the elites / leaders can freely operate for own interests
- The bigger the corporation, the more financial imbalance is produced on its specific location
- The more corporations dispose of money, the more they can lure and seduce protagonists
- The more corporations dispose of money, the more they buy and exploit global resources
- The bigger the financial power of corporations, the more they indirectly

govern the military

- The more banks have home repossessions, the more they influence the real estate market
- The more people pay for pensions, the more the banks dispose of money for more profit
- The more insurance companies dispose of money, the more they speculate with it for profit
- The more people believe in archaic religions, the more leaders can cheat and deceive them
- The more people think magically, the more they accept poverty, suffering and misery
- The more people are seduced with modern life style, the more corporations make money
- The shorter the life time of a product, the more corporations make money (obsolescence)
- The bigger the corporations and its expansion, the more the middle-class businesses shrink
- The more the middle-class businesses shrink, the more corporations can operate risk free
- The bigger the corporations, the more they control public education in their multiple interests
- The more people get irrelevant academic education, the more leaders can operate risk free
- The more people have a car, the more money flows to corporations and governments
- The more people lose their genuine inner being, the more corporations can make profit
- The more people are bombarded with lies and falsifications, the more they reject the truth
- The more people are neurotic, the more they accept neurotic, psychopathic, psychotic leaders
- The more people are cowards & hypocrites, the more they accept coward & hypocritical leaders
- The more people accept cowardice & hypocrisy, the more they can be exploited and abused
- The more people are deformed, distorted and dehumanized, the more they can be exploited
- The more people are desperate, the more they accept wars for capitalistic imperialism
- The more people have a fabricated enemy, the more they project their own evilness
- The more people can project their own evilness, the more they accept

leader's madness

- The more capitalistic imperialist and evil, the more the leaders can make money
- The more people have a reduced understanding, the more leaders can manipulate and lie
- The more this mad game goes on, the faster the planet is destroyed and humanity eliminated

→ Is there a way out of this network of interdependences and complex downward spirals?

6. Absence of Human Values

6.1. Basic Living as a Human Value

Healthy food	Billions do not have it. Part of industrialized food is not healthy.
Healthy drinking water	Billions do not have it. Immense illnesses due to dirty drinking water.
A home, shelter	Billions do not have it or have something of inhumane miserable quality.
Own bathroom	Billions do not have it.
Own kitchen	Billions do not have it.
Access to electricity 24/7	Billions do not have it: More than 1 billion use wood and coal (produces CO2) for cooking.
Connected with sanitation	Billions do not have it. Sewage goes to the sea and into nature.
Clothes and shoes	Billions only have an absolute minimum (not enough).
Goods for living	Billions only have an absolute minimum (not enough).
Work (for making a living)	Billions do not have work or are underemployed; can't live a proper life with it.
Doing business	Western world: too regulated. Small & medium sized businesses shrinking.
Education (basic, vocational)	Billions do not have it or only a minimum. Fully or partly illiterate. A holistic approach for personal growth and mastering life is excluded around the world.

6.2. General Values of Society

Sustainable life course	Worldwide very insecure. Billions do not have it.
Protection	Worldwide very insecure. Billions do not have it.
Social peace. Absence of crimes	Worldwide very insecure. Billions do not have it.
Justice (human rights)	Worldwide very deficient. Billions do not have it.
Healthy environment and nature	Worldwide in danger. Billions do not have it.
Fast access to Health Care	Basics must be free for citizens. Billions do not have it.
Public transport	Billions do not have it or only insufficient services.
Leisure and entertainment areas	Should have genuine and humane character. Billions do not have it.
Living culture	Must be authentic and promoting human values. Billions do not have it.
Genuine democracy	People must first be educated for it. Billions do not have it.
Fair, efficient governmental administration	Requires formation and principles of human values. Billions do not have it.
Fair, efficient government	Lack of integrity and extensive top-education of a majority of politicians.
Freedom of private movement	Destroys nature and resources. Creates imbalance. Billions pay for it.
Freedom to have a car	Destroys nature and resources. Creates imbalance. Billions pay for it.
Participation	People are not educated for competent participation. Billions do not have it.
Poverty support	Does not exist for billions; or only in a very limited extension.
Academic Education	Too much regulation. Very ideological concepts.
Resources (all kind of)	Extreme exploitation. Entire humanity in centuries will suffer from it.

6.3. Human Values

Inner life (mind)	Billions ignore it. Needs human education.
Spirituality	Extremely archaic. Needs human education.
Health (mental, physical)	Values highly ignored. Needs human education, healthy food, water, environment
Understanding	Billions ignore it. Needs human education.
Reliability	Billions ignore it. Needs human education.
Responsibility	Billions ignore it. Needs human education.
Truth	Billions ignore it. Needs human education. Needs a trustworthy environment.
Truthfulness	Billions ignore it. Needs a trustworthy environment.
Faithfulness	Billions ignore it. Needs a trustworthy environment.
Hope	For billions only superficial hope. Needs some realistic foundation.
Family	Billions ignore family values. Needs human education.
Parental education	Billions not prepared.
Love	Billions ignore it. Needs human education. Needs a trustworthy environment.
Friendship	Very superficial and temporary. Needs a trustworthy environment.
Respect	Billions ignore it. Needs human education. Needs a trustworthy environment.
Trust	Billions don't have it. Needs human education. Needs a trustworthy environment.
Self-realization	Billions don't have it. Needs human education.
Authenticity	Billions don't have it. Needs human education.
Sexual satisfaction	Billions don't have it. Needs human education.
Performance	Billions ignore it. Needs human education, effort and training.
Talents	Billions ignore it. Needs education and training.
Information	Billions are cheated. Must be correct, extensive and transparent including its network.

Freedom of speech	Billions abuse it. But not for propaganda, fabrications, deceit, lies, brainwashing.

7. Definitions of Sustainability

7.1. Explorations of the term Sustainability

We summarize the manifoldness of 'sustainability', discussed by several sources. [155]

O'Riorden (1985): "Exploration into a tangled conceptual jungle where watchful eyes lurk at every bend."

Spedding (1996): The remarkable number of books, chapters and papers, that even use 'sustainable' or 'sustainability' in the title but do not define either term.

Wilson (1992) stated: "The raging monster upon the land is population growth, in its presence; sustainability is but a fragile theoretical construct."

The definitions given below encompass all aspects of this subject. The areas of sustainable agriculture and sustainable development are dealt with in more detail later in the chapter:

1. Brundtland (1987): Sustainable development is development that meets the needs of the present without compromising the needs of future generations to meet their own needs. 1) The concepts of needs, in particular the essential needs of the world's poor, to which overriding priority should be given. 2) The idea of limitations imposed by the state of technology and social organization on the environments ability to meet present and future needs.
2. Harwood (1990): Sustainable agriculture is a system that can evolve indefinitely toward greater human utility, greater efficiency of resource use and a balance with the environment which is favourable to humans and most other species.
3. Pearce, Makandia & Barbier (1989): Sustainable development involves devising a social and economic system, which ensures that these goals are sustained, i.e. that real incomes rise, that educational standards increase that the health of the nation improves, that the general quality of life is advanced.
4. Conway & Barbier (1990): We define agricultural sustainability as the ability to maintain productivity, whether as a field or farm or nation, where productivity is the output of valued product per unit of resource input.
5. Daly (1991) then argued that: Lack of a precise definition of the term 'sustainable development' is not all bad. It has allowed a considerable

---

[155] http://www.ecifm.rdg.ac.uk/definitions.htm

consensus to evolve in support of the idea that it is both morally and economically wrong to treat the world as a business in liquidation.

6. Heinen (1994): No single approach to 'sustainable development or framework is consistently useful, given the variety of scales inherent in different conservation programs and different types of societies and institutional structures.

7. IUCN, UNEP, WWF (1991): Sustainable development, sustainable growth, and sustainable use have been used interchangeably, as if their meanings were the same. They are not. Sustainable growth is a contradiction in terms: nothing physical can grow indefinitely. Sustainable use is only applicable to renewable resources. Sustainable development is used in this strategy to mean: improving the quality of human life whilst living within the carrying capacity of the ecosystems.

8. Holdgate (1993): Development is about realizing resource potential. Sustainable development of renewable natural resources implies respecting limits to the development process, even though these limits are adjustable by technology. The sustainability of technology may be judged by whether it increases production, but retains environmental and other limits.

9. Pearce (1993): Sustainable development is concerned with the development of a society where the costs of development are not transferred to future generations, or at least an attempt is made to compensate for such costs.

10. HMSO (1994): Most societies want to achieve economic development to secure higher standards of living, now and for future generations. They also seek to protect and enhance their environment, now and for their children. Sustainable development tries to reconcile these two objectives.

The author mentions some other aspects of sustainability; we extract from the given source:

Types of Sustainability

- A sustainable system or process must be based on resources that will not be exhausted over a reasonable period.

- A sustainable system or process must not generate unacceptable pollution externally or internally

Biological Sustainability

- Individual species, ecosystems and habitats can be sustained as they involve reproductive and other essential processes - without which they would cease to exist

- Most biological systems have physical components, therefore there is considerable overlap between the use of biological and physical resources

Non Living Resources

- Some resources are limited; other resources if not used now, will not remain.

- Resources such as fossil fuels are totally changed when used and cannot be recreated on any reasonable time scale.

Living Resources

- The use of living resources may have to be considered over a relatively short period or be related to populations (plants and animals) capable of reproduction.

- This has given rise to the concept of sustainable harvesting, taking only such proportion of the population as can be continued over time, depending on reproductive rates in animals and seed numbers in plants.

Economics and Social Sustainability

- Theories regarding sustainable use of resources can be applied to economic sustainability, except that, in monetary terms, one resource can generally substitute another.

- The concept of economic sustainability is subject, on all levels, to different inputs and outputs.

- The economic sustainability of a nation is subject to the whole economy on local, national and international level.

7.2. Criteria for Sustainable Development

- *The critical question: For how many people is the planet sustainable?*
- *To find the right answer we must consider the bigger picture of sustainability:*

Critical: Humanity as a body in evolutionary development is extremely diverse and inert.

1. Humans need: work, food, water, energy, money, health care, sanitation, transport systems, medicine, detergents, recycling systems, and all kind of resources for construction and countless different products and services.

→ Sustainability must consider: The resources form part of a natural network and are limited!

2. Humans also produce manifold diverse contamination and pollution: waste, sewage, electronic scrap, nuclear waste, fine dust, gases, pharmaceutical and chemical elements, etc.

→ The sustainability of the planet's eco-systems and of the human body is limited and in mutual interaction!

3. The state of humanity and the planet today entails a long list of immense global problems. They are all linked together in a network.

→ Understanding of sustainability must also consider the interaction of all the enormous problems!

4. Humans are determined by their psychical-spiritual organism, with many single psychical functions needing to be formed. The aims of education must serve for a balanced life and for genuine human fulfillment.

→ Sustainability depends also on psychical-spiritual education and skills for mastering life and for work.

5. Close living together, especially in (mega-) cities, produces serious psychical and social problems; and reduces the opportunities for an authentic genuine life and development.

→ There are also social and environmental components that determine humane sustainability.

6. All significant religions are archaic and exclude the Archetypes of the Soul. The labyrinth of lies and misunderstanding of religion produce hostility, power fights, and wars – socially not sustainable anymore.

→ Sustainability also has a spiritual and religious dimension that must be considered.

7. The different political (ideological) systems around the globe produce enormous imbalance, hostility, misunderstanding, fights, riots, and wars.

→ Sustainability also has a political and ideological dimension that must be considered.

8. A few media corporate groups (10) with global operations brainwash 5-6 billion people. Most people are completely poisoned and deformed (dehumanized) in their genuine inner being.

→ Brainwashing and mentally deforming humans has a limited sustainability of mind and personhood.

9. The concentration of economical and industrial power (wealth, money, public debt), together with megalomania, psychopathy and imbalance of distribution produces enormous problems.

→ Sustainability of economy and industry depends on human factors and requires balance.

10. The rigidity, compulsivity, control obsession, standardization of everything, incompetence and arrogance of the state administration nearly everywhere enormously paralyzes and damages society's life.

→ State administrations have a negative impact in the sustainability of society's developments.

The Sustainability Questions

1. What types of goods are sustainable?
2. What kinds of production processes are sustainable?
3. What kinds of transport systems are sustainable?
4. What kind of education is sustainable for work and business?
5. What kind of education for mastering life is sustainable?

6. What kind of vocational education is sustainable?
7. What kind of teaching is sustainable?
8. What kind of wealth distribution is sustainable?
9. What kind of tourism is sustainable?
10. What kind of food production is sustainable?
11. What kind of water management is sustainable?
12. What kinds of devices (appliances) are sustainable?
13. What kind of energy production is sustainable?
14. What kinds of living human values are sustainable?
15. What kind of politics is sustainable?
16. What kind of economics is sustainable?
17. What kind of religion is sustainable?
18. What kind of public spending is sustainable?
19. What kind of pension regulation is sustainable?
20. What kind of marketing is sustainable?
21. What kind of entertainment is sustainable?
22. What kind of problem solving is sustainable?
23. What kind of unemployment politics is sustainable?
24. What kind of health care is sustainable?
25. What kind of penitentiary life is sustainable?
26. What kind of agriculture is sustainable?
27. What kind of livestock farming is sustainable?
28. What kind of fish exploitation and farming is sustainable?
29. What kind of transport of goods is sustainable?
30. What kind of raw material is sustainable?
31. What kind of electricity use is sustainable?
32. What kind of crude oil use is sustainable?
33. What kinds of materials and kind of toys are sustainable?
34. What kind of material for clothes is sustainable?
35. What kind of material for shoes is sustainable?
36. What kind of material for furniture is sustainable?
37. What kind of packaging is sustainable?
38. What kinds of urbanizations are sustainable?
39. What kind of political structures are sustainable?
40. What kind of propaganda is sustainable?
41. What kind of freedom of travel is sustainable?
42. What kind of family life is sustainable?
43. What kind of relationship is sustainable?
44. What kind of living love is sustainable?
45. What kind of peace is sustainable?
46. What kind of culture is sustainable?
47. What kind of managing humanity is sustainable?
48. What kind of political activities are sustainable?

49. What kind of communication is sustainable?
50. What kind of holidays is sustainable?
51. What kind of living (living a life) is sustainable?

There are more such questions!

➔ All these questions have an economic impact!
➔ The science of economics must ask and answer such questions!

7.3. Absence of Sustainability

	The Critical State	The Critical Development	Sustainable Renewal
State of Humanity	Unbalanced economy Poverty, Misery Illnesses, Hunger High Unemployment Extreme neg. psych. Effects	Increasing with Population growth Increasing costs and damages Places Humanity at risk of total collapse	No sustainable renewal Inner life of humans is never considered
State of the Planet	Contamination Climate Change Eco-systems Agricultural land Species Resources	Increasing with Population growth Increasing damages and costs Places Humanity at risk of total collapse	No sustainable renewal
State of the World	Urbanizations Traffic systems Very hostile relations Riots & wars	Increasing with Population growth Places Humanity at risk of total collapse	No sustainable renewal, Inner life of humans never considered
Society's Systems	Oil, Gas, Electricity and money Industry Power of the owners The inefficiency of Education & Culture Elite's interests	Increasing power concentration with Population growth Increasing power imbalance and costs Places Humanity at risk of total collapse	No sustainable renewal Inner life of humans never considered
Government	Psychopathy Megalomania Narcissism Neuroticism Blackmailed Lured, Chained Corruption Lies and deception Career maneuvers Power imbalance	Martial Laws Minute regulations Rigid punishment Menacing, deceiving Oppressing power Manipulations, lies Increasing waste of money and potentials Leads to wars and collapse	No sustainable renewal Inner life of humans never considered
Humans Psychical Spiritual Organism	Widely unknown Not formed, malformed, imbalanced, chaotic Ignored potentials Strongly rejected Therefore: no quality	Detached from truth Further growth of chaotic forming No understanding Increasing illnesses, Damages, hostility Increasing inability	No sustainable renewal Inner life of humans never considered e.g. in Education, Philosophy, etc.

	and no efficiency High compensation High fatalism Ignorance, lies	Increasing brainwashing Increasing costs Increasing hostility Increasing dehumanization	
Collective Unconscious	Energy surrounding humans: Explosive; Darkness Emptiness, guilt Aggressive, violent Destructive Cold, Despair, Fear Pain, Sadness Helplessness	Increasingly tense Already at 99% Imprisoning humans Paralyzing humans Separating humans from the 'spiritual Sun' Longing for punishment Forcing to destruction	Unknown Nothing
Religions Spirituality	Lies, Cheat, Distortion, Manipulations Myths Tales Legends Unknown authors No 'word of God' Ignoring psychical- spiritual Organism	Archaic, dogmatic and rigid; Authoritarian Increasing psychosis Ignoring psych. Organism Failed with the truth Waste of money	Nothing substantial Inner life of humans never considered
Archetypes of the Soul	Unknown Completely rejected, replaced by dogmas and myths, by psych. spiritual meanders	Actually not adaptable, completely hostile rejection Without: ends in chaos, total collapse	Unknown

7.4. Consequences of a Sustainable Society

What would happen with the Western economy if all people would change their lifestyle without losing life quality? The key would be: 'Change yourself and you change the economy.' A real economic principle is: The economic reality of a country (location) influences the lifestyle of people. We can also say it the other way round: Lifestyle influences the economic reality (due to increasing demand). The question is: How would a sustainable lifestyle of people influence the economy and economic life of a society? Here are some suggestions for a new lifestyle:

1.   Promote a lot your self-knowledge and psychical-spiritual development
2.   Elaborate your biography and get rid of unsolved past conflicts and pain
3.   Learn how to efficiently solve conflicts, problems, difficulties and crises
4.   Choose the right partner that shares with you growing and living with the soul
5.   Learn through courses before getting married and procreating a baby
6.   Write down your dreams every day and learn and practice dream interpretation
7.   Respect your energy and biorhythm and live with a smart self-management
8.   Talk daily minimum an hour with your partner and your children
9.   Learn to correctly meditate and meditate daily twice for 15 minutes
10. Never stop asking questions about life, love, trust, hope, belief and the truth
11. Live always rooted in the genuine human values and Archetypes of the Soul
12. Buy a car only when you absolutely need it for business or going to work
13. Don't let yourself be seduced for a new car and never overstrain your budget
14. Don't drive around with your car just for fun or for a bit of shopping
15. Always buy a car with cash and never with a loan or with leasing or renting
16. Consume 30-40% less petrol (by driving less, driving with care)
17. Use public transport whenever you can and accept walking up to 30 minutes
18. Reduce by 30% the amount of meat and fish that you consume

19. Use 20% less water (shower, washing, cleaning, garden, etc.)
20. Reduce lightening, heating, A/C and appliances by 30% (electricity, oil, gas)
21. Moderate if necessary: Smoke 50% less and / or drink 50% less alcohol
22. Use your credit/debit card only when you really need it; at least 75% less
23. Never contract a credit card from a shopping center or a petrol company
24. Get cash from the bank or the ATM of your bank (to buy everything with cash)
25. Pay all of what your credit card is charged every end of the month
26. Buy 50% less soda/beer/wine (alternatively drink tea at home)
27. Shop for goods at your local market or shops; and walk if possible
28. Buy local products such as vegetables, fruits, meat, fish, bakery products
29. Buy 75% less newspapers, magazines, stationery items (paper, ink)
30. Go on holiday in foreign countries only every 2-5 years; avoid mass tourism
31. Perfume/Toiletry: use 20-30% less (simply do not exaggerate the use)
32. Avoid getting a loan for consumption (work first to later get what you want)
33. Buy 90% less prepared (frozen) meals (cook your own meals)
34. Use detergents sparingly and medicine (psychotropic) when it is appropriate
35. Turn off appliances at home (TV, PC, Radio, etc.) when not used
36. Watch 50-80% less TV every day and examine the value of the content
37. Reduce waste by 50% (packaging, plastic, newspaper, magazines, paper, etc.)
38. Use the dishwasher and washing machine only when it's appropriate
39. Use your mobile phone and computer (Internet, Facebook) 75% less
40. Don't buy goods from countries that practice the death penalty, don't visit them
41. Buy natural and creative toys for your kids and never gadgets with batteries
42. Always be aware of possible accidents (driving, work, home, sport)
43. Live a healthy life style, eat and behave with intelligence and reason
44. Don't go shopping when you are hungry, frustrated or in a bad mood
45. Contract mortgages only with a low interest rate and at least 10 year fixed rate
46. Buy a home with at least 50% cash; never buy a holiday home with a mortgage
47. Don't buy consumer goods with a company credit, not even if free of interest
48. Contract insurance policies with a certain amount of own risk

49. Don't speculate (lottery, gambling, casino, investments, bets, etc.)
50. Go to shopping centers only when there is no local alternative for what you want
51. Every month, buy a book that improves your work, business, life and personality
52. Buy quality goods (products) considering their long term sustainability (value)
53. Buy decorations from local artists (handicrafts) and only local seasonal flowers
54. Drastically reduce buying useless cheap products that you will soon throw away
55. Prepare yourself with further education so you can start your own business
56. Start your own business very small and expand slowly with real growth
57. Daily thoroughly care for your teeth avoiding high costs 20-40 years later!
58. Avoid lying in the sun for more than one hour per day (risk of skin cancer!)
59. Always wash your hands very well when coming home and after the toilet
60. Eat sweets, chocolates and snacks moderately and not every day
61. All kind of drugs (cocaine, heroin, soft drugs, etc.) are absolutely taboo
62. If you have a garden, use some space for a vegetable and berry garden
63. Plant on your terrace or garden a lot of seasonal flowers and herbs
64. Spend part of your leisure for creative activities such as painting, handicraft, etc.
65. Go regularly for a long walk or for jogging or to the Gym (minimum twice weekly)

7.5. Sustainability and the Transport Systems

Let's take 'cars' as an example to show the complexity of economic sustainability:

- Road Traffic Accidents (RTA) result in 1.2 million deaths and 50 million injured every year.
- Over the last 50 years more than 60 (or: 100?) million people died and 2.5 billion people were injured due to RTA.
- Today, over 400,000 people die in Europe every year as a result of fine dust from road traffic; and millions more around the globe.
- Pollution from cars and lorry traffic: exhaust gases, including fine dust (diesel), fine dust by tires abrasion, fine dust by abrasion on driving surface, fine dust from brake shoes; and traffic noise.
- Pollution also from: Trains, aviation, sea vessels, wrecks, oil tankers, and military vehicles.
- There are an estimated 1.5-2 billion cars and other motor vehicles (e.g. lorries, vans, etc.) in use worldwide; all producing pollution, contamination, accidents, etc.
- Within the next 20 years an estimated 1.5-2 billion cars will be produced around the globe!
- Cars produced per year: 68-72 million.
- 1.5-2 billion cars and other motor vehicles (lorries, vans, etc.) are in use worldwide.
- Traces of more than 100 different (toxic) chemicals can be detected in new cars.
- Probably more than 1.5 billion people work within the 'car production' chain.
- The global annual cost of Road Traffic Accidents in the USA is almost $518 billion.
- 10% of all hospital beds are occupied by RTA victims.
- In Germany 55% of regular car usage is for holiday and leisure travel.

Car and lorry traffic pollution: 1) exhaust gases; 2) fine dust by tires abrasion; 3) fine dust by driving surface abrasion; 4) fine dust, from brake shoe. Traffic noise is also considered as extremely unhealthy emission.

Train pollution: Fecal fine dust, fine dust by rail abrasion and iron wheels. Traffic noise is also considered as extremely unhealthy emission.

Aviation pollution (civil, military, leisure): gases, noise, fuel and human waste pollution.

Wrecks from cars and lorries or trucks, all kind of transport vehicles, plus trains and airplanes leave behind dangerous metals and chemical elements.

Oil tankers, pipelines, and oil derricks produce – especially catastrophic accidents – produce an incredible amount of destruction of the world of animals and nature, including rivers, seas and oceans. Contamination of the soil, beaches and drinking water has dramatic long-term effects on nature and humans.

Special holiday pollution: A cruise ship produces the same amount of fine dust as 50,000 cars driving at 130 km/h. Therefore with approximately 230 cruise ships afloat at any one time globally, that is the equivalent of 11.5 million cars daily, 345 million monthly and 4.1 billion annually.

→ Enormous global demand of petrol, diesel, kerosene, oil
→ High speed trains consume enormous amounts of electricity

Negative implications of transport systems

- Road Traffic Accidents with millions of victims, injured and handicapped people
- Sea traffic accidents (oil tankers) producing mega damages
- Waste from vessels thrown into the sea (ocean)
- Car and lorry traffic pollution
- Train pollution
- Cruise ship and in general vessel pollution
- Wrecks of cars and lorries
- Oil tankers
- Noise pollution
- Negative impact on sea life and sea nature
- Navy (armadas)
- Enormous global demand of petrol, diesel, ceresin, oil, corn for ethanol
- Trains, especially high speed trains: high demand of electricity

The exaggerated road traffic produces greenhouse effect, allergies, respiratory disease, stress and stress reactions, irreversible global warming, heavy global environmental pollution, etc.

Tourism (980 million PAX in 2011) always includes traveling and therefore contributes enormously to global warming and climate change. Other damages and negative results are: temporary exorbitant use of water, hundred of tons of rubbish and huge amounts of sewage, destruction of environment and especially the natural recreation quality of nature, water pollution, traffic noise, misuse of cultural values, cheat, crimes (robbery, burglary), and masses of cars in tourist resorts (villages, towns, beaches, urbanizations', etc.).

Raw Material needed for Car Production

Glass, steel, plastic, copper, lithium, aluminum, iron, plastic steel, wood, cotton, rubber, coconut fiber, chemical elements, detergents, oil, electricity, water, rare elements, paint, labor colors, leather, and much more, etc.

The Complexity of the Car Industry

The car industry system includes many types of work; we offer here a brainstorming:

- Exploitation of raw material
- Elaboration of raw material
- Production and assembly of the parts of a car
- Exploitation of oil
- Refineries
- Manufacturing tools and machines for production
- Production of tires
- Production of spare parts
- Production of accessories
- Production of chemicals, colorants
- Production of special detergents and cleaning utilities
- Construction of buildings, offices, commercial premises, industrial premises
- Construction of parking areas, buildings, garages
- Parking businesses
- Furniture and equipment
- Security equipment
- Security companies
- Stationery
- Printing press
- Packaging
- High tech appliances

- Research and development
- Transport: tankers, ships, lorries, service cars, etc.
- Containers and storage units
- Car recycling
- Sales departments
- Accounting
- Satellites and communication systems
- Computers and printers
- Immeasurable amounts of cables of all kind
- Land
- Parking meters
- Traffic lights
- Repair services
- Road construction (including tunnels and bridges)
- Road planning and road repair
- Police
- Ambulance and Fire services
- Lawyers
- Courts, prisons
- Registration of fines
- Insurances
- Periodic car inspections
- Car wash services
- Petrol stations
- Administration (everywhere for everything)
- Driving schools
- Driving licenses
- Hospitals, clinics, doctors, rehabilitation
- Utilities for handicapped people (accidents)
- Management of car taxes
- Economic calculations and planning
- Bank services
- Tax collection with every movement of any piece
- Toll roads
- And much more …

All this is established everywhere around the globe for a product that has a life duration on average of 12-15 years with an immense loss of raw material, immense suffering, and immense environmental damages putting the ecosystems and the entire planet in danger. Above that it absorbs an estimated 20-25% of a monthly budget for the masses of people that have a car.

Collateral Factors

Some examples: Damages due to exploitation of prime resources produces (mines), destruction of environment, contamination due to chemicals and fine dust, poverty, exploitation of people, work accidents, illnesses (cancer), use of water, etc.

Probably more than 1.5 billion people are working (full time or part time) within this chain from raw material exploitation to the owner of a car, the car maintenance and final recycling of the cars.

There are predictions saying that in the year 2050 an estimated 3.5 billion cars will be needed and driving on earth. Is this sustainable?

Conclusion

→ If the car-system collapses, we have an estimated one billion people without work!
→ If the car-system collapses, many governments (state, province, local) will collapse.
→ If the car-system collapses, a majority of the wealth of super rich people will collapse.
→ If the car-system collapses, a majority of humanity will experience an existential earthquake.
→ If the car-system continues growing, the car system will destroy the planet.
→ The entire car system is the result of a 'car psychoses' and mad economic thinking.
→ The car psychosis and the mad economic 'rational thinking' dehumanize mankind.

But there is a solution, a multidimensional concept of global solutions. I have it on the table.

Diagram: Network of the Car System

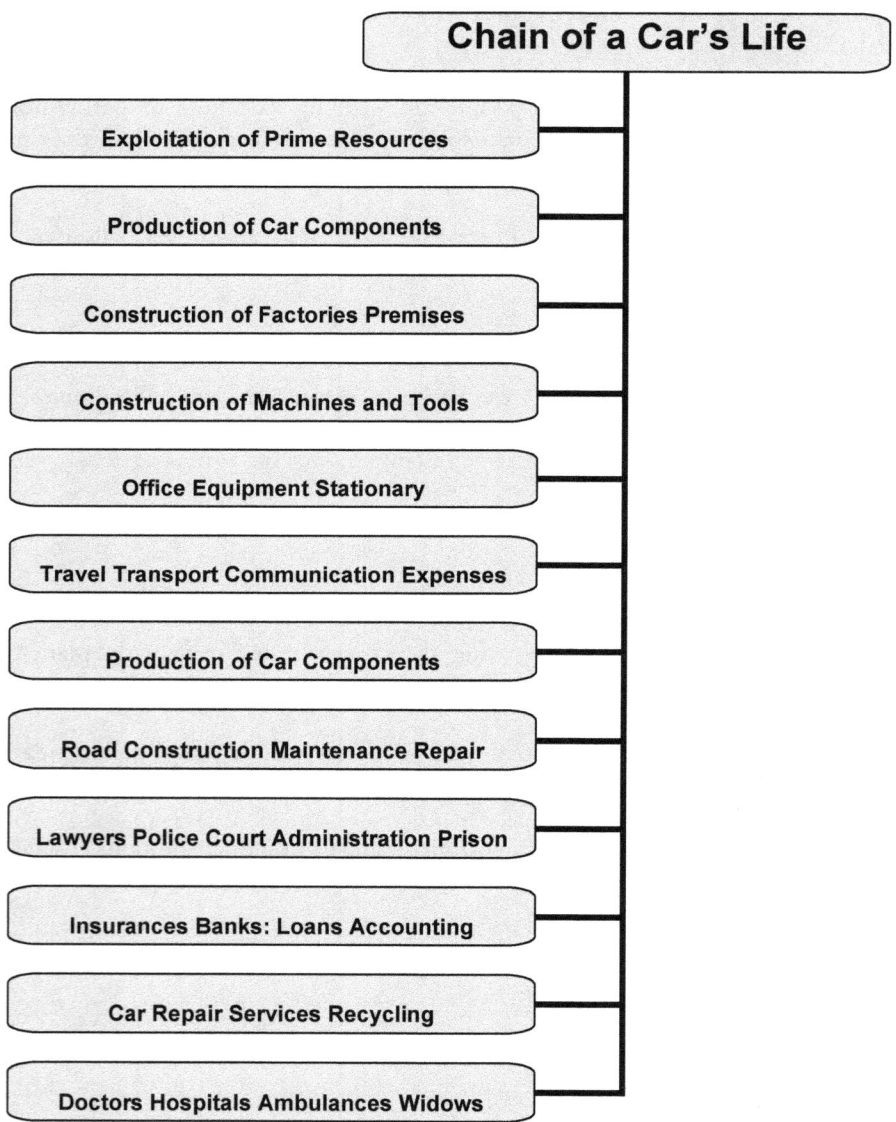

Chain of a Car's Life

- Exploitation of Prime Resources
- Production of Car Components
- Construction of Factories Premises
- Construction of Machines and Tools
- Office Equipment Stationary
- Travel Transport Communication Expenses
- Production of Car Components
- Road Construction Maintenance Repair
- Lawyers Police Court Administration Prison
- Insurances Banks: Loans Accounting
- Car Repair Services Recycling
- Doctors Hospitals Ambulances Widows

7.6. Austerity

The rejection and unwillingness of most people require austerity measures.

People in general reject:

- To learn and to appreciate learning opportunities (benefit from) for mastering life
- To learn and to appreciate learning opportunities (benefit from) for competent working
- To learn for professional flexibility and new orientations due to labor market changes
- To learn for avoiding accidents, illnesses, mental disease, psychosis, behavior disorder
- To practice self-knowledge, self-management and personal psychical-spiritual development
- To be aware of and to practice life long learning for personal growth and matters of life
- To read minimum one book per month for improvement of life and understanding of the world
- To be very alert and vigilant over brainwashing, manipulations, fabrications, lies, and deceit
- To exert and perform with permanent vocational education for success in business
- To change the understanding of the dehumanizing pension concept and to work lifelong
- To become prepared for making a baby and living marriage and a family life
- To learn dealing with personal energy, money and time aiming for sustainability and balance
- To become aware of and to appreciate, promote, strengthen and live genuine human values
- To learn and live genuine moral attitudes expressing love, care, trust, truthfulness
- To get rid of stupidity, naivety, credulity, superficiality, ego-centrism, narcissism, falseness
- To stand for peace, justice, sustainability and to reject hatred, violence,

abuse, riots, wars

- To become aware of compensatory and dehumanizing functions of exaggerated consumption
- To work hard for getting food, goods, entertainment, comfort, luxury, quality of life
- To pay for substantial knowledge, healthy life environment, healthy food, quality in general
- To respect the immense value of money for managing the holistic personal life course
- To take distance from the fast or speculative money and from permanent laziness to perform
- To extensively become aware of the dire state of humanity and the very damaged planet
- To learn how to contribute to the solutions of the big problems of society and humanity
- To learn about the horrible scam of religions and to search inside for the spiritual truth
- To change life style in order to find genuine satisfaction and complete inner fulfillment
- To give priority to a genuine way of life with a healthy environment including nature
- To respectfully live with the inner bio-rhythm, the rhythm of life, and the natural conditions
- To care for physical and mental health, for a responsible sexual life, for an inspiring social life
- To contribute to a real democratic society with activities, discussions, and high vigilance
- To promote local, regional, national, and global sustainable creation of society's life
- To become entirely responsible for the consequences of the way of living and growing

To achieve all-area sustainability austerity measures are necessary. People are extremely fastidious:

- Suffer from a car-psychosis: want to have a car although in most cases it is not necessary
- Are greedy to have the new model of a car although in most cases it is not necessary
- Want every year the new model of their mobile phone, computer or television
- Want every year the new model of any kind of clothes (fashion articles)

- Feel they are too good to get their hands dirty and to sweat during work
- Prefer not to work instead of working for low wages and learning through practice
- Want a good job, but have very low working attitudes and miserable skills
- Want to be paid well, but have no superior qualifications; in most cases very low skills
- Are too lazy to learn hard for a new job field and even to relocate in order to get a job
- Want higher education for free although they will have chances for a higher salary
- Want to possess (whatever good) without working for it (simply get it with consumer credit)
- Want a good life, but reject learning for mastering life and managing money and time
- Want happiness, but reject learning for personal psychical-spiritual development
- Prefer to pay weekly for their lottery ticket instead of working for money
- Want a job in the tourist industry, but do not learn a foreign language and adequate behavior
- Those who have a house with garden are too lazy to make their own vegetable garden
- Prefer to watch 4-6 hours of television instead of learning for new professional skills
- Are too lazy to learn how to cook and prefer to go to a cheap restaurant
- Prefer to spend money on drugs, alcohol and tobacco than for a healthy life style
- Don't care much for their health, illnesses and accidents; but want health care for free
- Always want to go out instead of taking time for the partner or their children
- Prefer to be ignorant, naïve and credulous instead of learning about the true realities
- Want an academic degree, but do not want to pay for it and study hard with serious attitudes
- Are stubborn and reject pioneering, vanguard and creative thinking and projects
- Want as much money as possible with as little work per week as possible
- Would never want to work 60 hours per week to build up a serious small business
- Their profit greed is focused on fast money and never on top service or quality
- Could walk or take public transport to go to work, but prefer to take their

car
- Are extremely lazy to walk half an hour or more to get what they want or need
- Fall in love and get married without considering that both have an inner life to be formed
- Women and men play with their partner's feelings and inner needs accepting all risks
- Women/men run for sex without true love to have their fast pleasure without commitment
- Have sex and procreate (unplanned) a baby without considering the manifold consequences
- Have children, but no time for them and treat them with an absolute ignorance and arrogance
- Always have their rigid opinion although it's only a cheap and superficial mindless talk
- Want a superficial life and don't ever take some minutes to contemplate about themselves
- With chips and beer they sit in front of the television without considering all the brainwashing
- God and J.C. shall solve their problems or it's destiny, instead of learning and acting
- Pray to J.C., but if he would live on earth today, they would destroy his business and life
- Are absolutely happy with an absurd belief because they reject profound self-knowledge
- Want a good life, but they never read a book for understanding life and the world
- Want to be retired at the age of 62-65 and live another boring 20-30 years as a maggot
- Delegate responsibility, including about happiness, success, work, money, life and health
- Can't wait for the weekend or special holidays always only thinking about fun and entertainment
- Admire all kinds of idiotic doing of others to avoid becoming aware of their own stupid behavior
- Try to solve all their problems with medicine, drugs, alcohol and suppression of their problems
- Identify themselves with celebrities instead of performing with their own potentials
- Do not want to learn from their mistakes (and damages), but prefer to put the blame on others
- Would never want to reduce their life style in the interest of decreasing

global contamination

- Want everything as cheap as possible, ignore the 3-4 billion people who work for it in misery
- Want a lot for free although it destroys businesses and above that they don't value what they get
- Want a supermarket with 1,000 goods and do not consider the irreversible natural damages
- Accept all kind of life lies, lies, cheat, deceit, and falseness and would never stand for the truth
- Want love and care and to be accepted, but are unable to love and care and to accept themselves
- Have very low personality qualities, but claim for manifold compensations with consumer goods
- Want to go on holiday to beaches and sea, to hang around, to drink alcohol, to have sex and fun
- They want all lights on at home, television and music on, but do not consider the nuclear waste
- Other cultures are always the evil ones, guilty for any criticalities; but they don't search for facts

→ There are an estimated 1.5 billion people with such attitudes and behavior in the Western world and billions more in the developing countries. These people destroy the planet with their existence! And today they are also a significant cause of war risks and ongoing wars since 1991.

→ The increase of the world population, alone since 1980 with estimated 3 billion people, requires a complete new understanding of how to govern a country, how to manage the economy, how to manage a society, how to educate people, and how to lead the citizens in their way of living.

→ There is only one solution: extreme collective austerity or putting all these people in closed communities where they must learn hard and work very hard, every day 12 hours during 6 days until they are responsible for themselves, for their life, for society, for the irreversible reduction of natural, raw and vivid resources, and for the planet and humanity.

Destructive Political and Economic Tools

- Mental control that is not realized by the people (media, propaganda)
- Polarizing the infinite realities into two opposite groups
- Ignoring or discrediting alternatives to the two opposite groups
- Memorizing facts, ideas and opinions in people's mind through repetition
- Annulling personality to lose one's own authenticity (to become robots)

- Putting up curtains of smoke or fog to hide the truth and cynical politics
- Lying, distorting, suppressing, luring, seducing, blackmailing, detracting
- Creating waves of false information and entertainment with hidden messages
- Reducing or prohibiting independence and weakening freedom
- Abusing words such as democracy, freedom, humanitarian, trust, hope, God
- Police, military and state administration are always on the 'right side'
- To everyday force people to focus on sensations (to dissipate relevant facts)
- Destroying, buying or killing those who have better alternatives, the truth
- Creating systems of attitudes and beliefs and training people to copy them
- Promoting individualism and consumption (compensations) to the extreme
- Standardizing, regulating, accrediting and controlling everything
- Creating manic 'hamster running wheel' behavior (endless concerns, preoccupations) for people
- Blame others to create an enemy – the bad and evil – for one's own good
- Promoting social pressure to think and talk the same way like everybody else does
- Eliminating reputation of a person by discrediting with any hair in the soup
- Disinformation must become the main 'food' people focus on (distraction)
- Permanent brainwashing to discipline the masses: already mental slaves
- To train and control the way of thinking through media information patterns
- Suffocating self-esteem and self-confidence through public education
- Creating poverty and unemployment to make people 'useless humans'
- Ignoring or suppressing creative and pioneering thinking that asks questions
- Demonizing ideologies that do not conform to the authority and privileged elites
- Creating assassination or terrorist attacks and blaming others for it (false flag)
- Valuing people only through superficial and external qualities, selected performances
- Relevant ethics, wisdom and intelligence in human matters are banned

8. Basic Methods of Economics

8.1. The Ignored Economic Reality

Economic Realities

A social science such as psychology, sociology, politics, education, and also economics is very complex. Therefore a first indispensable approach is to draw a systemic picture about this complex reality of a social science. The essential question is: What is inside, what is outside, and what is in significant interrelation between inside and outside?

The different economic worlds (entities) have completely different characteristics and operate in very different ways.

We have with the science of economics as offered from the classical books mainly from Western Universities about economics in essence:

- Price construction
- Scarcity
- Consumer behavior
- Rational decision making
- Sale patters
- Profit management
- Accounting
- Allocation
- Management decision
- Product characteristics
- Fresh and non-fresh goods
- Cost of time
- Market forces
- How markets work
- Elasticity
- Etc.

We must also structure the economic world and market into different categories such as:

- **Industry:** Food, water, raw material (resources), public transport, cars, aviation, communication (telephone), online (internet), pharmaceutics, electricity production, banking, media, health care, tourism, hospitality, etc.

- **Locations:** rural areas, villages, towns, big towns, cities, and mega-cities

- **Structures:** self-employed people, small and medium sized businesses, and the big corporations

- **Business Services:** Repair, legal services, doctors, psychologists, coaching, psychotherapy, marketing, art and craft, music, cleaning service, security guards, etc.

These four different areas economically operate in completely different ways. These areas consist in multiple essentially different factors and structures that the 'principles of economics' do not work in the same way in all areas. There are completely different 'principles', factors and correlations.

The quantity and quality is of very different 'class' and meaning. We observe that the entire body of theories in the mentioned study books about economics and economy only marginally or not at all analyze and elaborate the economic reality under such eminent differences. Therefore the world of economics is totally falsified and distorted in these study books (for millions of students). This is called 'economic thinking'. We assume that this is intentional to avoid transparency about the hidden ideology.

All mentioned authors discuss shortly the 'free market economy' and the 'command/planned economy'. With a smug smirking undertone they all praise the capitalistic economy. But the economic reality shows us that much more is planned on the stage behind the curtains than they tell us. All essential lines of economic production and development form part of a road map. The claim that the Western world operates with a 'free market' economy' is ridiculous and cynical.

Key Industries depending on Oil/Gas, Electricity, and Banks

Thesis: The key industries as listed above provide society with the goods people and the government want. These key industries are an immense source of high profit making

Conclusions about Profit

- The higher the collective demand, the higher the profit
- The higher the mass production, the higher the profit

- The higher the mass consumption, the higher the profit
- The lower the wages and low conditions, the higher the profit
- The lower the prices of raw material, the higher the profit
- The lower the environmental respect, the higher the profit
- The more extensive robot operations, the higher the profit
- The broader the mass media marketing, the higher the profit
- Corporate groups aim at any cost highest possible profit
- Corporate groups tend to expand and aim to increase profit
- The bigger the independence from governments, the higher the profit
- The less regulation, control and accountability the higher the profit

Economics and Policy

- Society works only with oil/gas, electricity and especially with the banks.
- If these industries depend on loans from banks, the banks have a say.
- The banks have a say over oil/gas industry and electricity industry.
- The owners of banks, oil industry and the electricity form a united power.
- This united power also holds power in most of the key industries.
- The rulers own the banks and the industry and therefore dictate to governments.
- An estimated 500-2,000 people rule the entire capitalistic coalition.
- It works only with an according education, brainwashing and manipulations.
- If there is little, low or no demand, then demand must be created or stimulated.

Conclusion

- ➜ A government with high debt is not free and is therefore not a democracy!
- ➜ There is no such thing as 'free market'; the road map on the hidden stage is what rules.
- ➜ Most of the protagonists on the stage of economics will die in the coming 20-35 years.
- ➜ Most of the protagonists on the stage of politics will die in the coming 20-35 years.
- ➜ The children of the protagonists will inherit a disastrous economy and world.
- ➜ The Western young generation (3-23 years old) is already significantly dehumanized.
- ➜ The truth is lost; the trust is gone; and all genuine inner human values are raped.
- ➜ Who will have the intelligence, wisdom, integrity, and the Spirit to rule

tomorrow?

8.2. Social Science and Variables

Economics claims to be a science. Mankiw & Taylor compare economics with biology and physics, and even compare the 'laws' of economics with the theory of gravity. [156]

Scientific thinking is a new way of thinking (as Mankiw & Taylor opinion): It is simply much deeper, much more precise, and much more interrelated thinking. A scientist is like a journalist. He observes something and describes it. A scientist's thinking goes deeper into the topic to get the best possible view and description over a reality. A scientist is required to describe things objectively and he can make his assessment to the facts or he gives advices and suggestions for certain aims.

The core question is: Is economics a science like physics? Are the topics of economics really like the physical world that can for example analyze and explain gravity, as Mankiw & Taylor categorically state?

Basic Understanding of Variables

- All chosen topics must have an importance in the world of economics. A topic must be exactly described with all its characteristics. The terms used (words) must be clear without ambiguity in their meaning. The importance must be explained. Doing wrong here, leads to all kind of mistakes in the scientific elaborations and conclusions.
- Variables can be any facts, factors, or additional interdependences. The facts, factors and interdependences must be clear without ambiguity in their meaning. The facts, factors, or additional interdependences must be comprehensible and reproducible.
- Variables are called also a 'constant' or a 'parameter': a variable has a quantity or quality of a fact or factor that is determined with a value range from zero to X. The meaning of a quality or quantity must be clear without ambiguity.
- A variable can determine a mini-fact ('thing') or a complex unity (a bunch of facts) determined as a 'variable'. A simple 'mini-fact' is for example 'egg',

---

[156] Mankiw (et al.), p. 22-23

'apple', 'human', 'dollar', the decision 'yes or no', 'worker' (labor), etc.

- A complex unity can be a basket of goods consisting of X determined goods, for example a basket contains 5 'things': meat, fish, bread, milk, and fruits. The meaning of the 'things' in the basket must be clearly determined.

- The variables can encompass a mini-area such as a school, a firm, a farm, a shop, a rural or urban area, a village, a town, city or mega-city, a nation, the entire world, and any field of topics. A variable is always isolated from its real context. The context must be clear.

- All scientific methods require a definition of variables and also always a hypothesis. All variables must be clearly determined. A hypothesis must be described in its context of real life and / or of another hypothesis. The interest and importance must be explained in the context of its reality in the world.

- Any thesis always first starts with a hypothesis that is founded on a premise, or any kind of evidence or determined meaning. Example: People need to eat a certain amount of different basic aliments; the variable can be: "The basket of goods that people need to eat for a healthy state (of body and mind)."

- Construction of a hypothesis: Variable A has a correlation with variable B (A and B, each with an extension). For example: Variable A = amount of money (i.e. Dollars, Euros) from zero up to X Dollars (Euros) spent during one month in Berlin for the determined basic basket of goods; and variable B = Basket of food with an exactly defined content (things and minimum amount per month) people need for a healthy body. The hypothesis: People need X Dollars (Euros) to get the basket for a month.

- A survey can be done in different places in a nation or in a place in a developing country. The results of different places (or entities) can be compared, which will lead to an additional result (and hypothesis or thesis).

- Multiple constructions: more than two, often up to 30 or more variables are determined in a network. Let's take these 5 goods of the basket of goods we determined the 5 'things': meat, fish, bread, milk, and fruits. We can understand these 'things' as 5 single variables, each with an extension of kilos and liters; which means we have now 5 variables. We also chose the variable 'wage per month', e.g. 600-800€, 801-1,000€, 1,001-1,200€, 1,201-1,500€, 1,501-2,000€ (etc.). We choose a) singles; b) couples; c) families with 1 child; and d) families with 2 children for a survey. Additionally we have the average price-variable for each 'thing', identified at the chosen location: 1 kg meat costs N, 1 kg fish costs F, 1 kg bread costs R, 1 liter milk costs G, 1 kg fruit costs M. We decide and declare: the chosen products are taken from medium quality products (and we explain clearly). The survey refers to Berlin metropolitan area and parallel to a village in a rural area in the South of Germany. With such a constellation we can find out how people make choices in basic foods, depending on money at their disposal per month, and their 'households' (amount and characteristics of people in a household).

- In a network of variables each variable can be measured with a given weight of relation to other variables; for example: People need more from this and less from that per month for their health: 1kg meat = weight 1; 1 kg fish = weight 4; 1 kg bread = weight 5, 1 liter milk = weight 3, and fruits = weight 2. This allows us in the end to interpret the balance of nutrition people chose depending on their wage and / or location and / or household (the people units as mentioned above).
- An extension of a variable can be a range of quality or quantity. A quality such as: village, town, and mega-city; or: single, couple, and family (1 or 2 children) understood as a way of living. A quantity can be measured in figures: dollars, amount, kilos, percents, absolute figures, size, etc.
- The mathematical formulas calculate increase, decrease, weight, and interrelations of variables.
- The diagrams and flowcharts show and compare visually figures of variables.
- The graphs show development and interrelations of figures with lines and / or patterns of points.
- Once chosen a population, for example 1,000 households with determined groups of single (250), couples (250), families with 1 child (250), and families with 2 children (250), each explored in 3 towns of similar size and characteristics, then we can also make a calculation (generalization) about the probability of any variation of all similar places in a nation.
- The practicability of such surveys is another matter. Obviously not everything is practicable for a survey. Therefore at the beginning of such a project the feasibility in the real world or in a constructed laboratory sample must be explored and determined.

There are countless possibilities to construct 'pictures' with interdependences of realities. Some examples:

Example 1: We have access to 100 chats (or private mails) of 1,000 people (of a certain age group) on a social website. We can count the words, then we group the words into meaning-unities, and then we can draw a picture about what preoccupies these people.

Example 2: We have access to the use of the credit card of 1,000 people of a certain age group, each with 50 movements per month. We also have the information of the type of shops where they have made a purchase. From there we can draw a picture about the lifestyle of the different types of people-groups.

Example 3: We have access to the Internet use of 1,000 people through the collected IP addresses they have visited during one month. We can draw a picture about the interests of these people, from there deduce their needs, interests, motives and ways of thinking.

Example 4: We have access to data about the books (content) 1,000 people of a certain age group have ordered online during one year. From there we can draw a picture about the interest and kind of thinking of this age group in a nation.

Example 5: We have access to data such as age, gender, marital status, wage, living location, kind of work/job, and the education of different age groups from 1,000 people. From there we can draw a picture of life courses and increase (or decrease) of life standard. The hypothesis could be: "the better the education, the higher is the wage with increasing age"; and this is more significant for singles than for families within the age group 30-35 than in all other age groups. Or: the factor education does not lead to very significant higher wages, especially without further education. We can create many more hypotheses within these variables.

The possibility to understand factors, facts, and interdependences is countless within economic variables and behavior of people. All variables have a meaning for humans, for consumers as well as for producers (sellers). In the end, the meaning and the interest in it for any market benefit (profit) is the core of every survey in the actual capitalistic economics.

Variables in Economics have Selected Importance

- Importance for self-employed businesses
- Importance for small businesses
- Importance for medium sized businesses
- Importance for big businesses (corporations)
- Importance for selected goods
- Importance for selected services
- Importance for selected urban areas
- Importance for selected age groups
- Importance for selected wage groups
- Importance for selected production entities
- Importance for exploitation of raw resources
- Importance for sale entities (sale business)
- Importance for shareholders
- Importance for specific lifestyle

- Importance for mind and soul
- Importance for physical health
- Importance for environment
- Importance for social peace
- Importance for future generations
- Importance for global developments
- Importance for humanity's evolution

→ In the majority of economic theories the importance is ignored and it is unclear for which field it is important or absolutely unimportant.

→ Some theories may be applicable for specific patterns (shopping, consumer behavior, production, or cost management) but for others not.

→ Some theories (models of graphs) are so idealized-that in the reality they become irrelevant (never work like shown in a graph).

8.3. Thesis and Theory in Social Science

Basic Understanding of a Social Science

- A scientific statement is always based on the actual available information about something.
- A description is a verbal way of saying what is observed about a thing or a pattern.
- A description can be a simple figure, e.g. the sum of counted specific goods.
- A diagram is a graphic description of something with different qualities and quantities.
- A theory is a description of a minimum of two variables in interdependence.
- Interdependences between variables can be measured with mathematical models
- Mathematical models can be shown with graphs, with lines, curves, and pattern of points.
- A mathematical model can calculate and sort out clusters forming affinities of variables.
- A mathematical model can make a multivariate analysis showing multiple interdependences.
- A mathematical correlation does not say which variable is cause and which one is effect.
- A mathematical correlation does not say which variable is producing an increase or decrease.
- A mathematically observed correlation can be caused by other unknown (or hidden) factors.
- A theory allows making predictions on a level of 100% or with a certain probability.

Mankiw justifies economic models: "The theory of consumer choice does not try to present a literal account of how people make decisions. It is a model. And … models are not intended to be completely realistic." [157]

Comment: A model has no value if it covers not even 20% of the corresponding reality, and especially if it ignores the immense varieties of all

---

[157] Mankiw (et al.), p. 389

consumer patterns. Economic models are not realistic or useful to understand and operate (theoretically) with consumer choices.

Mankiw understands economic analysis as: "Consumers are aware that their choices are constrained by their financial resources. And, given those constraints, they do the best they can to achieve the highest level of satisfaction. The theory of consumer choice tries to describe this implicit, psychological process in a way that permits explicit, economic analysis."

Comment: More stupid and incorrect is not possible to state "they do the best they can to achieve the highest level of satisfaction." Most consumers are not fully aware of their satisfaction. 'The highest level of satisfaction' is hype and is driven by a psychotic mind (of the author); it's simply stupid and untrue. The way economics understand the psychological process (in their models) is absolutely incompetent. The author's understanding of the mind (of psychology) is archaic and does not allow solid economic analysis.

There are two dangerous traps we found everywhere in the economic principles and theses:

a) If the meaning of a variable has a variety of connotations, then the interpretation leads to wrong description and wrong conclusions.
b) If between two variables there are significantly ignored factors possibly having an influence, then the interpretation leads to wrong description and wrong conclusions.
c) To get confirmed ideological interests, a complexity of variables can be manipulated, especially through ignoring factors that certainly have an (indirect) influence.

A verbal reduction of a statement using a mathematical model does not necessarily imply mathematics; but it can reflect a theory in the shortest way of description:

An example given by Mankiw & Taylor: [158]

$E = f(SS, Me, Tp, G, St, R, Gf, P, Ic, y)$
In words: The variable E is a function of the variables SS, Me, Tp, G, St, R, Gf, P, Ic, and y
Or: The factor E depends on SS, Me, Tp, G, St, R, Gf, P, Ic, and y
Remember: Such a description is not a mathematical formula!

---

[158] Mankiw (et al.), p. 25-26

For all students of economics some questions are of the highest importance when learning about the parameters (graphs):

- Why is it important to consider the parameter?
- What is the parameter (variable) about?
- What is the deeper meaning of a parameter?
- What is the connotation of a parameter?
- What is the meaning of a correlation?
- What exactly holds 2 or more variables together?
- What is the ideological premise of a parameter?
- What is the direct or indirect purpose of a parameter?
- What does a parameter not say?
- What could be a hidden or ignored relevant factor?
- Where does it lead if a parameter is multiplied by millions or billions?

8.4. Behind Statistics

Statistic Manipulations

Example (constructed): A touristic coast line area of 50km. Before the financial crisis in 2008 there were 100 hotels open all year long; let's say with an average of 200 rooms = 400 PAX, which is in total: 20,000 rooms or 40,000 PAX. In 2006 and 2007 they had an occupancy rate of 98% during high season. Every year 5 hotels had to close down. For the year 2012 they are only 60 hotels open for the summer season. At the same time the prices per PAX had to be reduced every year; in total up to 2012 of 40% reduction with an annual average of 100€ per PAX per night in the year 2008; means in the year 2012 the hotel prices have an average cost of 60€ per PAX per night. The occupancy rate was also reduced due to the crisis. Every year less tourists came to this coast and stayed for shorter periods. Above that, the tourists spent for extras on average every year 5% less during their stay. We can extend the situation with the fact that every year more hotels closed during the winter, up to 2012 in total 40% of the hotels, which did not happen at all before 2009.

In short: Every year (2009, 2010, 2011, 2012) the parameters declined: number of permanent closed hotels, number of open hotels during high season, amount of hotel beds, amount of PAX, prices per night, occupancy rates, duration of stays, and the spending of the tourists for extras during their stay in general.

The association of the hotels declared every year: "We can inform you with great optimism that the last year we had an occupancy of 85%"; the next year they declare: "… of 81%"; the following year they declare: "…of 76%"; and at the end of 2012 they will declare, let's say: "…of 71%". Obviously the figures are related to the total of open hotels. This is the way officials can operate with statistic figures.

The economically significant questions are: How much money per year has been spent in total from the tourists in this area? Additionally important is: How has this economically affected all tourism related businesses in the area? How has this affected the unemployment rate in the area? How has the quality changed to still make profit considering the maxim 'cost reduction'?

And also: How many business existences have been destroyed? How many relationships and family lives have been broken due to the money factor? How many of the resident young generation will have a dire future, has already lost any good perspective for their life? How many investors have made losses?

If such statistics do not consider all these questions and do not make the realities behind the figures transparent, then the economic (and political) approach of such statistics becomes a sham!

Critical Scientific Considerations

Variables are the basic 'building stones' of a social science.

A theory in a social science analyzes the movements from one variable in relation to another variable. The variables express a principle, rule, factor, thesis, hypothesis, or a theorem. Both variables (or more) have an extension (movement) of any kind, mostly expressed in a measure of absolute figures or in percentage terms, calculated with a mathematical formula, and visually shown in 'graphs'.

We elaborate in this book the basic terms and principles of economics: 'Economics I: Principles of Economics for Sustainable Development'. In the second volume 'Economics II: Microeconomics for Sustainable Growth' we elaborate the development of those economic theories that work with the given terms and principles, and that relate to the real world of business. We will discover that many variables get a completely different quality, movement, as well as meaning and function depending on the kind, size, and business location; and on human factors and aims (meaning) of human's life as well. With the third volume 'Economics III: Macroeconomics for a Sustainable Roadmap' we will critically enter into the big picture of the economy and we will explore the politicians' professional responsibility for the dire state of humanity, the world, and the planet.

We have already discussed the problem that all theories and statements of economics have an archaic understanding of human factors and that this leads to a wrong understanding of the real economic world and in the end to disaster.

Mankiw (et al.) elaborates these topics in the chapters 1, 2, 3, 4, 5, 7, 13, 14, 18, and 21. In these chapters we found 125 graphs.

With some different views and analytical approaches we observe with these

125 graphs:

- The presumption or assumptions are already declared as a result of scientific research.
- There is no principle or hypothesis carefully explored in the manifold real world of business.
- Not one graph represents a real result of a real scientific research that could be representative.
- All graphs are the result of a mathematical formula, constructed artificially from scientists.
- The mathematical formula expresses interdependence between 2 or more variables.
- The formula itself is constructed based on what the variables are measurably expressing.
- The formulas always catch an increase or decrease, or any other kind of (mutual) movement.
- Abstracting a variable from the complexity of its network can never lead to valid results.
- The graphs should give visual proof of the proven scientific principles, laws, and theories.
- The result can't be more valid than the presumption or assumption of a hypothesis.
- All the graphs with lines or curves are artificial calculations and do not represent reality.
- Without real data from the real world these graphs only confirm a mathematical possibility.
- The result depends on the function of the formula: there is always a calculated movement.
- In all formulas the indispensable factor 'probability' (for social sciences) is not included.
- Lack of the probability dimension leads to a cheat: 'relative' converts into 'absolute'.
- All formulas exclude the given variation (variance) of data's extensions in the many graphs.
- Excluding the variation field leads to absolute and unreal pictures and 'proofs'.
- Pure formulas have a self-confirming tendency (dynamics) within its own limits.
- A mathematical model or graph that does not show reality loses its validity for a thesis.
- There is no scientific research shown that gives proof of theses; reproduction is not possible.

- The more fake 'bricks' are put together to a complex theory, the more distorted is the result.
- Above that all theories lead to the divine aim: 'maximizing profit'; mentioned 10,000 times.

Conclusion

All these mathematical formulas and graphs suggest proof of the economic theses and are deemed of essential importance; but they are a disastrous scam!

The book by Mankiw (et al.), with 900 super big and overloaded pages requires a young and inexperienced student to spend a minimum of 1,000 hours to precisely and critically study all the explorations, the formulas, the several hundred graphs, the many (unreal) examples and exam questions, the author's conclusions, to understand the whole big picture, and to elaborate all the given exercises. Additionally the consultation of dictionaries and other sources are time consuming.

Above that we have to consider the age of the students: the majority are 18-21 years old. They all want to graduate and never want a confrontation with the professor's teaching. They all are absolutely unable to be fundamentaly critical and to uncover all the hidden scam mechanisms behind terms, principles, theories, and formulas or graphs. And in the end they are all infected from this junk and so become 'soldiers' of the economic 'army' to conquer the entire world and strive for the maximum profit. In the core it's all very similar to a religion: believe it, and when you believe it, then you will accept the given scientific proof; you don't even need proof anymore.

Imagine if all students would identify the economics' scam and then accuse their professor of being a scammer and their university or business school a scam training institution!

Another critical approach is: First came the capitalistic ideology. From there they created (built up, shaped) a market becoming more and more dominant (e.g. today's global corporations, banks). Then they observed the market and identified some principles, laws, interrelations, correlations, dynamics, and even some shameful effects that rose with the implementation of the ideology. Then they described all this as the modern 'natural market' reality being held together by 'the invisible hand'. From there to today they always confirm their ideology as 'natural' economic reality. That's how a false ideology, a sham or manipulation becomes an (natural) economic axiom or a principle like the law of gravity in physics.

The book from Mankiw (et al.) and the other classical books about economics used in our analysis here, are not introduction books; they are all capitalistic indoctrination books using all the tools of brainwashing and manipulation, and abusing their authoritative position and institutional support (university, business school) to shape and distort student's economic mind luring them with economic careers and excellent wages in the future.

The obsession and compulsion aimed at complete dominance over all humans and the entire markets is breathtaking in all the graphs and its theses; it's never Islamic attitude and never rooted in the Christian spiritual understanding of love, and it never came from the Asian, African or Latin-American spirituality. It eliminates with the power of a thousand nuclear bombs all spiritual values and human values existing on this planet.

8.5. Rules of Science

The 12 Rules

Complex statistical analysis can transform such a description into a mathematical analysis calculating the probability of each variable, the weight of each variable, and the correlation with its variation. Such mathematical models are always based on a probability and variation extension. The more complex the analysis is the more difficult becomes the interpretation. A mathematical analysis does not result in an interpretation of the meaning.

Top rule 1: The more imprecisely and incomplete the topics are described with its single factors (variables) in economic science, the more incorrect or vague is the hypothesis and therefore the mathematical result. Conclusion: a term must have an absolute clear and determined meaning.

Top rule 2: Interpretation is always about the meaning of a variable or of a result of statistical analysis; means: of the correlations with the variation of each variable and the probability and / or a weight. If two countries have a different basket of goods, then we can't correctly compare the mathematical result.

Top rule 3: Simple diagrams visualize one or two variables. More complex diagrams visualize more variables. The more a diagram simplifies complex interrelations, the less it can be used for a mathematical analysis with valuable interpretation (cause and effect of each variable) for decision making or advice.

Diagrams are a didactical tool. Purposes of diagrams are:

- Make visible sizes of sectors and variables and its range of qualities and quantities
- Give a general overview of interdependences of variables / components / fields / clusters
- Flowcharts can express decision making processes and further lines of action / problems
- Flowcharts can show sequences of a process and locations of interfering

factors
- Show the measured differences of interdependences
- Arrows show directions of movements of elements (e.g. money)
- Put different sizes (figures) of one or more variables in series or in separated fields
- Show if A increases, then B also increases; or the other way round
- Show if A increases, then B decreases; or the other way round
- Show that if C limits an increase, then B or A increase or decrease

Top rule 4: Economics always has to do with humans. In all processes humans are involved. Humans are everywhere the crucial factors. The more economics excludes the human factors, the more it fails in the description, analysis, interpretations, conclusions, and finally in the real world. The understanding of humans on the level of the 19th Century doesn't work anymore!

Top rule 5: A word can have very different meaning depending on the context: poverty in Germany is not the same like in India; a GDP from the UK is not the same like a GDP in an African country; society's well-being in Andalucía (Spain) is not the same as in New York (United States); unemployment rate in Spain is not the same like in Switzerland; one liter of drinking water in France is not the same like one liter of drinking water in Bangladesh, etc. An income of £200 or £500 does not facilitate making a good life in London, but in some areas of Africa it can allow a modest healthy life.

Top rule 6: The quality of one figure must be respected and never mixed with other figures that significantly have another quality. The nasty average blabber: There are 10 business people; one earns 50,000€; another 200,000€; another 100,000€, another 5,000€, five earn 1,000€ each, and another one earns a million euros per year. In the average they earn 136,000€ per year. An average only makes sense if the extremes are cut off and dealt with separately.

Top rule 7: Some words have an absolute clear meaning and this meaning should not be manipulated for statistics. If 5.35 million Spanish people are statistically unemployed, then this does not reflect reality: 4 million are working and make (some) cash for living. Others have fallen out of the statistic after 6 months and also work undeclared. Some participate in vocational further education that is paid for by the government. Some young people who left school do not register as they have no chance to get a (first) job anyway. Others are seriously ill for months and therefore are not registered as unemployed people; but they are unemployed. In the end we have maximum of an estimated 1.5-2 million unemployed people in Spain

(2012).

Top rule 8: The bigger a business the higher are the superior effects that change completely the understanding of the business's figures and reality. A big business with 500 employees is still a business. The Top 500 big corporations operating continentally or globally have immense, unprecedented power; especially as many of them are interconnected on the highest decision making level. This changes the economic function into a political function that must be considered in the macro-economy. The interpretation of figures in such a context must consider these superior new qualities.

Top rule 9: Positive statements are descriptive. They describe how a topic is. But many words in the science of economics have a crypto-normative value and function in the described picture or interpretation. This must always be considered and made clear. Taking a decision about the quality of a good is already a normative statement. Examples having an implicit positive or negative value are: lower (class), poverty, equity, scarcity, efficiency, depression, inflation, deflation, deficit, debt, standard (of living), (economic) growth, profit, increase (of GDP), market planning (communism), etc.

Top rule 10: Normative statements are prescriptive. They determine values and give rules how the world of something should be. Economic scientists must be aware that already the determination of what forms part of the economic is a normative statement. Interpretation of economic facts should separate between description, meaning, consequences, aims, and personal assessment.

Top rule 11: Economics always has normative implications. A pure positivistic understanding of the economy and the economic science leads to the destruction of the planet, ignoring the fact that being a human is a value itself and that economics is from humans and for humans. Society's well-being through increase of life standard is a normative decision and topic. A definition of life standard and life value by ignoring genuine human values of highest importance is meaningless.

Top rule 12: The abstract, descriptive, normative, political or mathematical correctness (truth) itself of something concerning the economic world is on its merits irrelevant. Only the reality shows the validity and with that the correctness (truth) and its relevance (importance) for humans.

If we consider the state of humanity, the world, and the planet today (2012), then we must conclude: a majority of the classic capitalistic economics' science is junk; similar to Christian religion with its 'Holy Bible'. Then again as 2.4 billion Christians like junk, they also like this economic junk. In both fields we have this 'invisible hand' operating with genius intelligence. The invisible hand has its fingers also in the methodology and theory of economic science.

9. Education for Life and the Economy

9.1. The Importance of Education

Thesis: Education is of fundamental economic interest. Everything in the real economic world is the result of education and learning, of the way people are shaped. The result can be calculated in trillions of Euros or dollars per year.

The Western science and real world of economics strongly focus on the factor of 'intelligence', 'human' (labor), 'satisfaction', 'happiness', and 'rational decisions'. They all confirm that education (especially professional education) is the super essential foundation for a well working economy and for economic growth; means: for all the production processes and the sale management. Therefore we must also have a look at public education.

We observe in the public education system up to academic level an immense lack of topics that are necessary to successfully realize a life and to efficiently operate in the economic world.

Key words and lack of topics in the public education system:

Diagram: Educational Goals

▪ Learning, studying attitudes	▪ In touch with nature
▪ Attitude for working daily	▪ Focus on sustainable decision
▪ Attitude for life long working	▪ Understanding the world
▪ Moral character, integrity	▪ Understanding politics
▪ Knowledge about inner life	▪ Understanding society
▪ Skills for mastering life	▪ Critical view over religions
▪ Communication skills	▪ Critical view over ideologies
▪ Reading to understand	▪ Critical about media content
▪ Ability to love and care	▪ Care for environment/nature
▪ Reliable and trustworthy	▪ Skills to manage people
▪ Living human values	▪ Skills to manage peace
▪ Living inner potentials	▪ Clear, complex perception
▪ Knowing the spiritual source	▪ Precise, analytical thinking
▪ Holistic personal growth	▪ Using spiritual intelligence
▪ Authentic being and living	▪ Picture: past-present-future
▪ Systematic self-knowledge	▪ Free of compensatory behavior
▪ Achieved inner fulfillment	▪ Pioneering, vanguard spirit

▪ Humble, decent, responsible	▪ Sexual satisfaction
▪ Interpreting one's dreams	▪ To stand for the truth
▪ Skills for family life	▪ Exploring the unconscious
▪ Sustainable personal lifestyle	▪ Conscious way of living
▪ Care for baby/child/teenager	▪ Fulfilled personal catharsis
▪ Inner archetypal experiences	▪ Ready for global renewal
▪ Generally critical, vigilant	▪ Free from brainwashing
▪ Physical health sustainability	▪ Inner male-female balance
▪ Mental health sustainability	▪ Meditating to understand

Public education is fundamentally regulated by governmental, private, and corporate accreditation bodies. The regulations do practically nothing to allow what is pioneering and vanguard, or include a critical and future perspective.

A short overview about the educational topics in education reveals:

- The education programs at universities have not significantly changed since 1960.
- The psychology programs at universities have not significantly changed since 1960.
- The concepts about 'human being' at universities have not significantly changed since 1960.
- The psychical-spiritual understanding of human life has not significantly changed since 1851.

Since Sigmund Freud and Carl G. Jung there is practically no pioneering research and knowledge developed in the social sciences about 'humans'. The unconscious world of humans, which forms a primordial role in humans' life, is completely ignored. The world of dreams, of meditation, of psychical and cosmic energy, and of the influences during prenatal time is absolutely neglected in the sciences of psychology and education. Philosophy and philosophical anthropology carelessly ignore these enormously important worlds. Humans' evolution has in the political and economic understanding, including in Christianity, zero importance and practically no psychical and spiritual understanding. And they all have absolutely no idea about the Archetypes of the Soul and the inner processes. That's an absolute disaster!

No wonder that the people working in the accreditation bodies for education are thoroughly incompetent in their tasks, mainly due to their own complete lack of psychical-spiritual knowledge and development. The criteria they have about what the right education is promote a world of ignorance, arrogance, neurosis, narcissism, compulsion, psychopathy, megalomania, and psychosis.

It is not surprising as again and also here the 'invisible hand' of the body behind the curtains of the visible stage rules the educational programs of the Western world.

A careful analysis of the accredited educational programs with their criteria, norms and rules, regulations and orders on hundreds of normative pages quickly reveals that the Western education as a whole is absolutely not sustainable considering the very fast changing world. Herein lies the fundamental causes of failure in economics and politics, and also in religions and the media. This vicious circle blocks everything: their programs do not allow human's evolution and therefore they are themselves not in a process of psychical-spiritual evolution; and logically they hinder any psychical-spiritual evolution of society and its economy. The question arises: human failure or deliberate planning?

The glorified lifestyle and life standard that the economy and its economic science, endlessly promote and repeat in their economic books become a joke if we consider the immense and unique value of humans' evolution. We must therefore assume that all these accreditation bodies are the normative tools of a hidden mission. They do not want a psychical-spiritual evolution. All they want is the total control of all humans, of all education and businesses, including control of all private matters and all people around the globe. Social science with its psychology and education, including economics and laws, is a very strong tool for this, their mission. Is there a hidden treaty between the Christian religion, economics, and the media?

→ Importance of Public Education

- Highest importance as education is the fundamental preparation for success in life, work, and renewal in a very fast changing world. Pioneering vocational education is fundamental.
- The immense problems of humanity and the planet can't be solved without fundamental renewal of education and especially a fundamental revision and re-construction of economics.
- Democracy and prosperity can never be better than the state of mind (and soul) of the collective and the way people do business. Professional competences of its leaders are indispensable.
- Work is a natural need of humans and improves satisfaction, self-esteem, and positive emotional state. Business success and professional satisfaction requires personality, knowledge and skills.
- Democracy can never be better than the state of mind of the working people, the small and medium sized businesses, and the quality of their performance.

→ Failure of Public Education

- The ignorance and exclusion of human's spiritual intelligence, emotional intelligence, intuition and creativity
- The lack of education for mastering life: money, self- and life management, relationship, marriage, family life, etc.
- The constrained and obsessive accreditations (standardizations) of public education (including social sciences such as economics and business in general)
- The centralization of public education with a highly rigid innovative inflexibility of institutions and curriculums
- The ignorance about human values such as love, care, truth, psycho-social security, inner roots of integrity (ethics)
- The disrespect for individual differences such as personality, character, performance, talents, inner potentials
- The paralyzing of teacher's creativity and inner dedication due to prescribed dominant intellectual curriculums
- The inability to rapidly respond to new educational needs related to fast changes in society and the world
- The incompetent and immature politicians and experts in the local and national departments of education
- The ideological interests that shaped curriculums, exam practices, principles of selection, school career and professional career
- The lack of complex thinking about life philosophy, spirituality, mind, environment, politics, media, consumption
- The performance criteria that ignore practical relevance, human values and a holistic humane education
- The absence of topics such as lies, cheat, deceit, falseness, narcissism, neurotics, psychopaths, brainwash, etc.
- The rigid, arrogant and authoritarian atmosphere towards children and adolescents in educational institutions
- The lack of joyful learning, creative learning activities, respect for the psychical-spiritual process of learning
- The lack of promotion of self-confidence, critical explorations of the world, respect for 'being a human on earth'
- The lack of promoting the genuine inner needs for working as a part of satisfaction, fulfillment and meaning of life
- The lack of pioneering spirit due to rigidity of fully standardized curriculums (e.g. businesses, social sciences) and the boring practical trainings

→ Public Education and general Goals of Renewal

- Strong focus on new learning, creative learning, pioneering spirit, analyzing and thinking in complex networks and with the biggest possible pictures
- Strong foundation and understanding of humans, human made problems, human values and humane life based on the psychical organism and on the Archetypes of the Soul
- New understanding of marriage, family, children's education, health, mastering conflicts and problems must become subjects and topics of science
- Knowledge must be developed and balanced with inner rooted spirituality, moral integrity, meaning of life, respect for humanity, nature, animals and the planet
- Peace, justice, hope, love, care, happiness, self-responsibility, truthfulness, reliability, trust, realistic faith must become subjects and topics of science
- Constructive behavior in the everyday life, in social life, in political participation, in the world of work and business must become subjects and topics of science
- Holistic and permanent all-embracing psychical-spiritual development aiming for inner satisfaction and fulfillment must become subjects and topics of science
- Inner rooted spirituality, moral integrity, meaning of life, respect for humanity, nature, animals and the planet
- Self-responsibility for positive attitudes for and high quality of working aiming much more than mere earning money

9.2. Public Education

■ **Benefits of Renewal and Strategic Considerations**

➔ **Money related Humane Benefit of a new Education**

- Less costly failure in educational career, life and love (marriage, family), work and business
- Less costly accidents, human made illnesses, mental disease, addictions, behavior disorder
- Less costly violence, crimes, victims of injustice, lies and cheat, brainwashing, manipulations
- Less costly damages of nature and environment, much less contamination and pollution
- Less costly blinded, lured, stupid and stubborn ways of living destroying human values and life
- Less costly abuse of all kind of energies and resources
- Less costly waste and contaminated sewage (going to the soil, drinking water, sea and oceans)
- Less high expenses for pharmaceutical products, health care and worthless products
- Less costly insurances and non-productive costs of all kind of human made damages
- Less costly car and air traffic, legal costs, police's and court's activities
- Less (complete elimination of) costly social unrest, rearmament and wars (for world dominance)
- Less costly political failure, mismanagement of resources, money and time
- Less indebtedness of governments, businesses and people (for compensatory consumption)

➔ **Suggestions for Innovation**

- All children and adolescents go to school from age 3 (pre-kindergarten) up to the age of 18.
- Promotion of talented children and adolescents are a matter of additional learning.
- Vocational schools and high schools start parallel at age 18 and last 2-3

years.

- Academic education starts with 20-21 and takes 3 years for a bachelor program (social sciences, economics and business).
- The political competences of public education must be decentralized and given to the local administration.
- Establishing private schools (on all levels) must become a 'free market' and be based on very general basic laws that determine maximum 50% of the super-essential subjects and topics of school books.
- A corresponding 'business license' with basic educational, health and business norms and rules is enough to be legally 'accredited' (officially recognized) as a private school, academy or university.
- Academic teachers must have responsible professional experiences in their fields of teaching and doing part time business (working) or being available as an expert (consultant, speaker) in any field of society.
- Academic programs (social sciences, business): Occasionally internship (partly paid for pocket money) must be part of or timely feasible during the higher educational period and offered by the business world.
- All teachers and professors must be graduated in 'Psychical-spiritual Education' and 'The state of Humanity and the Earth' as an academic further education program (courses) and for their own personal development.

➜ Free Market Competition

- Private public education on all levels is an economic contribution and boosts intelligence, quality, cultural preferences, local characteristics, and can adapt the demand of local citizens (e.g. immigrants, expats, and languages).
- Free market in the education sector hinders the elite's monster organizations to dominate the private education market with their mad capitalistic ideology.
- Free market with the right education and didactics promotes pioneering teachers, pioneering scholars, new pioneering businesses and in general experts of social sciences.
- Free market allows a private investor (individuals or a group of teachers) to establish a small school in a simple small business premises (and to grow with the years).
- The standard school books must have free-market options in at least 50% of the subjects and topics.
- Free market of public education is always a significant (small or huge) contribution to the local economy.

➜ Direct Cost Reduction

- The direct cost reduction is effective after the education career due to a significant reduction (35-50%) of failure in life and business, wrong doing, illnesses, accidents, damages of nature and environment, contamination, pollution, crimes, abuse of resources, etc.
- All these 'critical' costs are non-productive costs. Therefore there is, viewed in the long term, a highly significant cost reduction of non-productive expenses for the society (citizens, the economy).
- The yearly reduction of non-productive costs after the educational career due to the new humane education is much higher than the total costs for the public education (per year).

→ **Costs for Renewal**

- Restructuring the public educational system has no significant costs as the given institutions with their experts, employees and officers have to plan and implement it within their actual tasks and responsibilities.
- Psychical-spiritual development must become part of all kind of teacher traineeship and special further education programs; also for politicians responsible in education and educational administration.
- The longer educational career with the new topics produces 10-15% more public costs and a small reduction in tax income for the government (as with such a renewal of the public educational career system the young people will start working and therefore paying taxes 3-4 years later).

9.3. Academic Education (Social Science, Economics)

■ **Benefits of Renewal and Strategic Considerations**

➔ **Money related Humane Benefit**

- Less costly failure in educational and academic career, life and love (marriage, family), work, business, politics
- Less costly accidents, human made illnesses, mental disease, addictions, behavior disorder
- Less costly violence, crimes, victims of injustice, lies and cheat, deceit, brainwashing, manipulations
- Less costly damages of nature and environment, much less contamination and pollution
- Less costly blinded, lured, stupid and stubborn ways of doing business that destroys human values and life
- Less costly abuse of all kind of energy and resources as well as of power and academic privileges
- Less costly waste and contaminated sewage (going to the soil, drinking water, sea and oceans)
- Less high expenses for pharmaceutical products, health care and worthless products
- Less costly insurances and non-productive costs of all kind of human made damages
- Less costly car and air traffic, legal costs, police's and court's activities
- Less (complete elimination of) costly social unrest, rearmament and wars (for world dominance)
- Less costly political failure, mismanagement of resources, money and time
- Less indebtedness of governments, businesses and people (for compensatory consumption)

➔ **Suggestions for Innovation**

- Academic education starts with 20-21 and takes 3 years for a bachelor program (social sciences, business).

- The political competences of academic education must be decentralized and given to the local administration.
- Establishing private academies (universities) must become free market and based on very general basic laws determining maximum 50% of the super-essential subjects and topics.
- A corresponding 'business license' with basic educational, health and business norms and rules is enough to be legally 'accredited' (officially recognized) as a private business school, academy or university.
- Academic teachers (professors!) and the managers of such entities must have responsible professional experiences in their fields of teaching and doing part time business (working) or being at disposal as an expert (consultant, speaker) in any field of society.
- Academic programs (social sciences, business): Occasionally internship (partly paid for pocket money) must be part or have space of the higher educational period and offered from the business world.
- All teachers and professors must be graduated in 'Psychical-spiritual Education' and 'The state of humanity and the Earth' as an academic further education program (courses) and for their own personal development.

→ **Free Market Competition**

- Private academic education is an economic contribution and boosts quality, cultural preferences, local characteristics, and can adapt the demand of local citizens (e.g. immigrants, expats, and languages).
- Free market in the academic education hinders the elite's monster organizations to dominate the private academic education market with their ideology.
- Free market with the right academic education and didactics promotes pioneering professors, pioneering scholars, new pioneering businesses and in general top experts of social sciences, including business programs.
- Free market allows to a private investor (individuals or a group of teacher) to establish a small academy (university) in a simple small business premise (and to grow during the years).
- The traditional academic books with old fashioned theories and concepts must experience a complete renewal through free-market options in at least 50% of the subjects and topics.
- Free market of academic education is always a significant (small or huge) contribution to the local economy.

→ **Direct Cost Reduction**

- The direct cost reduction is effective after the education career due to a significant reduction (35-50%) of failure in life, politics, management and the world of businesses

- A renewed academic education contributes a lot in reducing social problems such as wrong doing, illnesses, accidents, damages of nature and environment, contamination, pollution, crimes, abuse of resources, etc.
- All these 'critical' costs are non-productive costs. Therefore there is, viewed in the long term, a highly significant cost reduction of non-productive expenses for the society (citizens).
- The academic contribution to yearly reduction of non-productive costs after academic career due to the new vanguard and pioneering education is much higher than the total costs for the academic education (per year).

→ Costs for Renewal

- Restructuring the educational system has no significant costs as the given institutions with its experts, employees and officers have to plan and implement it within their actual tasks and responsibilities.
- Psychical-spiritual development must become part of all kind of teacher traineeship and special further education programs; also for politicians responsible in education and educational administration.
- Due to the longer public education including high school, the students are much more mature for studying social sciences and therefore learn more efficiently. The new topics and pioneering research do not produce more (public) costs. There is a small reduction of tax income for the government (as with this new education structure the students will start working later and therefore paying taxes 3-4 years later compared to the educational system of today (2011).

9.4. Vocational Education

■ **Benefits of Renewal and Strategic Considerations**

→ **Money related Humane Benefit**

- Contribution to less costly failure in the job career, in life and love (marriage, family), in work and business
- Contribution to less accidents, human made illnesses, mental disease, addictions, behavior disorder
- Contribution to less violence, crimes, victims of injustice, lies and cheat, deceit, brainwashing, manipulations
- Contribution to less damages of nature and environment, much less contamination and pollution
- Contribution to less blinded, lured, stupid and stubborn ways of living destroying human values and life
- Contribution to less abuse of all kind of energies and resources
- Contribution to less waste and contaminated sewage (going to soil, drinking water, sea and oceans)
- Contribution to less expenses for pharmaceutical products, health care and inutile worthless products
- Contribution to less insurances and non-productive costs of all kind of human made damages
- Contribution to less car and air traffic, costs of layers, police's and court's activities
- Contribution to less (complete elimination of) costly social unrest, rearmament and wars (for world dominance)
- Contribution to less costly political failure, mismanagement of resources, money and time
- Contribution to less indebtedness of governments, businesses and people (for compensatory consumption)

■ **Suggestions for Innovation**

- Vocational schools start with 18 and last 2-3 years.
- The political competences of vocational education must be decentralized and given to the local administration.

- Establishing private vocational schools must become free market and based on very general basic laws determining maximum 50% of the super-essential subjects and school books.
- A corresponding 'business license' with basic educational, health and business norms and rules is enough to be legally 'accredited' (officially recognized) as a private vocational school.
- Vocational education must offer much more broaden training courses, each focusing on a larger spectrum of future labor career options.
- Teachers must have responsible professional experiences in their fields of teaching and doing part time business (working) or being at disposal as an expert (consultant, speaker) in any field of society.
- Vocational schools can and must offer modules of teaching to retired people with excellent working experiences and management responsibilities in the world of work.
- Earning pocket money must be part or have space of the vocational education period and offered from the business and labor world.
- All teachers must be graduated in 'Psychical-spiritual Education' and 'The state of humanity and the Earth' as an academic further education program (courses) and for their own personal development.

Free Market Competition

- Private vocational education is an economic contribution and boosts quality, cultural preferences, local characteristics, and can adapt the demand of local citizens (e.g. immigrants, expats, and languages).
- Free market in the vocational education hinders the elite's monster organizations to dominate the private vocational education market with their ideology.
- Free market with the right vocational education and didactics promotes pioneering teachers, pioneering apprentices, new pioneering businesses in the future and in general higher motivation for excellent performances.
- Free market allows to a private investor (individuals or a group of teacher) to establish a small vocational school in a simple small business premise (and to grow during the years).
- The standard school books must have free-market options in at least 50% of the subjects and topics.
- Free market of vocational education is always a significant (small or huge) contribution to the local economy.

We have a list of 100 new, pioneering and vanguard small businesses as an answer for a new sustainable economic market in the future. A small business must allow that a person or a family can live from the business. Western world: A net income of minimum 1500-2500€, means 30-60% of the turnover, is aimed. A business can grow and be expanded for 3-5 working places. Human values and new sustainable lifestyle is the core of new small businesses, marketing and success.

→ Direct Cost Reduction

- The direct cost reduction is effective after the education career due to a significant reduction (35-50%) of failure in life, work and business, wrong doing, illnesses, accidents, damages of nature and environment, contamination, pollution, crimes, abuse of resources, etc.
- All these 'critical' costs are non-productive costs. Therefore there is, viewed in the long term, a highly significant cost reduction of non-productive expenses for the society (citizens).
- The yearly reduction of non-productive costs after labor education due to the new humane education is much higher than the total costs for the public vocational education (per year).

→ Costs for Renewal

- Restructuring the educational system has no significant costs as the given institutions with its experts, employees and officers have to plan and implement it within their actual tasks and responsibilities.
- Psychical-spiritual development must become part of all kind of teacher traineeship and special further education programs; also for politicians responsible in education and educational administration.
- Due to the later start of vocational education, the apprentices are much more mature for labor education and therefore learn more efficiently. The new topics do not produce more (public) costs. There is a very small reduction of tax income for the government (as with this new education structure the apprentices will start working later and therefore paying taxes 3-4 years later compared to the educational system of today (2011).

9.5. Further Education (Life, Business)

- **A new Network of Private Businesses for Further Education is needed.**
- **The Benefits of Renewal for Economics and Society are immense.**

➔ Importance

- The adult generation today generally had no school career that prepared them for life, work and business with a strong focus on the human factors of all kind of individual, collective and global problems of humanity.

➔ Failure

- Billions of people have no knowledge, skills or methods to understand themselves and their life, their difficulties, their problems and conflicts.
- Billions of people are brainwashed, manipulated, suppressed and infiltrated by lies, cheat, fictions, illusions, seductions, false games, and a perverse and neurotic collective theater.
- Billions of people want to love and to be loved, want happiness and satisfaction, success and a secure life environment. But they all have no idea how to achieve such life aims.
- Billions of people are pushed into a mental and emotional chaos, into stress and fear, into countless meanders, into endless problems and conflicts without a chance to evade.
- Billions of people are treated like animals, like pure human biomass, partly lured with money and partly terrorized by poverty and misery. Nobody gives them hope and solutions.
- Religions failed. State schools failed. Politicians failed. Education failed. The lies replaced the truth. Every soul is abused and violated.
- Billions of people suffer from this frightening failure. They all have questions about life, love, relationships, spirituality, sexuality, dreams, emotions, feelings and inner conflicts on a daily basis.
- They need knowledge, skills, guidance and support to understand themselves, their life, and to master life for the fulfillment of their longing.
- All humans get messages from the inner Spirit through dreams. But billions can't interpret their dreams. They can't benefit from this spiritual power

that gives guidance and provides support.

- Therefore, further education about psychical-spiritual development (and understanding of humans and the state of humanity and the planet) is fundamental for all adults from age 18 as the preparation of all renewal, including new ways of living and understanding of human life.
- Further education is also strongly recommended for self-employed people and small businesses, including advanced business knowledge.
- Further education is indispensable for all people in responsible positions in politics, media, economy, industry, education, religion, etc.
- The inability of Institutions for Further Education to respond on new educational needs due to fast changes in society and the world

General Goals of Renewal

- Real preparation of the people for mastering life (the different life phases) and of elderly people for mastering their 'third age' life with very special topics
- Real preparations for marriage, family life, children's education, healthy ways of living, mastering problems and conflicts
- Real preparations for understanding oneself and humans, inner rooted spirituality, inner rooted moral integrity (ethics) and meaning of life
- Real preparations for more peace, justice, hope, love, care, respect for human values, efficient behavior, respect for human life and the planet (nature, animals)
- Real preparations for much better self-management, self-responsibility and personal psychical-spiritual and professional fulfillment, more business success, and especially a new understanding of life in general

→ Money related Human Benefit

- Less costly failure in educational career, life and love (marriage, family), work and business
- Less costly accidents, human made illnesses, mental disease, addictions, behavior disorder
- Less costly violence, crimes, victims of injustice, lies and cheat, deceit, brainwashing, manipulations
- Less costly damages of nature and environment, much less contamination and pollution
- Less costly blinded, lured, stupid and stubborn ways of living destroying human values and life
- Less costly abuse of all kind of energies and resources
- Less costly waste and contaminated sewage (going to soil, drinking water, sea and oceans)

- Less high expenses for pharmaceutical products, health care and inutile worthless products
- Less costly insurances and non-productive costs of all kind of human made damages
- Less costly car and air traffic, costs of layers, police's and court's activities
- Less (complete elimination of) costly social unrest, rearmament and wars (for world dominance)
- Less costly political failure, mismanagement of resources, money and time
- Less indebtedness of governments, businesses and people (for compensatory consumption)
- Much better health of elderly people and a fulfilled 'third age' life with substantial contributions to society

→ Suggestions for Innovation

- There are plenty of educational institutions dedicating fully to (private, professional) further education.
- There are also countless psychologists, psychotherapists, social educators, life coaches, sociologists, etc., that could extend their activities with further education programs.
- There are millions of retired top experts and professionals that could give all their knowledge and experiences to the younger generations.
- Obviously they need to get a new understanding of humans, of spirituality, of religions, of the state of humanity and the planet. With a one year program they would be well prepared for such a new professional field where they could work part time for years, even up to 90 years old or more with their specific characteristic 'wise man / woman'.

→ Free Market Competition

- The entire humanity needs a new generation of millions of professionals: mature teachers and educators, rock-solid in their moral character, with a high level of personal development, and with a genuine spirituality built up from their inner source of life to provide them with vanguard education based on the Archetypes of the Soul and the concept of Individuation.
- The state department of education does not have the maturity and competences, does not have the interest in such a holistic education with a thoroughly critical and profound thinking of their citizens. Therefore free market competition is the sole solution.
- A complex network of vanguard further education can create millions of jobs worldwide for corresponding experts (in psychology, education, spirituality, ethics, health, skills for mastering life, sociology, philosophical anthropology, life and business coaching, etc.).

➔ Direct Cost Reduction

- The positive consequences are in the fields of daily life, health, environment, contamination, politics, economy, industry, businesses, religion, media, etc., and therefore can reduce enormously non-productive costs and damaging (risky) investments or projects

➔ Costs

- The implementation of such educational programs has no significant costs as the given institutions and countless professionals can extend their activities. But it will create many new institutions of further education and therefore create up to 10 millions of jobs alone in Europe.
- Such new educational institutions can contribute significantly to the local economy.

9.6. Religion (Christianity)

→ Importance

Thesis: Christian religion is fundamentally education.

- Christianity is a religion, but also a cultural way of living and a way of thinking and understanding of human life and meaning of life.
- The Christian spirit has enormously shaped the Western world of economics.
- Religion is always an educational institution, mainly focused on teaching belief, but also focused on practical matters of human life (rules) and on social topics.
- Religion has a strong concealed influence in society, culture, politics, economy, and education.
- A complete understanding of all the aberrations, lies and patchworks is indispensable for aiming to form humans for the true meaning of life, the correct understanding of the Archetypes of the Soul, and with that of all innovations and implementations (renewal) in society.

→ Failure

- The archaic religions are the essential culprits of the actual state of humanity, the world and the planet.
- The structure of religious belief with all their lies and distortions logically always ends in aggression and wars.
- The very dark history of religions is not reconciled, not forgiven and not 'dead'.
- The estimated 3000 year-old mad games between religions are today as vivid as 800-1,000 years ago.
- A religious psychosis is essentially responsible for the economical disaster, the human made catastrophes, the wars, the soaring implementation of global dominance, the destruction of environment and the eco-systems, etc.
- Archaic religions are based on stupid, blinded, and brainwashed people.
- Archaic religions never want enlightened and happy people; people must suffer from inner deficits (since prenatal time) and from difficult and sad

life matters.

- Christians are not allowed to enjoy making love (or to enjoy themselves sexually) because the Churches need their guilt, their suffering, their longing for relief from guilt and inner pain.
- Christian religion as a hidden pact with the politicians and the economic institutions: the folks must be held down with rigid education, with brainwashing, poverty, permanent preoccupations, distrust between humans, general feeling of helplessness and being lost on earth, blindness, blind confidence, etc.
- There are people unlimitedly obsessed with their 'mission' from God and they believe to be chosen either to govern the entire world or to 'punish humanity' at all costs, even if only a few (hundred-) thousand 'chosen people' will survive.
- The roots of this incredible religious lunacy started with the legend of Abraham and Moses.

➔ General Goals of Renewal

- Relief of guilt and hate, elimination of insane historic (falsified) roots, reduction of tensions, decrease of hostility and distrust, elimination of prejudgments and wrong interpretations, rejecting the wrong doing.
- To understand the contribution of religions to the state of humanity and the planet and its human causes (since 3,000 years) eliminates prejudgments and the dark labyrinth without exit of the religions.
- Rigidity, stubbornness and arrogance of religious thinking must be eliminated through a complete new approach with the exploration of the inner genuine sources of religion.

➔ General Positive Human Effects

- Understanding the psychical-spiritual development as the true path for human's complete fulfillment
- Forming new drive, hope, inner energy, collaborations, strengthening people, building up the 'turning point' in the mind of people for a new life
- Better living together, more zest for life, constructive communication, respect and care, trust and real faith
- Finding the genuine human values and giving more care for it
- Authentic religious (spiritual) culture by forming the evolutionary human being
- Understanding of the archaic religious and political impact
- Giving the comprehensible orientation for the right doing in the future and the right understanding of the true religion
- Religion becomes evolutionary

→ Money related Human Benefit

- Less violence, less illnesses, less compensatory megalomania, fewer accidents, less compensatory consumption, less political hostility, less social hostility, less demonstrations, less repetition of the old provocative and reactive patterns, less propaganda, fewer need for management of local and international tensions, less political crisis meetings, complete absence of wars, fundamental increase of peace and justice on earth, much less wasting money for nothing better than the reasons that reactivate the old motives to go for war, etc.

→ Suggestions for Innovation

- The indispensable critical analysis is given from the author in separate programs. All office holders in religions must get further education as mentioned in this section above. There is no other institution at the moment that can teach the complete truth about religion than the one of the author. Graduated participants can spread the knowledge and train skills to the people of their professional field and to other office holders in the churches.

→ Free Market Competition

- Global centralized religions don't have any evolutionary learning dynamic.
- The religious institutions (Churches) have practically no disposition and ability to develop evolutionary innovations and implementations in teaching and practices.
- Dogmatism and fundamentalism represented with the centralized religious authorities form an invincible wall hindering the psychical-spiritual process towards God.
- They have all lost the inner path towards the highest Archetypes of the Soul and therefore they are madly cramped with their libido ties to 'Unholy Books'.
- The sole solution is a free market competition in the complete catharsis and renewal of religion achieving advanced teaching and practices.
- All incumbents can and must freely explore the inner mystery of humans with all the knowledge available today.
- They can share their inner experiences (of the Archetypes of the Soul) because these experiences are comprehensible and reproducible.
- They can all grow holistically and with that they will democratically execute catharsis and renewal of religion.

➔ Direct Cost Reduction

- If only Christianity with 2.2.-2.4 billion followers would learn and live this new path, the reduction of non-productive costs (costs for damages due to living an insane belief instead of the truth) would reach 3-5 trillion Euros (if not more) per year around the globe.

➔ Costs

- No significant costs; it's all simply a new orientation for all office holders and followers.
- As they all have to learn with books and further education, they will contribute to the economy instead of wasting their money for more and more destruction and dehumanization of human's soul and life.

9.7. Media: Educational Mission

→ **Importance**

Thesis: Media are fundamentally education

- The big media in the Western world have an immense educational influence on more than 5 billion people around the globe. They direct the lines of economic thinking and living.
- In the Western world we have 6-8 monstrous media corporate groups dominating the media world. The owners of these media networks are from the financial world; form part of the super-elite – the people behind the curtains of the visible stage.
- These super-elite also dominate the Western governments. They fabricated the economic crisis (2008) and they have the master plan for global governance.
- These media misinform, distortedly shape, radically brainwash, shamelessly mislead and thoroughly manipulate billions of people.
- Their positive mission should be: to enable people with correct and all-embracing information for mastering life and the right way to understand and solve collective problems and to develop new sustainable projects.
- Therefore the media are indispensable for the educational preparation of all innovations and implementations (renewal). Nothing else can reach nearly the entire world on a daily basis.

→ **Failure**

- Lies, cheating, deceit, brainwashing, manipulation, fake staging, misuse of power, propaganda
- Abuse of valuable words for supporting (proxy) wars (e.g. democracy, humanitarian mission)
- Ignorance and arrogance working as the tool of the Western corporate elite groups
- Suppression of human potentials and talents in all fields of economy, society and nations

→ **General Positive Human Effects**

- To form and shape new drive, hope, understanding, inner energy, trust, collaborations, strengthening people
- Building up the 'turning point' in the mind of people for a better living together
- More zest for life and constructive communication
- Finding the genuine human values and more care for it
- Promoting authentic culture, forming historic identity, responsibility for respect and care
- Understanding of the archaic religious and political impact
- Giving the comprehensible orientation for the right doing in the future
- Becoming aware of the essential matters of life and society, of the world of nature and animals

→ Money related Humane Benefit

- Fundamental changes in the world of media would produce: less violence, less illnesses, less compensatory megalomania, less accidents, less compensatory consumption, less political hostility, less social hostility, less demonstrations, less repetition of the old provocative and reactive patterns, less propaganda, fewer need for management of local and international tensions, less abuse of political or economic (industrial) power, less political crisis meetings, less stupid political projects, less control of citizens, etc.
- The unscrupulous abuse of the media power produces damages and costs on a level of billions of dollars; even trillions of dollars if they would stop promoting wars and heating up the masses for going to war.
- As there is no solution without the truth, the media would contribute in an incredible and very efficient way to solve the huge problems of humanity and the planet.
- The media could also benefit from distributing and broadcasting paid educational programs.
- Propaganda, falsifications and misleading marketing (abuse of human values) must be punished aiming for objective competences of people.
- Monster media dominance must be forbidden to let the inner potentials of people grow.
- Ideological and dogmatic brainwashing and manipulations must be forbidden to enable people for real contributions to society's problems.
- The unlimited arrogance of the media must be eliminated to enable people for a 'sustainable' life.

→ Suggestions for Innovation

- The media corporate groups are the indispensable tools for efficiently resolving the huge problems of humanity.
- As they don't want such solutions, they must be broken up and replaced with new media tools.
- All private TV and radio channels must become 'paid channels' with much less advertising.
- Marketing in general must be regulated in all media e.g. maximum 10% of the total pages and a size per advert of 1/8 page for each edition of newspapers and magazines.

→ Free Market Competition

- There is a legal free market competition, but only for those who have huge amounts of money.
- The corporations dispose of money to such an extent that most new small media projects are bound to fail.
- The standard media have become the extension of the life and family of billions of people.
- These media have become the authority for facts and the truth.
- How could a new media project with limited money reach millions, hundred of millions? Not possible!
- The owners of the media corporate groups are also the owners of industrial and economic corporate groups.
- The Western corporate groups are not interested in the truth – means: in educating people for the truth, for enlightenment, for educating people to live consciously, for an authentic self-realization, for inner human values, for a complex way of thinking, for any educational purpose making them free from greed and from compensatory consumption.
- The corporate media play the same game as the Christian religion: brainwashing and abusing people for their interests (to govern the world).
- A free media market competition is only possible with the break-up of the big media corporate groups (asset redistribution).

→ Direct Cost Reduction

- The contribution with all-embracing true information in all its manifoldness and with daily educational programs (reports) would produce a reduction of non-productive costs on a level of trillions of Euros per year around the globe.

→ Costs

- No significant costs; it's all simply a new orientation for all kind of media and programs, etc.

10. The Invisible Hand

It makes sense to understand the problems of global economics within a much bigger frame:

- Largest personal landowners
- The economic power of Christianity
- The economic power of the Anglican Church
- The power of the biggest banking centers
- The imperialistic warmongers

We want to have a closer overview about the biggest power centers on earth. Although we get information also from websites that are not completely free of conspiracies (or: hypotheses), we can formulate some economic theses that refer to the economic power of institutions with global dominance today.

It is not our intention to go into details of the 'body' of the invisible hand. Some information may have changed since the data was available. Other information needs a much deeper analysis or clarification of the real world behind the described facts. But we will formulate some conclusions related to economics and the economy. It may help to understand how far away all the scientific books (for students and professors) are from the economic reality. We present some statements from different sources as follows.

a) Largest Personal Landowners [159]

Landowner	Country	Acres
1. Elisabeth II	UK, Canada, Aust, NZ, and 18 others	6,600,000,000
2. King Abdullah	Saudi Arabia	547,000,000
3. Pope Benedict	Vatican & Catholic Church	177,000,000
4. King Mohammed	Morocco	175,665,040
5. King Bhumibhol	Thailand	126,792,000
6. Sultan Qaboos	Oman	76,000,000
7. King Gyanendra	Nepal	36,269,000
8. Kidman Holdings	Australia	24,000,000
9. King Adbullah of JOrdan	Jordan	22,076,000
10.AA Company of Brisbane	Australia	14,651,000
11.North Australian Pastoral	Australia	14,381,000
12.Terra Firma (formerly Packer)	Australia	12,800,000
13.Jimback Pastoral	Australia	11,303,000

[159] http://www.newstatesman.com/blogs/the-staggers/2011/03/queen-state-territories

14.King Wangckuck of Bhutan	Bhutan	9,479,360
15.Macdonald Holdings	Australia	7,572,000
16.Heyetsbury Beef	Australia	7,505,000
17.King Lestie 111	Lesotho	7,500,000
18.Brook Family	Australia	6,044,699
19.Colonial Agricultural Co.	Australia	4,539,000
20.Emir of Kuwait	Kuwait	4,403,000
21.King Mswati	Swaziland	4,290,000
22.James, Artkur & John Irving	Canada & US	3.600,000
23.Sheikh Hamad Bin Khalifa	Qatar	2,286,240
24.Tex Turner	US	2,000,000

"Queen Elizabeth II, head of state of the United Kingdom and of 31 other states and territories, is the legal owner of about 6,600 million acres of land, one sixth of the earth's non ocean surface."

"The Queen's land holding is worth a notional $33,000,000,000,000. [160] She is the only person on earth who owns whole countries, and who owns countries that are not her own domestic territory. This land ownership is separate from her role as head of state."

"Her holding is based on the laws of the countries she owns and her land title is valid in all the countries she owns. Her main holdings are Canada, the 2nd largest country on earth, with 2,467 million acres, Australia, the 7th largest country on earth with 1,900 million acres, Papua New Guinea with114 million acres, New Zealand with 66 million acres and the UK with 60 million acres. This makes her the richest individual on earth by land holdings".

The British crown and its wearer, Elizabeth II. Her legal title runs thus: "By the Grace of God, of the United Kingdom of Great Britain and Northern Ireland and of Her other Realms and Territories Queen, Head of the Commonwealth, Defender of the Faith".[161]

b) The Economic Power Centers of the World [162]

- City of London is the world's financial capital [163]
- Washington DC is the world's military capital [164]

---

[160] http://www.whoownstheworld.com/about-the-book/largest-landowner/

[161] http://www.newstatesman.com/blogs/the-staggers/2011/03/queen-state-territories

[162] http://stateofglobe.com/2011/05/21/washington-dc-city-of-london-og-vatikanet-er-egne-stater/

[163] http://en.wikipedia.org/wiki/Corporation_of_London

- The Vatican is the world's religious capital [165]

"Those three cities belong to no nation and pay no taxes." [166] [167] The three city states rules the world together. [168] The Western Rating agencies are also tools of this centralized power for global governance.

The following citations are from the same source:

"All these three geographic limited places are sovereign entities in the countries ... the three cities (in the cities) are privately held corporations/city-states, physically located in a nation ... The English king William II ... in 1694 transferred the British Empire's central bank the Bank of England to private interests. This became the start of the private banking system and gave the private owners ever greater power over the world ... The truth seems to be that Vatican since 1215 had a hand on the wheel in England. Their seat is the global financial main 'fortress' Crown of London, which is located in City Of London. Thus, in reality the British Empire is a continuation of the Roman Empire ... Almost all of the Founding Fathers of the United States used the title 'Esquire', which is a household title in London. Used by men on a certain level ... Do we have any reason whatsoever to think that the Popes since 1215 ever have given up the control Pope Innocent III got over the British Empire?"

"The colossal wealth of the Vatican includes enormous investments with the Rothschild's in Britain, France and the USA and with giant oil and weapons corporations like Shell and General Electric. The Vatican's solid gold bullion, worth billions is stored with the Rothschild controlled Bank of England and the US Federal Reserve Bank ... The Catholic Church is the biggest financial power, wealth accumulator and property owner in existence, possessing more material wealth than any bank, corporation, giant trust or government anywhere on the globe." [169] [170]

"The City State of London is the world's financial power center and the wealthiest square mile on the face of the Earth.
It houses the Rothschild controlled Bank of England, Lloyds of London, the

[164] http://en.wikipedia.org/wiki/District_of_Columbia_Organic_Act_of_1871
[165] http://stateofglobe.com/2011/05/21/washington-dc-city-of-london-og-vatikanet-er-egne-stater/
[166] http://jubilee2012.50webs.com/the_hidden_empire.htm
[167] See also: http://www.rumormillnews.com/cgi-bin/archive.cgi?noframes;read=139227
[168] http://www.carlg.org/eng3kronstater.html
[169] http://jubilee2012.50webs.com/the_hidden_empire.htm
[170] http://stateofglobe.com/2011/05/21/washington-dc-city-of-london-og-vatikanet-er-egne-stater/

London Stock Exchange, all British banks, the branch offices of 385 foreign banks and 70 US banks. It has its own courts, own laws, own flag and own police force … It is also the headquarters for world wide English Freemasonry, and for the world wide money cartel known as The Crown."

"Contrary to popular belief, The Crown is not the Royal Family or the British Monarch. The Crown is the private corporate City State of London. It has a council of 12 members who rule the Corporation under a Mayor, called the Lord Mayor … the District of Columbia is located on 10sq miles of land in the heart of Washington. The District of Columbia flies its own flag, and has its own independent constitution."

"When Congress passed the act of 1871 it created a separate corporation known as THE UNITED STATES and corporate government for the District of Columbia. This treasonous act allowed the District of Columbia to operate as a Corporation outside the original constitution of the United States and outside of the best interests of American Citizens … The United States has always been and still is a British Crown colony … Most US citizens believe that the United States is a country and that the President is the most powerful man on earth. The United States is not a country, it is a Corporation. And the President is President of the Corporation of the United States. He and his elected officials work for the Corporation, not for the American people. Since the United States is a Corporation, who owns the Corporation of the United States?" See also another source:[171]

c) The Military Power

Since the end of World War Two the United States has: [172] [173]

➔ Endeavored to overthrow more than 50 foreign governments, most of which were democratically elected.
➔ Grossly interfered in democratic elections in at least 30 countries.
➔ Waged war/military action, either directly or in conjunction with a proxy army, in some 30 countries.
➔ Attempted to assassinate more than 50 foreign leaders.
➔ Dropped bombs on the people of some 30 countries.
➔ Suppressed dozens of nationalist movements around the world.
➔ Has spent over 50 trillion dollars on Israel alone.

[171] http://www.thehalsreport.com/2010/07/d-c-london-and-vatican-city-do-they-rule-the-world/
[172] See: Schellhammer: Economics III
[173] http://www.foreignpolicyjournal.com/2010/10/02/the-secret-to-understanding-us-foreign-policy/

➔ Has masterminded and dictated politics throughout the European Union.

The rearmament and wars since 1990 has swallowed in the Western world more than 50 trillion dollars (counting all capitalistic countries), including supportive 'services' that are not calculated within the defense budgets of the capitalistic nations. Such enormous financial concentration directed to selected specific economic fields changes the entire picture of an economy and also changes the economic dynamics in a society's life and in its economy. Logically such developments completely change the 'welfare' and life standard of entire folks. One can include or exclude in this figure the very costly fields of long-term collateral damages.

We also must include the future costs of such evil doing: millions of people in the Balkans, in Iraq, in the entire Arab world, in Afghanistan, and Pakistan will not forget these diabolic nations for the next 300 years. And this means uncountable trillions of dollars and the values of the scarce raw resources irreversibly lost for the future generations. There is no study book about economics that analyzes such long-term economic effects! How is it possible that billions of people trust in such politicians and rulers, and give them permission to act in such blinded, destructive and very shortsighted ways? The answer lies in the accredited education and religion of the Western world.

Sicker and madder societies, cultures and religions are not possible!

Imagine: If these $50 trillion would have been invested in healthy food, efficient large area wide networks of public transport, a holistic and efficient education of all people (all ages), a healthy environment, in programs to drastically reduce all kind of accidents and human made illnesses, in pioneering and vanguard businesses providing hundreds of millions of sustainable jobs, in 'green' energy, in global peace-making programs, in programs to drastically reduce crimes, etc.

Thesis: Military activities and wars destroy or distort all principles and theories of economics and with that the economic development of nations in the interest of real 'welfare'.

d) The Power of Rating Agencies

The Rating agencies are another tool – better 'visible hand' – that rules the governments within the frame of a mission behind the curtains: 'the invisible hand'.
The basically important function in a society has converted into an instrument to exploit governments, economies, and to destroy entire countries with the

indispensably following bailout programs.

- Standard & Poor's
- Moody's
- Fitch
- And many more

We must see the monetary tools as part of a dangerous chain: there are several kinds of wars that come before a real war starts: activities of secret services, economic war, trade war, psychological war, blackmailing governments, false flags, proxy wars, and then the real war.

Hundreds of millions of people work hard and they hope for a good or a better life standard, especially for their children. They trust in authorities. Deep inside they want genuine human values. They want work and happiness, sustainable happiness. They want peace, love, and hope.

The financial systems, the governments, and the corporations take away all the opportunities they could have for a better life standard and a higher life quality with genuine human values and a healthy environment. Over the past 30 years they have taken away around 50 trillion dollars for their sick mission. The monetary system takes away the money; the governments control their life even within their home; they want to control their car movements, their emails, their internet activities, their chatting and mobile phones messaging and all activities on social networking websites; they have destroyed more than 50 million jobs; they have taken away homes from millions of individuals and families; and the Christian religion with more than 2.4 billion followers steals their soul with false promises.

Above that the US-Army and NATO (the Western world) have destroyed and continue destroying other nations and their infrastructure, have killed millions, have injured millions more, have made millions of children become orphans and women become widows, and have destroyed and contaminated huge lands of these nations for a hundred thousand and much more years during the last 20 years.

If we include Africa, Asia and Latin America the Western economic apparatus (network of corporations) has exploited billions of workers, has put billions of people into dire poverty, have taken away from them their agriculture and fish resources and many other resources, and with economics even control the governments of these countries; and they continue doing so every day – not to talk about the dire state of the planet with irreversible global destruction of the eco-systems and species, of the water resources and the natural environment of humans.

The professors and experts of economics call this 'the rational decision making'. The capitalistic economics is a brutal scam! Together with the Christian religion it is the most evil and biggest scam in the history of mankind!

Where will this lead the entire humanity in 35-40 years? The lesson from the Titanic is: The captain will die, the officers will die, the workers will die, and everyone will go under including all the people in the luxurious suites: the kings, the aristocrats, the billionaires, the rich people, the presidents, the ministers, the politicians, the CEOs, the managers, the Pope, the Cardinals, the Bishops, and all the superior office holders in the Christian Church and in the secret clubs.

Does it really bother anyone? Maybe the entire body of all souls on this earth will get another opportunity in 200,000 years to restart their psychical-spiritual evolution beginning as monkeys or pre-hominids on another planet in the Universe.

The glorification of the Western standard of living with its immense abundance of goods conceals the fact that all our wellbeing and material 'happiness' is entirely at the cost of an evil exploitation of billions of people in Asia, Africa, and other developing countries. The Western corporations have destroyed entire countries and resources around the globe, and have thrown billions of people in dire poverty and misery (including millions of children), and above that have contaminated more than half of the planet to an irreversible state today. [174] This is hubris as never seen before!

Above that the concentration of money in the Western world, in the hands of a few individuals and corporations, is now destroying their own countries and people, putting hundreds of millions of Europeans and Americans into poverty, unemployment or underemployment. To protect themselves they now are implementing systems of total control of all citizens' personal life with new laws that not even the worst tyrant has ever implemented. It is an unbelievable disgrace, how the science of economics ignores all of these facts. But since economics is a 'science' we can only deduce that all this is intentional, not a mistake, not through nescience, and certainly not by accident.

Final Conclusion

---

[174] http://www.mastersdegree.net/truth-about-tech/ and
http://www.theglobaleducationproject.org/

→ The economic consequences and implications are immeasurable and unimaginable!

→ The body of the 'invisible hand' is in the general frame identified.

→ The institutions on the stage behind the curtains are identified.

→ The 'invisible hand' is absolutely not an irrational and inexplicable power like a ghost.

→ The study books about economics reflect the people managing these power centers.

→ The study books about economics reflect the way of thinking of these power centers.

→ The study books about economics reflect the mission these power centers have.

→ There must a reason why such economic structures are not presented in books about economics.

→ The reason must be of most frightening dimension humans have ever created.

→ The people managing these power centers are not important; important is their mission.

→ The mission must have a power of such intensity that it can't be explained with greed or psychopathy.

→ The mission is older than 2,500 years; goes back to the earliest times of the Old Testament.

→ Islam as religion, culture, and economics does not form part of this mission.

→ Asian culture, economics, and religion (e.g. Buddhism) do not form part of this mission.

→ Such a global mission with unimaginable power must have a mission authority and a project authority.

→ There must be a book or document containing the mission; it's the holiest book since ever.

→ There must be a book containing the roadmap since centuries and a script for the actual theatre.

→ The working on the mission with its sanctum goes beyond the times of the Roman Empire.

→ Each generation of mission authority and project authority simply brings forward the project.

→ Western governments, state presidents, prime ministers, Kings and Aristocrats have no say.

→ State presidents, prime ministers, Kings, and Aristocrats are only paid protagonists of this mission.

→ The mission is rooted in the Genesis I, verse 28; there are the roots of the psychotic lunacy.

→ Huge parts of the world do not conform to this mission and project; and they never want.

→ A confrontation between the Christian-imperialistic world and the rest of the world is unavoidable.

→ Working on the mission is of higher importance than achieving the end-goal.

→ The complete elimination of humanity is unimportant; working on the mission is itself the goal.

This science is indeed the worst scam in the 21st Century and the worst evil doing in the history of mankind! And all accredited universities, the professors, the heads of universities, the experts of economics, the authors of economics, the academic teachers of economics, and the financial institutions know it very well. Even the politicians and governments in Europe and the United States, including the British Royalty, the Pope and his cardinals must know it. But all these responsible authorities keep their eyes closed as they have immense wages and additionally an extravagant bonus.

Impeachment

Disgraceful and infamous all of you, economists as well as politicians and clergy, – beyond what Hitler and his henchmen have done! The ones are cowards, the others are hypocrites; both are the worst actors of crimes against humanity and the creation! This is pure regicide and deicide! You all must be impeached and penalized! This doesn't fall under my authority; but for the regicide and the deicide, this falls fully under my judicial authority.

Literature – Economics I, II, III

Antonioni Peter, Flynn Sean Masaki: Economics for Dummies. Wiley 2011. Chichester, West Sussex, England.

Arum Richard, Roksa Josipa: Academically adrift. Limited Learning on College Campuses. University of Chicaco Press 2011. Chicago. London.

Brandon Craig: The Five-Year-Party. Benbella Books 2010. Dallas.

Chinn Menzie D., Frieden Jeffry A.: Lost decades. Debt Crisis and the long recovery. W.W. Norton & Company 2011. London.

Colander, D.C.: Microeconomics. 8th edition. McGraw-Hill 2010. New York.

Dasgupta Partha: Economics. Oxford University Press. 2007. New York.

Hacker Andrew, Dreifus Claudia: Higher Education. Times Books Henry Hold 2010. New York.

Haralambos Mike, Holborn Martin: Sociology. 7th edition. Collins 2008. London

Kamenetz Anya: DIY U Edupunks, Edupreneurs, and the Coming transformation of Higher Education. Chelsea Green Publishing 2010. White River Junction VT.

Krugman Paul, Wells Robin, Graddy Kathryn: Essentials of Economics. Worth Publishers 2011. New York.

McConnell Campbell R., Brue Stanley L., Flynn Sean M.: Macroeconomics, Principles, Problems, and Policies. 19th edition 2012. McGraw-Hill. New York.

McDowell Moore, Thom Rodney, Frank Robert, Bernanke Ben: Principles of Economics. 2nd European Edition. McGraw-Hill Higher Education 2009. Berkshire.

Mankiw N. Gregory, Taylor Mark P.: Economics. 2nd edition. South-Western Cengage Learning. 2011. Hampshire. United Kingdom.

Meadows, Donella, Randers Jorgen, Meadows Dennis: Chelsea Green Publishing. 2004. Vermont.

Palmer Parker J., Zajonc Arthur: The Heart of higher Education. Jossey-Bass 2010. San Francisco.

Smith Adam: The Wealth of Nations. First copy 1776. Edition 2010. Simon and Brown. www.simonandbrown.com

Other Publications (English, German) from Dr. Edward Schellhammer: www.edwardschellhammer.com